Upgrading to
MS-DOS 5®

Brian Underdahl

Publisher: Lloyd J. Short

Associate Publisher: Karen A. Bluestein

Acquisitions Manager: Terrie Lynn Solomon

Product Development Manager: Mary Bednarek

Managing Editor: Paul Boger

Indexer: Jeanne Clark

Book Design: Scott Cook

Production Team: Jeff Baker, Scott Boucher, Martin Coleman, Sandy Grieshop, Betty Kish, Sarah Leatherman, Howard Peirce, Bob LaRoche, Cindy L. Phipps, Tad Ringo, Lisa A. Wilson

To my wonderful Darlene and my little pal Wolfie.

Product Director
Timothy S. Stanley

Production Editor
Lori A. Lyons

Editors
Don Eamon
Norene Lewis

Technical Editor
David Knispel

Editorial Assistant
Patricia J. Brooks

Composed in Garamond and MacMillan
by Que Corporation

Brian Underdahl

Brian Underdahl is an independent consultant and author in Reno, Nevada. He studied electrical engineering at the University of Minnesota. Brian is a coauthor of several Que books, including *Using Symphony, Special Edition* and *Using 1-2-3 Release 3.1*, 2nd Edition. Brian provides programming services and support to companies and individuals throughout the United States.

TRADEMARK
ACKNOWLEDGMENTS

Q ue Corporation has made every effort to supply trademark information about company names, products, and services mentioned in this book. Trademarks indicated below were derived from various sources. Que Corporation cannot attest to the accuracy of this information.

1-2-3, Lotus, and Symphony are registered trademarks of Lotus Development Corporation.

AutoCAD is a registered trademark of Autodesk, Inc.

COMPAQ Personal Computer DOS Version 4.00 is a trademark, and COMPAQ and COMPAQ DeskPro 386 are registered trademarks of COMPAQ Computer Corporation.

CompuServe Information Service is a registered trademark of CompuServe Incorporated and H&R Block, Inc.

DeskJet, LaserJet, QuietJet, and ScanJet are trademarks of Hewlett-Packard Co.

DESQview, QRAM, and Quarterdeck QEMM/386 are trademarks of Quarterdeck Office Systems.

IBM ProPrinter, OS/2, Quietwriter, and Systems Application Architecture (SAA) are trademarks, and IBM PC XT and PS/2 are registered trademarks of International Business Machines Corporation.

DUMP.EXE is a trademark of Phoenix Technologies Ltd.

EPSON is a registered trademark of Epson Corporation.

Hercules Graphics Card is a trademark of Hercules Computer Technology.

Microsoft Windows is a trademark, and GW-BASIC, Microsoft Excel, Microsoft QuickBASIC, Microsoft Word, MS-DOS, and XENIX are registered trademarks of Microsoft Corporation.

Mouse Systems is a trademark of Mouse Systems Corporation.

NU and Norton Utilities are registered trademarks of Peter Norton Computing.

PC Tools is a registered trademark of Central Point Software.

PostScript is a registered trademark of Adobe Systems, Inc.

Q&A is a registered trademark of Symantec Corporation.

WordPerfect is a registered trademark of WordPerfect Corporation.

WordStar is a registered trademark of WordStar International Incorporated.

Trademarks of other products mentioned in this book are held by the companies producing them.

TABLE OF CONTENTS

Introduction

MS-DOS Version 5 (referred to in this book as DOS 5) represents a major advancement in operating systems for the IBM-PC and compatibles. DOS 5 is fully compatible with programs that ran under earlier versions of MS-DOS and PC DOS, but includes many advanced features—some of which take advantage of the increasing power and sophistication of today's PCs.

Upgrading to MS-DOS 5 introduces the new features and enhancements to DOS 5. This book provides an overview of DOS 5, while concentrating primarily on those areas that have changed. Instead of comprehensive coverage of all aspects of DOS, this book focuses on the new features of DOS 5. *Upgrading to MS-DOS 5* shows you how to take maximum advantage of the opportunities available when you upgrade your operating system.

As this book presents DOS 5's new features, you are given tips to help you understand the best ways to use those enhancements. You learn about the different types of memory DOS 5 can use and how you can optimize your system. You see how to configure your PC using CONFIG.SYS and AUTOEXEC.BAT. You see the advantages of the new DOS 5 Shell, learn how to use macros to customize DOS 5, examine the new and enhanced DOS commands, learn how to use the exciting, new full-screen DOS editor, and look at the modern QBasic interpreter.

Who Should Read This Book?

Upgrading to MS-DOS 5 shows you what you need to know to upgrade to DOS 5 and provides tips on making the most of your time and money.

Many different types of people will consider making the upgrade to DOS 5: the long-time PC users who already have been through a DOS version upgrade; and PC users who never have considered changing to another DOS version, but are trying to decide if DOS 5 is worthwhile. In addition, many different types of PCs exist, from ten-year-old IBM-PCs to the new 80486-based systems.

Regardless of your experience level and the type of PC system you use, *Upgrading to MS-DOS 5* is intended to help you decide if DOS 5 is for you.

PC Users Who Have Upgraded in the Past

DOS has gone through several versions since IBM released the PC in 1981. If you're an experienced upgrader who has upgraded your PC's operating system in the past, you probably want to know what features are new and how they affect you. You want to know about the new configuration options that, on many systems, can be used to provide up to 100K of additional usable memory. You also want to know about the new full-screen editor, using DOSKEY macros to customize DOS commands, the many new or enhanced DOS commands, and the QBasic interpreter.

All of these subjects are presented here in a lean, trim package that gets to the heart of what DOS 5 can do for you. You will see the reasons to make the upgrade and find out how to optimize your system.

PC Users Who Have Not Upgraded but Are Thinking about DOS 5

If you have never upgraded your PC's DOS software, the idea of making the move to DOS 5 may seem a little intimidating. How do you begin and what choices should you make? Do you have to upgrade to DOS 4 before you can upgrade to DOS 5?

Upgrading to MS-DOS 5 is intended to answer your needs. Although this book concentrates on features that are new or enhanced in DOS 5, features that were added or changed in DOS 4 also are covered if they continue to have importance in DOS 5 (many PC users never upgraded to DOS 4).

You also find coverage of items such as the new on-line help system, which can provide expert answers without making you go back to your DOS manual. This book also offers suggestions for DOS macros you can create that will make DOS 5 easier to use.

Using the information in this book, even inexperienced DOS users can make the most of DOS 5's enhancements. This book clearly identifies those enhancements that require advanced hardware so that you are able to determine if your system can take advantage of these enhancements.

What Is Covered in This Book?

Upgrading to MS-DOS 5 is designed to answer questions you may have as you install, configure, and use DOS 5.

Descriptions of Enhancements to DOS 5

DOS 5 includes many enhancements, such as several new commands, additional options for many of the existing commands, and a completely new Shell program. This book shows you what those enhancements are and gives you examples so that you can learn how to use them to your advantage.

This book also examines new features of DOS 5 that, in many cases, eliminate the need for many of the extra programs PC users have needed in the past to perform functions. For example, the new UNDELETE and UNFORMAT commands can help you recover from errors that formerly required utility programs such as the Norton Utilities or PC Tools.

Tips on System Customization and Optimization

DOS 5 offers many opportunities for customization and optimization that were not available to the PC user in previous versions of DOS. You can, for example, place much of DOS itself, device drivers, and some programs into high memory (if available on your system), thereby freeing up conventional memory. You also can customize the defaults for DOS commands and create new commands. The DOS Shell can be configured for many different combinations of screen resolution and color scheme.

This book shows you tips on how to make DOS 5 work in the way you want. You learn how to make the changes that will make your PC easier and more pleasant to use. In Chapter 6, for example, you see several suggestions on using DOSKEY macros to replace or enhance existing DOS commands.

Computer Systems That Can Run DOS 5

If you have been using a previous version of MS-DOS or PC DOS, you should be able to upgrade to DOS 5 without any difficulty. DOS 5 is an upward compatible enhancement of earlier versions of DOS and should be able to run any programs that also ran under one of those earlier versions.

Upgrading to DOS 5 requires a certain minimal level of hardware and software in your current configuration. You must, for example, have at least DOS 2.11 currently installed. In the unlikely event you're still using DOS 1.25 or some other very early version, you first have to upgrade to a more modern version before installing DOS 5. In addition, upgrading to DOS 5 requires the following hardware:

- At least 256K of memory.

- If you're upgrading a hard disk system, at least 2.8M of free disk space.

  DOS 5's installation program saves your old version of DOS so that you can return to it if problems occur during installation. Depending on the version you're upgrading from, saving these old files can require between 1/2M and 1 1/2M of disk space. You'll be able to recover this space after you're satisfied with DOS 5, but you must have the space available before you try to install DOS 5.

- If you're upgrading by installing DOS 5 on a floppy disk system, you'll need seven 5 1/4-inch or four 3 1/2-inch disks for DOS 5 itself.

- Hard disk system installations also require two blank 360K floppy disks (or one higher density floppy disk) that will be used during the installation process. These are called UNINSTALL disks and are used to reinstall your previous version of DOS if problems occur during installation.

Although not required, you should have enough blank disks for a complete backup of your hard disk before installing DOS 5. The SETUP program even includes an optional step that backs up your files before proceeding with installation. You should take the opportunity presented, especially if you have been lax in making sure you have current backups.

Nearly all IBM-PCs and compatibles should be able to take advantage of the upgrade to DOS 5. DOS 5 provides new power and enhancements that will make using a PC easier than ever.

The Details of This Book

Now that you have an idea of what's included in *Upgrading to MS-DOS 5*, it's time to have a closer look at the new DOS 5 features that are covered.

Chapter 1, "Introducing DOS 5," provides a short introduction to the enhancements included in DOS 5.

Chapter 2, "Upgrading to DOS 5," takes you through the steps of actually installing DOS 5 on your system.

Chapter 3, "Customizing Memory Usage with DOS 5," covers the different types of memory DOS 5 can use and the hardware requirements necessary to take advantage of them. You also learn how to optimize your system's use of available memory resources.

Chapter 4, "Configuring DOS 5," introduces you to factors you need to consider as you configure DOS 5 for your system. You learn, for example, why you may want to use the CONFIG.SYS INSTALL command instead of loading certain programs in AUTOEXEC.BAT.

Chapter 5, "Interfacing with the DOS 5 Shell," introduces the DOS 5 Shell. You learn how to use the Shell, what features the Shell provides, and how to customize the Shell.

Chapter 6, "Using DOS 5 Macros," covers a new program, DOSKEY, that provides a DOS command line macro capability and advanced command buffer options. A number of sample macros are provided—to be used as is, and as ideas on which you can build.

Chapters 7 through 10 cover the new commands and the enhancements to existing commands. You learn how to recover accidentally deleted files using the new UNDELETE command, how to make the DEL command safer, how to use DIR's new options, how to change any file attribute using ATTRIB, how to "lie" to programs about the DOS version by using SETVER, and much more.

Chapter 11, "EDIT: Using the Full-Screen Editor," introduces you to the new, full-screen editor, EDIT. As a modern replacement for EDLIN, EDIT offers mouse support, on-line help, and word processor-like editing of your files.

Chapter 12, "QBasic: A Revised BASIC," looks at QBasic, the new version of the BASIC language included in DOS 5. You see how QBasic improves greatly on both BASICA and GW-BASIC.

The Command Reference covers commands that are enhanced or new since DOS 3.3. The commands, which are arranged in alphabetical order, are shown with syntax, applicable notes, and examples. The Command Reference provides a quick, easy-to-use reference on these commands.

Learning More about DOS 5

This book provides only an overview of the features new to DOS 5 and does not cover all areas of DOS. After you decide to upgrade to DOS 5, you may be interested in purchasing other Que books on this subject, including *MS-DOS 5 QuickStart*, *Using MS-DOS 5*, *MS-DOS 5 Que Cards*, and *Que's MS-DOS 5 User's Guide, Special Edition*.

Conventions Used
in This Book

Certain conventions are followed in this book to help you more easily understand the discussions, use of commands, and syntax lines.

Special Typefaces and Representations

In most cases, the keys on the keyboard are represented as they appear on your keyboard, with the exception of the arrow keys. Arrow symbols and their corresponding terms, such as "up arrow" or "up-arrow key," have been used.

Ctrl-Home indicates that you press the Ctrl key and hold it down while you also press the Home key. Other hyphenated key combinations, such as Ctrl-Z or Alt-F1, are performed in the same manner.

Words or phrases that are defined for the first time appear in *italic* characters. Words or phrases you are to type appear in **boldface** characters.

Uppercase letters are used to distinguish file names and DOS commands. Uppercase letters usually are used in the examples for what you type, but you can type commands in either upper- or lowercase letters. For a few commands, the case of the letters makes a difference. When the case is significant, the difference is specifically mentioned in the discussion of the command.

All screen displays and on-screen messages appear in the following special typeface:

```
This is a screen message
```

Command Syntax

The notation for issuing commands and running programs appears, in fullest form, in lines such as the following:

*dc:pathc***CHKDSK** *filename.ext /switches*

In any syntax line, not all elements of the syntax can be represented in a literal manner. For example, *filename.ext* can represent any file name with any extension. It also can represent any file name with no extension at all. To activate the command CHKDSK.COM, you must type the word **CHKDSK**. To use the CHKDSK command with the /V (verbose) switch, you can type the following:

CHKDSK /V

Any literal text that you type in a syntax line is shown in uppercase letters. Any text that you can replace with other text (variable text) is shown in lowercase letters.

As another example, note the following syntax line:

FORMAT d:

The representation means that you must type **FORMAT** to format a disk. You also must type the drive represented by **d:**. However, **d:** can be replaced by any disk drive and therefore is in lowercase. If **d:** is to be drive A:, you would type the following:

FORMAT A:

Mandatory versus Optional Parts of a Command

Not all parts of a syntax line are essential when typing a command. You must be able to distinguish mandatory parts of the syntax line from those that are optional. Any portion of a syntax line that you see in **boldface** letters is mandatory; you must always give this part of a command. In the preceding example, to issue the FORMAT command, you must type the word **FORMAT** as well as substitute the drive letter you want for **d:**.

Not all items in a command line are always mandatory. Portions of a syntax line that you see in *italic characters* are optional; you supply these items only when needed. In the CHKDSK example, you substitute for *dc:pathc* the appropriate disk drive and path name. You substitute for *filename.ext* a file name or other item. You use the appropriate character or characters for */switches*. If you do not type an optional item, DOS will use its default value or setting for the item.

In most cases, the text also helps you distinguish between optional and mandatory items, as well as those mandatory items that are variable.

Introducing DOS 5

C hapter 1 looks at the enhancements included in DOS 5 and explains how these enhancements can benefit you and improve the operation of your PC.

As you read Chapter 1, keep in mind that many different types of PCs are capable of running DOS 5. Some of the new features may not apply currently to your system, but this book will try to specify when a special feature requires more than just a basic PC. You are encouraged to read those sections that may not apply to your system—you may find the excuse you need to update your hardware.

Although some of DOS 5's new features benefit only owners of more advanced PCs, most of the enhancements are available to every PC user. The next sections briefly describe DOS 5's enhancements, which include the following:

- Advanced memory management
- A new shell program that provides some of the features of Windows 3.0
- A DOS macro capability
- Support for higher capacity disks

- Many command enhancements

- A complete on-line help system

Later chapters show you in detail the advantages of these new features.

Memory Management

How you benefit from DOS 5's improved memory management capabilities depends largely on what type of PC you have and how your PC is configured. Memory management benefits can be broken down into the following types:

- Benefits all PC users

- Requires at least an 80286-based PC with extended memory

- Requires an 80386- or 80486-based PC with extended memory

Memory Benefits for all PCs

The first 640K of memory in a PC, known as *conventional memory*, is always in high demand. All DOS programs require conventional memory in order to run. Because many applications programs have continued to grow as new features are added, available space in conventional memory has become quite precious.

One program that always used some of the available conventional memory is the DOS kernel—that part of DOS needed to keep the system running. One of the reasons many PC users never upgraded to DOS Version 4 was that the DOS 4 kernel used about 10K more conventional memory than DOS 3.3. DOS 5, even though it has many new, additional features, splits the difference in memory usage between DOS 3.3 and DOS 4. DOS 5's kernel, therefore, uses only about 5K more conventional memory than DOS 3.3.

If your hard disk is larger than 32M, you may be able to save an additional 6K of conventional memory with DOS 5 compared to DOS 4. More details on this can be found in the section "DOS 5 Supports Large Disks without Requiring SHARE."

Memory Benefits for Systems with Extended Memory

PCs using 80286, 80386, or 80486 processors often have additional memory, called *extended memory*, which is addressed above the 8086 and 8088 processors' 1M address limit. DOS 5 can use this extended memory to great benefit by placing part of the DOS kernel in a special area of extended memory, called the *High Memory Area* (HMA).

Placing the DOS 5 kernel in the HMA frees up between 38K and 45K of additional conventional memory. COMMAND.COM, the DOS buffers, and part of HIMEM.SYS also can be loaded into the HMA with the DOS kernel. The following table shows typical figures for available conventional memory for PCs with the HMA available.

DOS version	Conventional memory available
3.31	504K
3.31 + Windows 3.0	494K
4.01	494K
4.01 + Windows 3.0	483K
5.0	610K
5.0 + Windows 3.0	580K

Note: Chapter 3 covers in detail the many memory types available with DOS 5. For now, keep in mind that you need extended, not expanded memory to use the HMA.

Memory Benefits for 80386 or 80486 Systems

If you have an 80386- or 80486-based PC, DOS 5 offers yet another type of memory management—*Upper Memory Blocks* (UMBs). UMBs are portions of the reserved address space between the 640K DOS address limit and the 1M upper address limit of the 8086 and 8088 processors. By using a program called EMM386.EXE with DOS 5, you can place device drivers and TSR programs into Upper Memory Blocks instead of in conventional memory.

You therefore have even more available conventional memory while still having access to the services provided by these device drivers and TSR programs. For example, placing Microsoft's mouse driver, MOUSE.COM, into the UMBs saves about 18K of conventional memory.

> *Note:* Chapter 3 also describes how you can make use of UMBs on 80286 PCs by using programs from other manufacturers that complement DOS 5.

Other Memory Enhancements

DOS 5's EMM386.EXE program adds support for the VCPI (Virtual Control Program Interface), a memory management specification used by some programs such as Lotus 1-2-3 Release 3.0 (but not Release 3.1).

In addition, EMM386.EXE now supports the VDS (Virtual DMA Services) 1.0 specification. This specification was produced by Microsoft and IBM to support some of the advanced features of systems that can have multiple bus masters, including IBM's PS/2 microchannel architecture (MCA) machines.

Regardless of the type of processor or the amount of memory in your PC, DOS 5's advanced memory management capabilities give you more features and more conventional memory. This, however, is just the first of many DOS 5 benefits.

The DOS 5 Shell

DOS 5 includes a completely new shell program that brings a Windows 3.0 type interface to every PC user. You can use a mouse or the keyboard in the DOS 5 shell to easily perform nearly any DOS task.

A *shell* program, such as the DOS 5 Shell, is intended to make the PC easier to use by changing your interaction with the computer from command-line orientation into a visual, graphical interface. If you want to see which files are in a directory, for example, you move the cursor until that directory is highlighted in the tree structure. When the directory is highlighted, the files contained in your selected directory are listed. Figure 1.1 gives an example of how this shell directory looks.

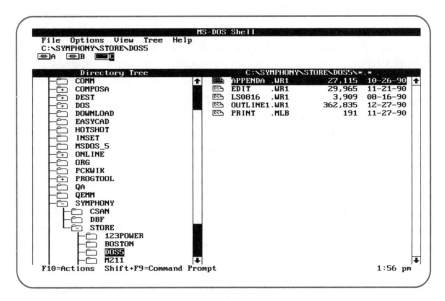

Fig. 1.1. *An example of the DOS 5 Shell.*

The DOS 5 Shell makes seeing your files easier and also simplifies many common tasks such as running programs, copying or moving files, and moving around in your directories. Because the DOS 5 Shell uses visual cues instead of verbal commands, the program is easy to learn and easy to use—you just select options from menus.

DOS 5 provides on-line help for the shell program, as it does for its other enhancements. Instead of trying to find commands in a manual, you can find the answer with the touch of a key.

Although the DOS 5 Shell makes life much easier by giving DOS a visual interface and on-line, context-sensitive help, two other features also add greatly to its value.

Task Swapping

How many times have you been using a program on your PC when you suddenly realize you need some information you can get only from another program?

Suppose that you are writing a letter to your favorite aunt, when you realize that her birthday is some time in the near future. You cannot remember the exact date; but, luckily, you have a database with everyone's birthday listed. The problem is that you cannot access the database from your word processor. Even if you could, you first have to save your 10-page letter. Your only choice is to save the letter, exit from your word processor, load the database program, load the birthday database, and search for Aunt Darlene's record. After you find the record and check the date, you have to exit the database program, reload the word processor, and then reload your letter.

The DOS 5 Shell gives you another option—*task swapping*. If you are running your word processor under the DOS 5 Shell, you can press a "hot key" combination to switch between your word processor and the database program. With another hot key press, you can jump right back where you were in your letter.

Hot keys are key combinations, such as Alt-S or Ctrl-W, which you define. The hot keys tell the Shell to switch directly to the program associated with the hot key. If you assign Alt-S to Symphony and Ctrl-W to Microsoft Word, for example, pressing Alt-S switches you to Symphony. Similarly, pressing Ctrl-W switches you to Word.

Associating Files with Programs

Most of the time, you use a particular type of file only with a particular program. For example, you usually don't load Lotus 1-2-3 worksheets into Microsoft Word. To work with a file, however, you usually first must load the program (such as 1-2-3) and then issue a command telling the program to load the file. Working with files would be easier if you could just select the file and let the computer determine which program is needed.

That's the idea behind the DOS 5 Shell's ability to associate files with programs. You can tell DOS 5 that all files with a DOC file extension are Microsoft Word files. When you select a file with a name like BUDGET.DOC, the Shell will load Word and tell Word to load

BUDGET.DOC. After you are familiar with using the DOS 5 Shell, you will wonder how you ever got along without this feature.

If this short look at some of the DOS 5 Shell features has interested you in this enhancement, you can find more information about the Shell in Chapter 5.

Macro Capability

At times you probably would like a few extra DOS commands to make your work easier. Or you sometimes need to repeat a series of steps several times and would like to cut down on the number of keystrokes you have to execute.

With the addition of DOSKEY, DOS 5 has become much easier to customize. DOSKEY is a special program that provides macro capabilities to the DOS 5 user. As Chapter 6 details, DOSKEY enables you to decide how DOS commands should work. With DOSKEY, you can create new commands and keep a record of commands you have issued so that you can reuse them.

DOSKEY is such an important enhancement to DOS 5 that suggestions for using DOSKEY are given throughout this book. Follow these suggestions and use them as ideas for developing your own DOSKEY macros.

New and Enhanced Commands

Because DOS 5 has so many new or enhanced commands, most of this book is devoted to telling you about them. The following list includes these commands:

APPEND	ASSIGN	ATTRIB	BACKUP
BUFFERS	CHKDSK	COMMAND	COMP
DEL	DELOLDOS	DEVICEHIGH	DIR
DISKCOPY	DOS	DOSKEY	DOSSHELL
DRIVPARM	EDIT	EMM386	ERASE
EXPAND	FASTOPEN	FIND	FORMAT

GRAPHICS	HELP	INSTALL	KEYB
LOADFIX	LOADHIGH	MEM	MIRROR
MODE	QBASIC	REM	REPLACE
RESTORE	SETVER	SHARE	SYS
TIME	TREE	UNDELETE	UNFORMAT

As you learn more about DOS 5, you will see that the important benefits offered by these DOS command enhancements not only make DOS 5 much easier and safer to use, but also act as replacements for many of the utility programs currently on the market. In fact, some of the new commands in this list are popular utility programs Microsoft has licensed from other manufacturers. (So upgrading to DOS 5 may even save you money.)

Other Features Available with DOS 5

Several other features offer potential benefits to those considering upgrading to DOS 5.

The QBasic Interpreter

The BASIC programming language has always been a part of PCs. IBM included BASIC on its first PC, and most systems have included a closely related version since then. With the upgrade to DOS 5, Microsoft includes a new version of BASIC that enables you to take advantage PC hardware like the VGA display and the mouse, which were introduced long after BASICA and GW-BASIC.

QBasic provides DOS 5 users a much friendlier programming environment. The QBasic editor (EDIT) supports a mouse, allows full-screen editing, and has complete cut-and-paste capabilities. QBasic also has on-line, context-sensitive help that enables you to write your own QBasic programs without ever looking in a manual.

The QBasic editor is so capable and easy to use that it even serves as a full-screen editor, replacing the DOS EDLIN line-oriented editor program. After you use EDIT to modify a batch file, you will appreciate the advantages of using EDIT rather than EDLIN.

Chapter 11 gives an in-depth look at EDIT, and Chapter 12 shows how QBasic compares to BASICA and GW-BASIC.

DOS 5 Supports Large Disks without Requiring SHARE

SHARE.EXE is a program that enables DOS to support file and record locking. SHARE was created to protect files on a PC when more than one program attempted to access the same files at the same time. Although this sounds like the type of program you may see on a networked PC, in which several computers access the same database files at the same time, SHARE was designed to protect files on a single system running two or more programs at once. For example, multitasking software such as Windows 3.0 may allow two copies of a database program to access the same database at the same time.

Designers of DOS 4 gave SHARE another task. Before DOS 4, hard disks were limited to 32M in a single volume (except in the case of a few special OEM versions of DOS such as Compaq's 3.31). If you had a 40M hard disk, you were required to divide it into two logical drives—C: and D:, for example. DOS 4 removed the 32M limit on the size of a single volume, but required you to use SHARE if you formatted your hard disk in the new, larger size. Although you could load SHARE.EXE automatically in CONFIG.SYS, the process still was a nuisance and a waste of precious memory if you were not using software that required SHARE's services.

DOS 5 recognizes that formatting a hard disk larger than 32M does not necessarily mean you need file and record locking. SHARE has been returned to the status of an optional command that you can use if required by your applications programs. Chapter 4 gives more information on using SHARE.

DOS 5 Supports 2.88M Floppy Disks

DOS has evolved partly in response to changes in PC hardware. When DOS was introduced, PCs used single-sided, 5 1/4-inch floppy disks with 160K capacity. Soon thereafter, double-sided floppies with 320K capacity became the standard. DOS V2 added support for 9-sector instead of

8-sector formatting and the 360K disk replaced the 320K disk. DOS 3, introduced along with the IBM-AT, made 1.2M the standard. When the first laptop PCs with 3 1/2-inch disks appeared, DOS 3.2 added support for the 720K 3 1/2-inch size. With DOS 3.3, 1.44M, 3 1/2-inch disks also were added.

DOS 5 makes the first addition to the list of supported disk sizes since DOS 3.3. The 2.88M, 3 1/2-inch disk that DOS 5 supports is compatible with the earlier, lower density 3 1/2-inch disks, but holds as much data as 18 of the 160K disks used with the first IBM-PCs.

Chapter 7 discusses how the FORMAT command has been enhanced in several ways to provide support for this new, higher capacity disk. Like the existing 3 1/2-inch disks, the 2.88M disks are double-sided with 80 tracks. The primary difference is that 2.88M disks have 36 sectors per track instead of 18 sectors per track for 1.44M disks, and 9 sectors per track for 720K disks.

On-Line Help Available with All DOS Commands

DOS commands always have required the user to learn a sometimes cryptic set of switches or parameters in order to use those commands in any but the most basic manner. Although these options have provided useful and powerful alternatives, they also have made it difficult for anyone except the most dedicated to make full use of the commands.

> *Tip:* Switches or parameters are the additional information you type following a DOS command. Suppose that you enter the following command:
>
> **DIR** **.COM /W*
>
> **DIR** is the command, **.COM* is the first *parameter* (or set of variable information), and */W* is a *switch* (or method the DIR command should use to process the parameter). The terms switch and parameter often are interchanged even though they actually have slightly different meanings.

The three basic variations of the DIR command are not difficult to remember: DIR for the full, scrolling directory listing; DIR /W for the abbreviated, wide listing; and DIR /P for the full, paged listing. DIR and other commands now have a long list of switches that may be difficult to remember, particularly if you use the command only now and then.

Taking a cue from the many available PC utility programs, creators of DOS 5 added an on-line help feature for all DOS commands. You now can find out how to use a DOS command without pulling out your DOS manual and searching for the switches and parameters used with that command. You only need to type the command name and follow it with /? (forward slash and question mark) to see an explanation of the command without actually executing the command.

Figure 1.2 shows how the on-line help system works with the FORMAT command. When you type **FORMAT /?**, the FORMAT program provides the help you need to determine that a proper switch to format a 360K diskette in a 1.2M drive is /4, which formats a 360K floppy disk in a high-capacity drive. You can use other switches as well, but /4 is an acceptable choice for now. Chapter 7 examines a few of the other switches used with the FORMAT command.

```
C:\>FORMAT /?
Formats a disk for use with MS-DOS.

FORMAT drive: [/V[:label]] [/Q] [/U] [/F:size] [/B | /S]
FORMAT drive: [/V[:label]] [/Q] [/U] [/T:tracks /N:sectors] [/B | /S]
FORMAT drive: [/V[:label]] [/Q] [/U] [/1] [/4] [/B | /S]
FORMAT drive: [/Q] [/U] [/1] [/4] [/8] [/B | /S]

  /V[:label]   Specifies the volume label.
  /Q           Performs a quick format.
  /U           Performs an unconditional format.
  /F:size      Specifies the size of the floppy disk to format (such
               as 160, 180, 320, 360, 720, 1.2, 1.44, 2.88).
  /B           Allocates space on the formatted disk for system files.
  /S           Copies system files to the formatted disk.
  /T:tracks    Specifies the number of tracks per disk side.
  /N:sectors   Specifies the number of sectors per track.
  /1           Formats a single side of a floppy disk.
  /4           Formats a 5.25-inch 360K floppy disk in a high-density drive.
  /8           Formats eight sectors per track.

C:\>
```

Fig. 1.2. On-line help for the DOS FORMAT command.

On-line command help is not intended to be a substitute for the DOS command reference manual. Experienced DOS users can see in the FORMAT example that some of the available switches need more information than on-line help provides. When short descriptions are all you need, on-line help saves valuable time. If you're an experienced DOS user, the listing of the switches and parameters may be just enough to jog your memory.

Novice DOS users also can benefit from on-line help. Notice that in figure 1.2 the help information starts with the explanation of the FORMAT command: `Formats a disk for use with MS-DOS`. If you wonder whether you have chosen the correct command, simply follow the command with /? to see the explanation without actually executing the command. The explanation should clarify whether the command is appropriate. In most cases, you don't have to go to your DOS manual. You also don't have to worry that you may choose the wrong command.

Additional Help Available

Although each command in DOS 5 has on-line help, DOS 5 also includes a program that gives you even more help deciding which command to use. The following list shows how the command HELP explains each of the DOS commands.

Table 1.1
Command Descriptions

Command	Explanation
APPEND	Allows programs to open data files in specified directories as if they were in the current directory
ASSIGN	Redirects requests for disk operations on one drive to a different drive
ATTRIB	Displays or changes file attributes
BACKUP	Backs up one or more files from one disk to another
BREAK	Sets or clears extended CTRL+C checking
CALL	Calls one batch program from another

Command	Explanation
CD	Displays the name of or changes the current directory
CHCP	Displays or sets the active code page number
CHDIR	Displays the name of or changes the current directory
CHKDSK	Checks a disk and displays a status report
CLS	Clears the screen
COMMAND	Starts a new instance of the MS-DOS command interpreter
COMP	Compares the contents of two files or sets of files
COPY	Copies one or more files to another location
CTTY	Changes the terminal device used to control your system
DATE	Displays or sets the date
DEBUG	Runs Debug, a program testing and editing tool
DEL	Deletes one or more files
DELOLDOS	Deletes old DOS files after DOS 5 installation
DIR	Displays a list of files and subdirectories in a directory
DISKCOMP	Compares the contents of two floppy disks
DISKCOPY	Copies the contents of one floppy disk to another
DOSKEY	Edits command lines, recalls MS-DOS commands, and creates macros
DOSSHELL	Starts MS-DOS Shell

continues

Table 1.1 *(Continued)*

Command	Explanation
ECHO	Displays messages or turns command-echoing on or off
EDIT	Starts the MS-DOS Editor, which creates and changes ASCII files
EDLIN	Starts EDLIN, a line-oriented text editor
EMM386	Turns on or off EMM386 expanded memory support
ERASE	Deletes one or more files
EXE2BIN	Converts EXE (executable) files to binary format
EXIT	Quits the COMMAND.COM program (command interpreter)
EXPAND	Expands one or more compressed files
FASTOPEN	Decreases the amount of time needed to open frequently used files and directories
FC	Compares two files or sets of files and displays the difference between them
FDISK	Configures a hard disk for use with MS-DOS
FIND	Searches for a text string in a file or files
FOR	Runs a specified command for each file in a set of files
FORMAT	Formats a disk for use with MS-DOS
GOTO	Directs MS-DOS to a labeled line in a batch program
GRAFTABL	Enables MS-DOS to display an extended character set in graphics mode
GRAPHICS	Leads a program that can print graphics
HELP	Provides help information for MS-DOS commands

Command	Explanation
IF	Performs conditional processing in batch programs
JOIN	Joins a disk drive to a directory on another drive
KEYB	Configures a keyboard for a specific language
LABEL	Creates, changes, or deletes the volume label of a disk
LOADFIX	Loads a program above the first 64K of memory, and runs the program
LH or LOADHIGH	Loads a program into the upper memory area
MD	Creates a directory
MEM	Displays the amount of used and free memory
MIRROR	Records information about one or more disks
MKDIR	Creates a directory
MODE	Configures system devices
MORE	Displays output one screen at a time
NLSFUNC	Loads country-specific information
PATH	Displays or sets a search path for executable files
PAUSE	Suspends processing of a batch program and displays the message `Press any key to continue...`
PRINT	Prints a text file while you are using other MS-DOS commands
PROMPT	Changes the MS-DOS command prompt
QBASIC	Starts the MS-DOS QBasic programming environment

continues

Table 1.1 *(Continued)*

Command	Explanation
RD	Removes (deletes) a directory
RECOVER	Recovers readable information from a bad or defective disk
REM	Records comments (remarks) in a batch file or CONFIG.SYS
REN or RENAME	Renames a file or files
REPLACE	Replaces files
RESTORE	Restores files that were backed up using the BACKUP command
RMDIR	Removes (deletes) a directory
SET	Displays, sets, or removes MS-DOS environment variables
SETUP	Installs MS-DOS 5 on an existing DOS system
SETVER	Sets the version number that MS-DOS reports to a program
SHARE	Installs file-sharing and locking capabilities on your hard disk
SHIFT	Changes the postion of replaceable parameters in a batch file
SORT	Sorts input and writes results to the screen, a file, or another device
SUBST	Associates a path with a drive letter
SYS	Copies MS-DOS system files and command interpreter to a disk you specify
TIME	Displays or sets the system time
TREE	Graphically displays the directory structure of a drive or path

Command	Explanation
TYPE	Displays the contents of a text file
UNDELETE	Restores files that have been deleted
UNFORMAT	Restores a disk erased by the FORMAT command or restructured by the RECOVER command
VER	Displays the MS-DOS version
VERIFY	Turns disk-write verification on or off
VOL	Displays a disk volume label and serial number
XCOPY	Copies files (except hidden and system files) and directory trees

After you determine which command you need, you can use the HELP command or the /? parameter for more detailed information. The following commands, for example, give you exactly the same information:

XCOPY / ?

or

HELP XCOPY

As you can see, DOS 5 tries to make using DOS much easier by providing several different ways to get assistance.

Summary

This chapter briefly covered a number of features and enhancements available with DOS 5. Advanced memory management, a highly improved DOS shell, macro capability, commands enhancements, and on-line help are some features that may enable you to use your PC more easily and effectively. The following chapters show you how to make the most of your DOS 5 upgrade.

Upgrading to DOS 5

Chapter 2 discusses the new features you use to upgrade to DOS 5. First, you examine upgrading from a previous version of DOS. You then cover floppy and hard disk considerations. You see how the new installation program makes upgrading DOS 5 both easy and painless. This chapter also discusses some of the advancements DOS includes automatically. Finally, you see a new feature of DOS 5—how to uninstall the program if necessary.

Before Upgrading to DOS 5

Installing DOS 5 using the SETUP program is quite simple. SETUP guides you through the installation process, examining your system's configuration and asking you to verify it's conclusions about your system. Most of the installation proceeds automatically and you simply change disks when prompted. Before you begin, however, you need to perform certain tasks to prepare for upgrading.

Determining Your Current DOS Version

Before you can upgrade your system to DOS 5, you must make sure that you have at least DOS Version 2.11 installed. To determine your current DOS version, enter the following command at the DOS prompt:

VER

DOS responds by displaying a message such as the following:

```
MS-DOS 3.10
```

If the version number displayed is 2.11 or higher, you can install DOS 5. If your DOS version is lower—1.25, for example—you cannot upgrade directly to DOS 5. In this case, you need to obtain and upgrade to a version of DOS earlier than DOS 5 (at least 2.11 or later), and then upgrade to DOS 5.

> *Note:* If you have a version of DOS prior to 2.11, contact the manufacturer of your computer. The manufacturer may offer the version of DOS 5 that accompanies a new computer (called the OEM Version or Retail version). Upgrade to DOS 5 using this version.

Determining Memory and Space Requirements

Next, you must make sure you have 256K or more conventional memory, and, if you're installing DOS 5 on a hard disk, at least 2.8M free disk space. To determine the amount of conventional memory and available disk space, enter the following command:

CHKDSK C:

> *Note:* This command assumes that you have a hard disk (you can ignore the disk space requirement if you're upgrading a floppy disk system) and that drive C: is the drive you use to boot your system. If you boot from another drive, substitute the correct drive letter in place of the C:.

The CHKDSK command responds by displaying several pieces of information regarding the size of the user files, total bytes of memory, and bytes available on disk (depending on your current DOS version, the wording may vary slightly, but will be similar). You should have at least the following memory and available disk space:

```
262144 total bytes memory
2800000 bytes available on disk
```

DOS 5 requires 256K or more of memory. If the figure shown for total bytes memory is smaller than 262,144, you cannot install DOS 5 unless you add additional conventional memory to your PC. Your computer manual should contain a section on installing additional RAM (memory), or you may need to contact your computer dealer for assistance.

If you don't have enough available space on your hard disk, you have to make space available before installing DOS 5. You may need to clean up the old files on your hard disk.

Note: Although DOS 5 requires approximately 2.8M of free space to be installed on a hard disk, not all of that space is necessary after installation. Part of the installation process backs up your existing DOS version to a new directory. These files can be deleted after you determine you don't need to uninstall DOS 5. A number of the files copied to your hard disk during installation also are of little use unless you're using foreign languages and may be deleted if you don't need them. After installing DOS 5, you see a file called README.TXT in your DOS directory. This file, which you can read using EDIT, describes the various files you may want to delete.

Floppy Disk Considerations

You should use the DISKCOPY command to back up the original upgrade disks before you begin installation.

Installing DOS 5 on a PC without a hard disk requires a total of four 3 1/2- or seven 5 1/4-inch blank disks to hold your installed copy of DOS 5. Label the blank disks with the following labels:

5 1/4-inch double-density disks:

> Startup
> Support
> Shell
> Help
> Basic/Edit
> Utility
> Supplemental

3 1/2-inch double-density disks:

> Startup/Support
> Shell/Help
> Basic/Edit/Utility
> Supplemental

You do not need to format the disks before you install DOS 5 because DOS will format the disks if necessary.

Hard Disk Considerations

DOS 5 is supplied on either three 3 1/2- or six 5 1/4-inch disks. Most of the files are compressed to save disk space and to reduce the number of times you must change disks during the upgrade. You must remember that the installation process uncompresses the files and that they cannot be used in their compressed format. Don't try to bypass the SETUP program, or you will find yourself with a disk full of unusable files.

Before you begin the installation, you should use the DISKCOPY command to back up the upgrade disks. You should do this regardless of whether you're upgrading a hard disk or floppy disk system. After you back up the upgrade disks, you can proceed with installing DOS 5.

As far as the installation process is concerned, you gain no advantage in using high-density disks because they will be formatted double-density, regardless. The one exception to this is the Uninstall disk that SETUP creates for hard disk systems. You can substitute a single high-density disk for two double-density disks when creating the Uninstall disk. After you install DOS 5, you can create a high-density system disk if you prefer. The installation program, however, creates only double-density disks.

Upgrading without Changing Hard Disk Structure

Prior to DOS Version 4.01 (or Compaq's DOS 3.31), you had to partition a hard disk that was larger than 32M into logical drives of 32M or less. DOS 5 no longer requires this partitioning but is compatible with hard disks with logical partitions. You can, therefore, install DOS 5 without changing your hard disk's structure.

DOS 5 must, however, be installed on the active, primary partition of the hard disk (usually drive C:). If your old version of DOS is not installed in this partition, you first must copy your old DOS files to the active, primary partition. After you install DOS 5, you can move all of the files except the system files (IO.SYS, MSDOS.SYS, and COMMAND.COM) back to the other partition.

Changing Hard Disk Structure

As you are installing DOS 5, you may want to change your hard disk's structure for several reasons. If you have been using an earlier version of DOS that doesn't allow a partition size over 32M, you may want to change to a single, large partition that matches the physical size of your hard disk.

If your existing primary, active disk partition is too small (less than 2.8M), you must change the disk's structure before installing DOS 5.

Regardless of your reason for changing the partition structure of your hard disk, you have several steps to perform in preparing to upgrade to DOS 5.

You must install DOS 5 on floppy disks using the /F argument with the SETUP program.

This step is absolutely necessary if you plan to change your hard disk's partition size to one larger than that supported by your current version of DOS—you no longer will be able to access the larger partition with the old DOS version.

You should back up the files contained on the hard disk.

Make sure you have enough blank disks for backing up your files and recovering from installation problems. If you're upgrading a hard disk PC, you need two double-density or one high-density disk during installation to create the Uninstall disk. As noted earlier, if you're changing your hard disk's partition size, you need to install DOS 5 on floppy disks first, so you also need four 3 1/2- or seven 5 1/4-inch floppy disks for that purpose.

You can use either the DOS 5 SETUP program option to back up all of your previous files, or you can use your current DOS version's BACKUP command if you want to do a partial backup. You can save time and reduce the number of disks by backing up your data files and then re-installing your programs using the original program disks.

If you decide to back up all of your files, the SETUP program will give you an estimate of the number of disks you need. You also can make your own estimate before running SETUP by using the CHKDSK C: command. Don't forget to add the files contained on your hard disk's other partitions if you currently have the disk partitioned as multiple logical drives.

To calculate how many disks you need for backing up your hard disk, type the command **CHKDSK**. Write down the number of bytes CHKDSK shows for user files (these are the files that will be backed up). To determine the number of disks, divide the number you wrote down by the number of bytes contained on the disks you will use for your backup. As a rough estimate, you can use the following chart:

Size	Capacity	Bytes
5 1/4"	360K	368,640
5 1/4"	1.2M	1,228,800
3 1/2"	720K	737,280
3 1/2"	1.44M	1,474,560

If CHKDSK indicates 14,003,712 bytes in user files, for example, you need thirty-eight 360K, twelve 1.2M, nineteen 720K, or ten 1.44M disks. You always should have a few spare disks before you start—after you start backing up your files, you cannot change disk sizes.

Repartition your hard disk.

You should use the same software and version that created the current disk structure in order to remove that structure. If you used the FDISK command included in your current DOS version, for example, you should use the same version to remove the disk partition.

After the existing partition or partitions have been removed, place the DOS 5 STARTUP or STARTUP/SUPPORT disk in drive A: and reboot your PC. (Note: This is the disk you created when you installed DOS 5 on the floppy disks.) When you see the DOS command prompt, type the following command to start the DOS 5 FDISK program:

FDISK

> *Note:* If you are using 5 1/4-inch floppies, remove the STARTUP disk and replace it with the SUPPORT disk after you reboot and before you issue the FDISK command. Place the STARTUP disk in drive A: before issuing the FORMAT command.

Follow the prompts to create a single DOS partition or at least create an active, primary partition of at least 3M.

After changing the hard disk's partition size, you next must use the FORMAT command to format the new disk partitions.

> *Note:* If you have more than one hard disk in your system, be certain that FDISK completes successfully before you attempt to format drive C:. If you removed the existing DOS partition from drive C: but did not create another, DOS assigns drive letter C: to your former drive D:. If you type the DOS command **DIR C:** (after changing drive C:'s partition size but before using the FORMAT command) and files are displayed instead of an error message, you should run the FDISK command again to make sure drive C: has an active, primary DOS partition.

You need to restore the files you backed up.

Next, place SETUP disk #3 (if you are using 5 1/4-inch floppies) or disk #2 (for 3 1/2-inch floppies) in drive A:

At the DOS prompt, type the following command and follow the prompts:

> **A:HDRSTORE**

You will need your backup disks and will be swapping them as files are restored.

After your files are restored, enter the following commands to rename CONFIG.SYS and AUTOEXEC.BAT:

> **REN C:\CONFIG.SYS CONFIG.OLD**
> **REN C:\AUTOEXEC.BAT AUTOEXEC.OLD**

Finally, replace the disk in drive A: with your backup copy of SETUP disk #1 from the DOS 5 installation disks.

To complete your upgrade to DOS 5, type the following command and follow the screen prompts.

> **A:SETUP**

You now are ready to install DOS 5 on your hard disk.

Upgrading Made Easy

As you install DOS 5, you have to make a number of decisions relating to the DOS environment you will have when the install program finishes its work.

Using the SETUP Program on a Floppy Disk System

To begin the upgrade on a floppy disk system (after you make backups of the upgrade disks and label the disks as mentioned previously), follow these steps:

1. Switch on your system.

2. After the system boots, place the backup of your SETUP Disk 1 in drive A:.

3. Enter the command **SETUP /F**.

Follow the instructions on the screen and change disks when instructed. Make certain that you always insert the proper disk. You also may want to use write-protect tabs on the upgrade disks to prevent damage to them in case you make a mistake.

Note: If you are installing DOS 5 on a floppy disk system, you may want to use the new /MSG switch with COMMAND when you boot your system to ensure that DOS will give you complete error messages. You should include this command in your CONFIG.SYS file using the following syntax:

SHELL=COMMAND.COM /MSG /P

Using the SETUP Program on a Hard Disk System

Make sure you know where you want DOS 5 to be installed. On a hard disk, you most likely want to use a directory such as C:\DOS. You also need to know the type of display monitor you have (such as CGA, EGA, or VGA). The SETUP program will try to determine your monitor type and most likely will guess correctly, but knowing what monitor you have enables you to verify the program's choice.

Now you're ready to install the DOS 5 upgrade by following these steps:

1. Boot your computer.

2. Place SETUP disk #1 in drive A: and make sure the drive door is closed.

3. Type the command **A:SETUP** and press Enter.

The SETUP program now examines your system and then asks you to verify what it has found. Before any part of DOS 5 actually is installed, you also are given the opportunity to back up your existing files. Use the blank, formatted disks you collected for your backup and follow the instructions on the screen.

After your backup is complete, the SETUP program instructs you when to change disks. As installation continues, you are instructed to insert your UNINSTALL disk. This is a very important part of installing DOS 5 because this disk will be used to recover from any installation problems and provides the means to uninstall DOS 5 if necessary. Be sure to watch and follow the instructions very carefully!

The SETUP program also asks if you want to automatically start the DOS 5 Shell. The DOS 5 Shell is a graphical user interface that simplifies many DOS tasks, and often is much easier to use than the DOS command line. The Shell includes a task swapper that enables you to jump easily from program to program, displays your disk's directory structure in an easy-to-understand format, and supports a mouse as well as a keyboard. (Chapter 5 covers the Shell in detail.) SETUP adds a line to your AUTOEXEC.BAT file to start the DOS shell. If you later decide not to use the DOS shell, you can edit AUTOEXEC.BAT and remove the DOSSHELL command.

The SETUP program also offers a minimal installation option, /MIN, that you can use if you don't have enough space available on your hard disk. Unless absolutely necessary, however, you should avoid using the SETUP /MIN option. A minimal installation does not replace your existing DOS version's files—except for the three system files necessary for your PC to boot DOS V5.

After performing a minimal installation, your system can boot DOS 5, but cannot use any external DOS comands such as FORMAT, CHKDSK, or BACKUP. Any attempt to use these commands is greeted with the message `Incorrect DOS version`.

You may want to use the minimal installation option for two possible reasons. If your PC has a very small capacity hard disk and you cannot free enough space for a standard installation, the minimal installation option enables you to install DOS 5 using only those features and commands that will fit in the available space. You can, for example, decide to forego the DOS 5 Shell and QBasic to save about 800K of disk space.

You also can use the minimal installation option if your hard disk currently is partitioned with a primary partition too small to enable DOS 5 to be installed. Although you can repartition your hard disk as mentioned earlier in this chapter, you may decide that backing up all of your files, repartitioning your hard disk, and then restoring the files is too time-consuming. In this case, the minimal installation option would enable you to prepare your system so that it can boot using DOS 5. You then can copy the balance of the DOS 5 files to available space either in the primary partition or to one of the other existing partitions and then add a PATH command in AUTOEXEC.BAT that points to the location of those files.

To perform a minimal installation, follow these steps:

1. Install DOS 5 on floppy disks (see directions earlier in this chapter).

2. Using the SETUP disk, enter the command **A:SETUP /MIN** and follow the instructions on the screen.

3. Replace the existing DOS files in your DOS directory (usually C: \DOS) by copying the files from your set of DOS 5 working disks.

   If you have limited space, copy only the files you determine are necessary—you still will be able to use any other DOS commands by running them from the floppy disk.

> *Note:* Because the DOS files on the SETUP disks are in a compressed format, you cannot use the COPY command to place the files on your disk. Rather, use the EXPAND utility to uncompress and copy the files. EXPAND.EXE is found on disk #6 of the 5 1/4-inch disks or disk #3 of the 3 1/2-inch disks.

4. Rename AUTOEXEC.BAT and CONFIG.SYS as AUTOEXEC.OLD and CONFIG.OLD, respectively, using the REN command. Next, rename AUTOEXEC.NEW and CONFIG.NEW as AUTOEXEC.BAT and CONFIG.SYS.

5. Remove any floppy disks and reboot your system to load DOS 5 into memory.

As an alternative to the minimal installation, you may choose to install to floppy disks. You then may boot the computer with the floppy DOS 5 version and use the SYS command to transfer the operating system and COMMAND.COM to the hard disk. Then you may use the COPY command to copy the desired DOS programs to the hard disk.

Handling Installation Problems

Although it's very unlikely that you'll have any problems installing DOS 5, there's always the possibility that a disk could be damaged, your power could fail, or your system just won't run DOS 5 properly. The UNINSTALL disk created by the SETUP program is updated during installation and is used to recover from any problems. If errors occur, a message on your screen will instruct you to place the UNINSTALL disk in drive A:. Be sure to follow the instructions on your screen carefully, and you should be able to recover from most problems with little difficulty.

Note: The DOS 5 SETUP program creates either one or two disks, which you label as UNINSTALL disks. If you use a 5 1/4-inch, double density disk, SETUP creates two UNINSTALL disks—otherwise you have a single disk. Regardless of the capacity of the disk you use, you must use a disk that is compatible with your A: drive, because the UNINSTALL disk is used to boot your PC if you have a problem during the installation of DOS 5.

Uninstalling DOS 5

If you decide that you want to give up the many new features and enhancements that have been added to DOS 5, which is very unlikely, the SETUP program makes uninstalling DOS 5 easy. Just insert the UNINSTALL disk in drive A: and reboot your system. Follow the screen instructions to restore your previous version of DOS.

Before you decide to uninstall DOS 5, however, you should consider the following important points:

1. If you have reformatted, repartitioned, or used the DELOLDOS command to remove the old version DOS, you cannot uninstall DOS 5. Before performing any of the previous steps, verify that all programs you use work correctly with DOS 5.

2. DOS 5 has a new command, SETVER, which is designed to allow old programs that require a specific DOS version to run under DOS 5. These programs typically will give you a message such as `Incorrect DOS version` and refuse to run. Instead of giving up on DOS 5, see the discussion of SETVER in Chapter 10. You should find that DOS 5 can run any existing DOS program without problems.

3. DOS 5 provides many new features and enhancements. Unless you try these new features, you will never know how important they can be to your productivity and enjoyment of your PC.

Summary

In Chapter 2, you had a brief look at what you need to do to upgrade to DOS 5. Installing DOS 5 is only the first step. You will see in upcoming chapters that you can make many changes after you have completed the installation to optimize and customize your PC's setup.

Customizing Memory Usage with DOS 5

Chapter 3 covers the different types of memory available. You learn how to place device drivers, TSR programs, and much of DOS itself into high memory, thereby freeing conventional memory for your applications programs. The chapter also describes DOS 5's support for expanded memory.

Before You Begin

Changing your PC's memory usage can provide many benefits, but you accidentally may make changes that can prevent your system from functioning properly. Before you experiment with your system's configuration, therefore, take the following precautions:

- Always make certain that your hardware supports a feature before trying to include that feature in your system configuration. If your system has an 8088 or 80286 processor, for example, you will not be able to use features requiring an 80386 or 80486 chip.

- Prepare a bootable floppy disk before you make any changes to your configuration. Doing so enables you to boot your PC from the floppy, even if your system locks up when trying to boot from the hard disk. To create a bootable floppy, place a new disk in drive A: and type the following command:

FORMAT A: /S

Although this bootable disk will contain only the files IO.SYS, MSDOS.SYS, and COMMAND.COM, the disk can be used to boot your PC. You may copy additional DOS files to the disk, but you don't need to.

In determining which additional files you may want to copy to your floppy disk, consider those programs that can help you recover from any problems you may encounter. The following lists provide recommendations of files you may find useful, depending on the capacity of the floppy disk.

If you are using a 360K disk, the following files can be useful (in addition to IO.SYS, MSDOS.SYS, and COMMAND.COM):

BACKUP.EXE
CHKDSK.EXE
EDLIN.EXE
FDISK.EXE
FORMAT.COM
MEM.EXE
RESTORE.EXE
SYS.COM

If you are using a 720K or larger disk, you may want to include the following files:

ATTRIB.EXE
BACKUP.EXE
CHKDSK.EXE
DISKCOPY.COM
EDIT.COM
EDIT.HLP
FDISK.EXE
FORMAT.COM
MEM.EXE
MIRROR.COM
QBASIC.EXE
RESTORE.EXE
SYS.COM
UNDELETE.EXE
UNFORMAT.COM
XCOPY.EXE

Understanding CONFIG.SYS and AUTOEXEC.BAT

When you turn on or reboot your PC, your PC immediately searches the root directory for CONFIG.SYS and AUTOEXEC.BAT. These two files are optional, but serve an important purpose: they enable you to customize your system's operation.

CONFIG.SYS normally contains commands and directives that either cannot be typed at the DOS command line, or that should be used only once per session.

AUTOEXEC.BAT is a batch file, and therefore contains commands that you can type at the DOS command line. Chapter 4 covers CONFIG.SYS and AUTOEXEC.BAT in depth.

Understanding COMMAND.COM

COMMAND.COM is a special DOS program that reads and determines how to process your commands. COMMAND.COM often is referred to as the "command processor" and has a special DOS environment variable, COMSPEC, which points to its location. Although you can replace COMMAND.COM with another command processor, the MS-DOS command processor always is called COMMAND.COM.

When you type a command at the DOS prompt, COMMAND.COM examines what you typed and tries to determine how your input should be processed. In DOS versions prior to DOS 5, your input first was compared to a table of commands internal to COMMAND.COM. If a match was found, the matching internal DOS command was executed. If no match was found, DOS attempted to run an external program (one other than COMMAND.COM). In DOS 5, COMMAND.COM has been modified so that it first attempts to find a DOSKEY macro before looking at the internal command table (see Chapter 6 for more on DOSKEY).

Because COMMAND.COM processes your commands, the program must be loaded whenever you boot your PC. Otherwise, you receive the message `Bad or missing command interpreter` and your system quits.

Reviewing DOS 5 Memory Types

It's important that you understand the types of memory available in PCs. All PCs have conventional memory—extended, expanded, and reserved memory may be available depending upon your hardware and software. Past versions of DOS only supported conventional memory, but DOS 5 uses all types of memory if you have the right configuration.

Memory Terms

The following sections describe the types of memory important to users of DOS 5. The terms that refer to these memory types can be confusing, partly because they are so similar. The following table is included to remind you how each type of memory is described.

Table 3.1
Descriptions of Memory Terms

Memory Term	Description
Conventional	The first 640K of memory addresses on a PC. Available on all PC processors: 8086, 8088, 80286, 80386, 80386SX, and 80486.
Expanded	Paged memory used to provide extra memory for data. Also called LIM 3.2 or LIM 4.0 EMS memory. Can be installed using an expanded memory board on 8086, 8088, and 80286 PCs. Can be emulated on 80386, 80386SX, and 80486 PCs.
Extended	Memory that is addressed in a linear fashion above the 1M memory address limit. Available only on 80286, 80386, 80386SX, and 80486 PCs.
Reserved	Memory located above the 640K conventional memory and below the 1M address.

Memory Term	Description
XMS	Extended Memory Specification. A memory management specification for extended memory. HIMEM.SYS is the DOS 5 XMS memory manager. Available only on 80286, 80386, 80386SX, and 80486 PCs.
HMA	High Memory Area. The first 64K block of extended memory that is managed under XMS. The place where the DOS kernel is loaded when the DOS=HIGH directive is used. Available only on 80286, 80386, and 80486 PCs.
UMB	Upper Memory Blocks. Unused blocks of memory in the reserved memory area that can be used to load device drivers and TSR programs. EMM386.EXE is the UMB provider supplied with DOS 5. Available only on 80386 and 80486 PCs unless you obtain another UMB provider.

Conventional Memory

Personal computer capabilities have increased greatly in a relatively short time. Today's PCs, with 32-bit processors and megabytes of memory, have power that only the mainframe computers of the 1980s could provide. One limitation from the first design of the IBM-PC still exists: a 640K limit on conventional memory. DOS 5 can stretch this limit.

Early versions of DOS could address only 1M of memory because the Intel 8086 and 8088—the top microprocessors at the time—had only 20 address lines. Because the addressing function is binary (consisting of two states), 20 address lines can access 1,048,576 bytes, or 1M (two to the 20th power bytes). The later 80286 and 80386 have more than 20 address lines and can address far more memory than 1M.

Designers of early versions of DOS allocated 640K of the 1M of memory for applications programs, which seemed an adequate amount of memory at the time. The remaining 384K was reserved for various device drivers, ROM (read-only memory), graphics adapters, and other functions.

When the 80286 and 80386 microprocessors began to appear in PCs, DOS already had a huge installed user base. To accommodate the larger memory capacity of the newer CPUs, DOS would have had to abandon the installed base of users with 8086- and 8088-based PCs. DOS designers chose not to change the basic arrangement of DOS and to keep DOS uniform with the installed user base.

Two basic methods were developed to give programs access to the extra memory available with the more advanced microprocessors. The first method uses *extended memory* addressing. The second method accesses memory through a device driver and is called *expanded memory*. Currently, DOS supports the XMS (eXtended Memory Specification) standard for extended memory and the EMS (Expanded Memory Specification) standard for expanded memory.

Expanded Memory

Expanded memory enables even the 8086 to take advantage of more RAM. Some DOS programs (such as 1-2-3 Release 2.2) access the contents of expanded memory, or EMS, in real mode as addresses within the first 1M of memory. Using expanded memory, any CPU in the 8086 family can break the 1M memory barrier.

Expanded memory is accessed through a device driver as though the expanded memory were a device. The device driver "pages" (or temporarily assigns) expanded memory into part of the reserved memory. The portion of expanded memory is called a *page* and the portion of high conventional memory (located in reserved memory) is called a *page frame*. More than one memory page is associated with a page frame.

When the CPU addresses the page frame, the CPU actually accesses the values in a page of expanded memory. The expanded-memory device driver locates unused portions of reserved memory in 16K blocks and uses the blocks for page frames. To access all the pages of expanded memory, the driver must swap pages of memory in and out of the available page frame. When a program needs to access a page of expanded memory that is not in the page frame, the device driver must swap the new page into the page frame (and the old one back to expanded memory if any changes were made).

This swapping of page frames is a processing overhead that extended-mode addressing does not have. Because of this, most programs and device drivers that can use extended memory perform slightly better using expanded memory.

Expanded-memory operation, however, offers the capability for specially designed programs to enable even the older 8086 and 8088 processors to access more than 1M of memory through page frames.

Two different versions of EMS exist. LIM 3.2 and LIM 4.0 both use the paged switching of expanded memory. LIM 4.0, which is supported by DOS 5, provides for more flexible page-frame location and greater expanded-memory access. You still can use a LIM 3.2 expanded-memory board and driver with DOS 5, but because of the advantages mentioned for LIM 4.0, you may want to obtain the most recent version of the LIM software from the manufacturer of your expanded memory board.

The advanced memory-management features of the 80386, 80386SX, and 80486 processors emulate an expanded-memory adapter board. DOS 5 provides expanded-memory support for these processors through EMM386.EXE, a LIM 4.0 device driver. DOS 5 does not provide LIM 4.0 drivers for the expanded memory boards that often were installed in PCs with 8086, 8088, and 80286 chips because such drivers are specific to the particular expanded memory board.

Extended Memory

As a result of having 20 address lines, the Intel 8088 and 8086 processors, for which DOS was designed, can address 1M of memory. The Intel 80286 processor has 24 address lines and can address 16M of memory. The newer 80386, 80386SX, and 80486 have 32 address lines and can address 4G (gigabytes) of memory. Regardless of the processor, however, the first 1M of this address range addresses the system's conventional memory. Addresses above 1M are called extended-memory addresses. Any memory at these extended addresses is called extended memory and is unavailable on systems with 8086 and 8088 processors.

The 80286, 80386, 80386SX, and 80486 processors address conventional memory as the earlier 8086 does, by using an internal operating mode called *real mode*. In real mode, the microprocessors are restricted to the same 1M address range as the 8086. The newer microprocessors enter another mode (called *protected mode*) to address the extended-memory locations.

DOS became a standard before the advent of protected mode and cannot effectively take advantage of protected mode's extensive address range. Some DOS programs and device drivers, such as 1-2-3 Release 3.1, Windows 3.0, and SMARTDRV.SYS, can use extended memory. The programs switch the CPU from real mode to protected mode. These DOS programs and device drivers cooperate in extended memory use, but many older programs that use extended memory may not.

Protected mode and extended memory have some disadvantages when used with a real-mode operating system such as DOS. The switch from real to protected mode is not easy for a programmer to code. Programs that use extended memory must check carefully to determine which programs are using which extended memory. Additionally, programs that use protected mode and extended memory require the more modern 80286, 80386, 80386SX, or 80486 processors.

High Memory Area

The first 64K of extended-memory space is called the *High Memory Area* (HMA). (Note: The HMA officially starts at FFFF:10h and ends at FFFF:FFFFh, making it 64K-16 bytes in length.) If your PC has extended memory and you include the HIMEM.SYS device driver in your CONFIG.SYS file, the HMA becomes available. The HMA is unique because programs can be executed in HMA while in real mode (unlike the rest of extended memory, which requires protected mode).

At this time, only a few programs besides DOS 5 use the HMA. Later in this chapter, you learn how DOS 5 can place most of the DOS kernel into the HMA, freeing up a considerable amount of conventional memory.

XMS Memory

The HIMEM.SYS device driver manages extended memory according to a set of rules called the Extended Memory Specification or XMS. XMS includes the reserved memory between 640K and 1M, the HMA (the first 64K of extended memory), and the balance of extended memory (also called extended memory blocks).

XMS enables DOS programs to utilize extended memory found in 80286, 80386, 80386SX, and 80486 machines in a consistent manner. With some restrictions, XMS adds almost 64K to the 640K that DOS programs can access directly. XMS also provides DOS programs with a standard method of storing data in extended memory.

Reserved Memory

DOS addresses the first 640K of conventional memory as low memory and the remaining 384K as reserved memory. Until now, however, DOS was unable to make use of reserved memory. As you will see in the section on HIMEM.SYS, DOS 5's new features enable you to place device drivers and *terminate-and-stay-resident* (TSR) programs, such as Microsoft's MOUSE.COM mouse driver, in the Reserved Memory.

Accessing reserved memory requires an *Upper Memory Block* (UMB) provider. DOS 5 includes a UMB provider, EMM386.EXE. In order to use UMBs with DOS 5's UMB provider, you must have an 80386- or 80486-based PC, memory available between the 640K and 1M addresses, and include both the HIMEM.SYS and EMM386.EXE device drivers in your CONFIG.SYS file. (HIMEM.SYS and EMM386.EXE are required because EMM386.EXE remaps XMS memory to provide UMBs.)

Although the earlier versions of DOS have not been able to use reserved memory, several utility programs including QRAM, QEMM386, and 386MAX have provided this feature for some time.

Shadow RAM and UMBs

Because the memory addresses between 640K and 1M were inaccessible to DOS programs prior to DOS 5, many PC manufacturers developed a technique called *shadowing*. Using this technique, PC users can copy the information in the system ROM to RAM memory in the reserved memory address range. Accessing information in RAM usually is faster than accessing memory in ROM, so a slight performance gain is realized.

Because DOS 5 can make UMBs available in the reserved memory area and, as a result, free up conventional memory, ROM shadowing and UMBs now compete for the same memory space. Because of this, you probably should disable ROM shadowing if you intend to use UMBs. The section "Using HIMEM.SYS" describes one method for doing this; your PC's reference manual or manufacturer may offer another method.

UMBs on 8086, 8088, and 80286 PCs

Many 80286-based PCs (and some 8086 and 8088 PCs as well) have memory installed in the reserved memory space between 640K and 1M. DOS 5, however, does not provide the means to convert this memory into usable UMBs. The UMB provider supplied with DOS 5, EMM386.EXE, requires an 80386, 80386SX, or 80486 PC. You can, however, make use of memory located in the reserved space and provide UMBs for your device drivers and TSR programs even though DOS 5 doesn't provide this service.

One helpful product is QRAM by Quarterdeck Office Systems. QRAM can be used as a replacement for HIMEM.SYS and provides the HMA (if you have more than 1M of RAM), UMBs, and XMS extended memory. QRAM also includes other drivers that enable you to use EGA or VGA video memory and, if you have a LIM 4.0 expanded memory board, to use part of your expanded memory in place of UMBs.

Understanding MEM *(also DOS 4)*

All DOS versions include a multipurpose utility program called CHKDSK that, along with information about disk space utilization, gives a limited report on your PC's memory. The following example shows a typical CHKDSK display.

```
Volume Fixed C      created 10-13-1989 2:32p
Volume Serial Number is 1594-6E14

 67860480 bytes total disk space
    73728 bytes in 2 hidden files
   147456 bytes in 62 directories
 54530048 bytes in 1409 user files
    14336 bytes in bad sectors
 13092864 bytes available on disk

     2048 bytes in each allocation unit
    33135 total allocation units on disk
     6393 available allocation units on disk

   655344 total bytes memory
   190176 bytes free
```

As you can see, CHKDSK provides very little information about your system's memory. Only conventional memory is included in CHKDSK's report, and to see even that information requires waiting while the program searches your entire disk to gather disk space and file information.

As programs have become more complex, memory requirements have grown dramatically. With conventional memory limited to 640K, more and more programs rely on expanded and extended memory to provide the working room they need. Users of such programs need more information than CHKDSK provides.

Microsoft, therefore, introduced a totally new program, MEM.EXE, which was designed to provide in-depth information on memory availability and usage. The following sections examine these features of MEM and show you how to use them to your advantage.

The following syntax is used with the MEM command:

    MEM */PROGRAM*

    or

    MEM */DEBUG*

    or

    MEM */CLASSIFY*

/PROGRAM or /P displays programs loaded in memory. /DEBUG or /D displays programs, internal drivers, and other information. /CLASSIFY or /C, like /P and /D, lists programs in memory, but makes the distinction of whether a program is loaded in conventional memory or upper memory (UMB).

Available Memory

MEM replaces CHKDSK's very limited memory report with a more comprehensive report suited to today's larger programs. In addition to reporting on conventional memory, MEM also displays information on both expanded and extended memory if either or both are available on your system.

The following listing shows an example of a typical display produced by typing the command **MEM**, with no parameters:

```
 655360 bytes total conventional memory
 655360 bytes available to MS-DOS
 190208 largest executable program size

1048576 bytes total EMS memory
 442368 bytes free EMS memory

3538944 bytes total contiguous extended memory
      0 bytes available contiguous extended memory
 630784 bytes available XMS memory
        MS-DOS resident in High Memory Area
```

Because MEM displays much more information than CHKDSK, each section is examined separately to help you understand the report.

The first section reports on conventional memory—generally the first 640K of RAM in your system. This report should provide the same information as CHKDSK. In the above example, the report shows 655360 bytes total conventional memory or 640K. (1K equals 1024 bytes, therefore, 640K equals 640 times 1024 or 655,360 bytes.) The second line shows that all of the 640K is available to DOS, and the third line shows that 190,208 bytes are available for the largest executable program. In this case, 465,192 bytes have been used by DOS device drivers, the command processor, and other programs loaded into conventional memory.

The second section of MEM's report shows statistics on EMS (or expanded) memory. This section appears only if you have loaded an expanded-memory driver, which conforms to Version 4.0 of the Lotus-Intel-Microsoft Expanded Memory Specification (LIM EMS 4.0). EMS memory—sometimes referred to as paged memory—is used by many popular programs, including Lotus 1-2-3 Versions 2.x. In this example, **MEM displays** 1048576 bytes total EMS memory **and** 442368 bytes free

EMS memory. **All members of the Intel microprocessor "family," from the 8088 to the 80486, can support EMS memory.**

> *Note:* EMS memory may not be installed on all systems. Additionally, the expanded memory in many PCs conforms to earlier versions of the LIM specification and will not be included in DOS 5's MEM report.

The third section of the MEM report examines a system's extended memory. In the example shown, **MEM reports** 3538944 bytes total contiguous extended memory, 0 bytes available contiguous extended memory, **and** 630784 bytes available XMS memory. **You should not be alarmed by the** 0 bytes available contiguous extended memory **message—the HIMEM.SYS driver converts all extended memory into XMS memory. Although quite a bit of XMS memory seems to be missing, it really isn't. Some of the XMS memory is used by the expanded memory manager (converted by EMM386.EXE, as reported in the second section of the report) and some is allocated to the SMARTDRV.SYS disk cache program.**

Finally, **MEM reports** MS-DOS resident in High Memory Area. **The CONFIG.SYS directive DOS=HIGH places DOS in the high memory area and frees additional conventional memory for applications programs.**

The MEM /PROGRAM Switch

Although the basic MEM memory report is much better than CHKDSK's, by adding the /PROGRAM switch (which you can enter as /P) to the MEM command, you get a much more comprehensive report showing the address, name, size, and type of all programs loaded in conventional memory. The following listing demonstrates a typical MEM /PROGRAM report:

```
Address  Name   Size   Type
-------  ----   ----   ----
000000          000400 Interrupt Vector
000400          000100 ROM Communication Area
000500          000200 DOS Communication Area
```

continues

Address	Name	Size	Type
000700	IO	0009B0	System Data
0010B0	MSDOS	0014A0	System Data
002550	IO	00BCB0	System Data
	HIMEM	000440	DEVICE=
	EMM386	001A40	DEVICE=
	RAMBIOS	0035F0	DEVICE=
	SMARTDRV	004CE0	DEVICE=
		0005D0	FILES=
		000100	FCBS=
		000200	BUFFERS=
		0001C0	LASTDRIVE=
		001040	STACKS=
00E210	MSDOS	000080	--Free--
00E2A0	MOUSE	0047C0	Program
012A70	MSDOS	000040	System Program
012AC0	COMMAND	000930	Program
013400	MSDOS	000040	--Free--
013450	COMMAND	000200	Environment
013660	COMMAND	000040	Data
0136B0	MSDOS	0000C0	--Free--
013780	DOSKEY	000FC0	Program
014750	INSET	000110	Environment
014870	INSET	00BF60	Program
0207E0	SYMPHONY	000110	Environment
020900	SYMPHONY	050350	Program
070C60	COMMAND	000110	Data
070D80	COMMAND	000930	Program
0716C0	COMMAND	000100	Environment
0717D0	MEM	000110	Environment
0718F0	MEM	013480	Program
084D80	MSDOS	01B270	--Free--

```
 655360  bytes total conventional memory
 655360  bytes available to MS-DOS
 190208  largest executable program size

1048576  bytes total EMS memory
 442368  bytes free EMS memory
```

```
3538944   bytes total contiguous extended memory
      0   bytes available contiguous extended memory
 630784   bytes available XMS memory
          MS-DOS resident in High Memory Area
```

> *Note:* The optional /PROGRAM and /DEBUG switches produce a MEM report too large to display on a single screen. Although you can pause the display by using the MORE filter, it's better to redirect the report to your printer by adding >PRN to the command, or to a file so that you can examine the report with the help of an editor such as EDIT.

The MEM /PROGRAM report shows a considerable amount of information about the programs loaded into your system's conventional memory. This report, for example, starts by displaying the beginning address of the system interrupt vector table.

> *Note:* All of the addresses and sizes are shown in hexadecimal notation (base 16). The interrupt vector table, for example, has a listed size of 000400. You can use the QuickBasic interpreter to convert these numbers to decimal (base 10) notation. Converting this to base 10 shows that the interrupt vector table uses the first 1024 (1K) bytes of memory.

The listing includes several interesting items. HIMEM is listed as a device driver. This makes sense because one line in the system's CONFIG.SYS file shows `DEVICE=C:\DOS\HIMEM.SYS`. The rest of the installed device drivers, EMM386, RAMBIOS, and SMARTDRV also are shown in this area. By examining the size shown for each device driver, you can determine how much conventional memory each is using. This information can be quite useful if you are running out of memory room for some of your applications.

Notice that farther down the program, MOUSE is listed at address 00E2A0. This program's listing shows that MOUSE is a TSR program. The report also reveals that the MOUSE program uses 18,368 bytes of memory. This shows that if you load your mouse driver program automatically, even when the program isn't needed, you may be wasting memory.

Several blocks of memory are listed as --Free--. When these blocks are located anywhere except at the end of the list, they represent small blocks that are unused, but unavailable.

Following the program listing, MEM displays the same information shown in table 3.1.

The MEM /DEBUG Switch

Another MEM option, /DEBUG (which can be entered as /D), provides even more detail in some areas than the /PROGRAM option. In particular, the sections labeled as IO are expanded to show more about the various device drivers. The following listing shows the expanded device driver information provided by the MEM /DEBUG switch.

```
000700    IO       0009B0    System Data
          CON                System Device Driver
          AUX                System Device Driver
          PRN                System Device Driver
          CLOCK$             System Device Driver
          A: - C:            System Device Driver
          COM1               System Device Driver
          LPT1               System Device Driver
          LPT2               System Device Driver
          LPT3               System Device Driver
          COM2               System Device Driver
          COM3               System Device Driver
          COM4               System Device Driver

0010B0    MSDOS    0014A0    System Data

002550    IO       00BCB0    System Data
          HIMEM   000440     DEVICE=
            XMSXXXX0           Installed Device Driver
          EMM386  001A40     DEVICE=
            EMMXXXX0           Installed Device Driver
          RAMBIOS 0035F0     DEVICE=
            VGA BIOS          Installed Device Driver
          SMARTDRV 004CE0    DEVICE=
            SMARTAAR          Installed Device Driver
```

The /DEBUG switch also causes MEM to display information about any EMS handles, as shown in the following sample report.

```
Handle    EMS Name    Size
-------   --------    ----
      0               060000
      1               010000
      2               024000
```

Although much of the information, such as the EMS handle information, is of little use to the average user and also well beyond the scope of this book, the /DEBUG and /PROGRAM switches do provide a means of examining system resource usage in a much more detailed manner than was available previously. Through careful examination of these reports, you probably can discover areas in which you can save some memory for your applications.

The MEM /CLASSIFY Switch

The last MEM switch, /CLASSIFY, is a new switch added in DOS 5. This switch probably is the most useful of the three switches, especially if you are using an 80386SX, 80386, or 80486 computer. The /CLASSIFY switch shows you each file loaded in memory, how large the file is in decimal values, Kilobyte values, and in hexadecimal. The following listing shows the output created using the /CLASSIFY switch:

```
Conventional Memory :

Name            Size in Decimal          Size in Hex
------------    --------------------     -----------
MSDOS           13024      ( 12.7K)         32E0
SETVER            416      (  0.4K)          1A0
ADAPTEC           176      (  0.2K)           B0
HIMEM            1184      (  1.2K)          4A0
EMM386           8400      (  8.2K)         20D0
MOUSE           14320      ( 14.0K)         37F0
SMARTDRV        19696      ( 19.2K)         4CF0
ANSI             4192      (  4.1K)         1060
COMMAND          2768      (  2.7K)          AD0
FASTOPEN         1312      (  1.3K)          520
```

```
       DOSKEY                4128      (  4.0K)         1020
       FREE                    64      (  0.1K)           40
       FREE                    64      (  0.1K)           40
       FREE                585296      (571.6K)        8EE50


    Total  FREE :          585424      (571.7K)


    Upper Memory :


       Name              Size in Decimal         Size in Hex
    - - - - - - - - -     - - - - - - - - - - - -   - - - - - - - - -

       SYSTEM              163840      (160.0K)        28000
       MIRROR                6512      (  6.4K)         1970
       FREE                    64      (  0.1K)           40
       FREE                 26128      ( 25.5K)         6610


    Total  FREE :           26192      ( 25.6K)


    Total bytes available to programs (Conventional+Upper) :
                           611616      (597.3K)
    Largest executable program size :
                           585088      (571.4K)
    Largest available upper memory block :
                            26128      ( 25.5K)


       655360 bytes total EMS memory
       245760 bytes free EMS memory

      7733248 bytes total contiguous extended memory
            0 bytes available contiguous extended memory
      5177344 bytes available XMS memory
            MS-DOS resident in High Memory Area
```

When you use the /CLASSIFY or /C switch, you are shown files loaded in conventional memory and upper memory. Although most of the files are loaded in conventional memory, one memory-resident program, MIRROR, is loaded in upper memory. The MIRROR program was placed in upper memory using the LOADHIGH command.

Even with MIRROR loaded in upper memory, you have enough room to load in upper memory another file of up to 25K in size. You can, for example, use the CONFIG.SYS DEVICEHIGH statement to place SMARTDRV.SYS in upper memory. Placing SMARTDRV.SYS in upper memory would free nearly 20K of conventional memory.

After you display the programs loaded in memory, you are shown a report of the total combined conventional and upper memory available. You also are shown the largest amount of conventional memory in which the program can run, as well as the largest amount of upper memory.

Finally, the last lines are the same as when using MEM without switches. A report shows EMS memory, extended memory, and XMS memory, if any. You also are shown that MS-DOS is placed in the HMA.

The next section of this chapter covers techniques for optimizing memory usage. Later in the chapter, you see how to use these techniques with the information MEM provides.

Optimizing Your System's Memory Use

DOS 5 provides you with many options. Those options dealing with optimizing memory usage often take advantage of built-in features of today's more advanced processors and, in many cases, are not available to users whose systems have the older 8086 and 8088 processors. The physical limitations of the older processors prevent them from doing some of the things that must be done to provide these advanced features.

Although this section deals primarily with the methods DOS 5 provides for making the largest possible amount of memory available, you should keep in mind that some tradeoffs exist. Sometimes, for example, memory space gained at the expense of execution speed is a poor bargain. Allocating a certain portion of memory to utilities such as buffers or disk caches may be wiser than going for that last byte of free memory. Similarly, using some memory for your favorite TSR programs may make sense, if you find this improves your productivity. Fortunately, with DOS 5 you often can have the advantages of larger available conventional memory and also the performance and convenience enhancements of disk caches, device drivers, and TSRs.

Using HIMEM.SYS

HIMEM.SYS is an extended memory manager. As mentioned in the earlier sections describing the types of memory, extended memory is available only on systems using an 80286, 80386, 80386SX or 80486 processor. If your PC has an 8086 or 8088 processor, you will not be able to take advantage of the feature HIMEM.SYS offers. You may want to read this section, though, to learn what direction DOS is taking.

When extended memory first became available on PCs, no formal rules existed specifying how extended memory should be allocated. Unlike conventional memory, which was governed by DOS and therefore had specified methods for using memory, developers made their own rules for extended memory—rules that frequently were incompatible. If this situation had not changed, extended memory would have been of little benefit to anyone.

Fortunately, software developers agreed upon an eXtended Memory Specification (XMS) that standardized the way programs use extended memory, in much the same way that the earlier Expanded Memory Specification (EMS) standardized the use of expanded memory.

As an extended memory manager that conforms to the XMS standard, HIMEM.SYS manages the allocation of XMS memory to programs and device drivers. One of the very important areas of XMS memory is the High Memory Area (HMA).

The HMA is quite important in DOS 5 because HIMEM.SYS can make this memory function as an extension of a PC's conventional memory. Using HIMEM.SYS may make 620K of conventional memory available for applications programs.

HIMEM.SYS Installation

Installing the HIMEM.SYS driver is simple. Just include the following statement in your CONFIG.SYS file:

DEVICE=HIMEM.SYS

On most systems, of course, the DOS files are placed in a directory—typically C:\DOS. Instead of the preceding line, you can use the following command:

DEVICE=C:\DOS\HIMEM.SYS

Note: The *C:* portion of this CONFIG.SYS entry is optional, but serves the purpose of documenting the entry.

HIMEM.SYS Switches

In most situations, you don't need to use any of the optional switches. HIMEM.SYS provides the XMS support to extended memory programs and device drivers without them. For complete system optimization, however, the following switches are invaluable.

/HMAMIN

The /HMAMIN=m switch enables you to specify the minimum amount of memory a device driver or a TSR program must use before HIMEM.SYS allows them to use the HMA. You can set the minimum memory usage between the default of 0K and 63K.

This switch enables you to control which programs use the HMA. Programs smaller than the size you specify will not be loaded into the HMA.

Suppose that you have two TSR programs which will run correctly in the HMA. One of these programs, TSRCALC.EXE, requires 52K of memory for loading and execution. The other program, TSRJOKE.EXE, requires 23K of memory. Through experimentation you find that after loading DOS into the HMA (see "Placing DOS in High Memory" a little later in this chapter), you only have enough HMA space for one of the two programs. Because TSRCALC.EXE uses 52K and TSRJOKE.EXE uses 23K, loading TSRCALC.EXE into high memory and TSRJOKE.EXE into conventional memory leaves more conventional memory available. The following CONFIG.SYS line ensures that a TSR program must use 52K of the HMA in order to be loaded into high memory:

DEVICE=C:\DOS\HIMEM.SYS /HMAMIN=52

/NUMHANDLES

The /NUMHANDLES switch sets the maximum number of extended-memory block handles that can be used at one time. If you try to run too many programs simultaneously that use extended memory, you may need to increase the number of handles from the default setting of 32. You may select any number between 1 and 128, and because each handle uses only 6 bytes of memory, little penalty occurs for setting the number high. Suggesting the optimum number of extended-memory block handles is difficult because a program may use one handle or several. Increasing the number of handles to 64, for example, uses only an extra 192 bytes of memory.

To change the number of extended-memory block handles to 64, create the following CONFIG.SYS command line:

DEVICE=C:\DOS\HIMEM.SYS /NUMHANDLES=64

/INT15

The /INT15=xxxxK switch allocates extended memory for the Interrupt 15 Interface to software that uses Interrupt 15 to access extended memory. Programs such as Paradox, Oracle, QEMM, and Turbo EMS use this method. The value you specify (xxxxK) indicates the amount of extended memory you want HIMEM.SYS to make available to this type of program.

> **Note:** You may need to use the particular software's options to indicate how much extended memory is available through the Interrupt 15 Interface.

To make 512K of extended memory available through the Interrupt 15 Interface, use the following syntax:

DEVICE=C:\DOS\HIMEM.SYS /INT15=512

The need for the /INT15=xxxxK switch is likely to diminish as more software producers adopt the XMS standard for accessing extended memory.

/MACHINE

The /MACHINE:xxxx switch specifies which A20 handler is to be used. In some PCs, the system BIOS requires special handling if extended memory is to be used reliably. HIMEM.SYS includes the necessary programming for a number of PC systems.

> **Note:** As mentioned earlier in this chapter, 8086 and 8088 processors have 20 address lines. These address lines are numbered A0 through A19. The A20 address line is available only on systems with an 80286 or higher processor. Its presence indicates a machine that can use extended memory. The A20 address line, which is used to address memory above 1M, is controlled by the A20 handler; this is the reason for the /MACHINE switch.

If table 3.2 lists your PC, you should include the proper HIMEM.SYS /MACHINE:xxxx switch in your CONFIG.SYS file.

Table 3.2
Specifying the A20 Handler To Be Used

BIOS number	Name	Machine or BIOS
1	at	IBM AT
2	ps2	IBM PS/2
3	pt1cascade	Phoenix Cascade BIOS
4	hpvectra	HP "Classic" Vectra (A and A+)
5	att6300plus	AT&T 6300 plus
6	acer1100	Acer 1100
7	toshiba	Toshiba 1600 and 1200XE
8	wyse	Wyse 12.5 MHz 286 m/c
9	tulip	Tulip SX
10	zenith	Zenith ZBIOS

continues

Table 3.2 *(Continued)*

BIOS Number	*Name*	*Machine or BIOS*
11	at1	IBM PC/AT
12	at2	IBM PC/AT (alternative delay)
13	philips	Philips
14	fasthp	HP Vectra

To create the command for CONFIG.SYS, you may use either the BIOS number or the name. If your system is an IBM-PS/2, for example, you may use either of the following lines in CONFIG.SYS:

DEVICE=C:\DOS\HIMEM.SYS /MACHINE:2

or

DEVICE=C:\DOS\HIMEM.SYS /MACHINE:PS2

/A20CONTROL

You must specify whether the /A20CONTROL switch is :ON or :OFF. If you specify :ON, HIMEM.SYS takes control of the A20 address line, even if another program already was controlling it when HIMEM.SYS was loaded. Using the :OFF parameter enables HIMEM.SYS to take control of the A20 address line only if no other program was controlling it when HIMEM.SYS was loaded. You should not use the /A20CONTROL switch with the :ON parameter selected, because allowing two programs to control the use of extended memory is likely to cause problems.

The following is an example of the /A20CONTROL switch with the :OFF parameter selected:

DEVICE=C:\DOS\HIMEM.SYS /A20CONTROL:OFF

/SHADOWRAM

On many systems, the computer's ROM BIOS chips are copied to RAM during the boot process because accessing RAM usually is much faster than accessing ROM. When this is done, the memory area used is part of the UMBs. To save this memory area for device drivers and TSR programs, you can issue the following command:

DEVICE=C:\DOS\HIMEM.SYS /SHADOWRAM:OFF

HIMEM.SYS then prevents the ROM from being copied into RAM. Because most programs make at least some use of the ROM BIOS, however, using this switch will reduce your PC's performance. /SHADOWRAM:ON is the default setting.

/CPUCLOCK

A provision is built into HIMEM.SYS in case this device driver causes your system clock to slow down. If you find that your computer operates at a slower speed after installing HIMEM.SYS, consider using /CPUCLOCK.

To use this switch, add /CPUCLOCK:ON to the DEVICE=HIMEM.SYS statement in your CONFIG.SYS file. The default is /CPUCLOCK:OFF.

Now that you know the syntax for using HIMEM.SYS, you can examine what this program can do for you as a DOS 5 user.

Placing DOS in High Memory

Although most of the discussion about memory and HIMEM.SYS has concentrated on device drivers and TSR programs, DOS 5 has another memory trick—placing much of DOS itself in high memory.

As DOS has become more "feature rich" during its evolution from a relatively simple disk-operating system to the complexity of DOS 5, fitting everything into a small portion of conventional memory has become increasingly difficult. Even small items such as the text screens for on-line help take some room. At the same time, applications programs continue to demand more and more memory. By placing DOS into high memory, you can have the advantages of DOS 5's new features and provide considerably more memory for your other programs.

MS-DOS is made up of three main programs: the two system programs IO.SYS and MSDOS.SYS, and the command interpreter COMMAND.COM. As you use your PC, COMMAND.COM may be reloaded several times during a session, as some of the memory it uses is released for use by applications programs and then reclaimed when they terminate. Part of COMMAND.COM, though, must remain in memory all the time. In effect, COMMAND.COM is a TSR program that loads its transient portion as needed. When you think of DOS in this way, you can see the potential benefits of placing the TSR portion of COMMAND.COM into the HMA. This is exactly what DOS 5 enables you to do.

DOS HIGH for COMMAND.COM

Whether you can place DOS into HMA depends on several factors. All the conditions listed below must exist before you can place DOS into the HMA.

- The system must have an 80286, 80386, 80386SX, or 80486 processor. 8086 and 8088 processors cannot place DOS in the HMA.

- The system must have memory to provide the HMA. A PC with 640K does not have high memory.

- HIMEM.SYS (or another high memory provider) must be loaded in CONFIG.SYS.

- The DOS version must be 5.0 or later.

- The command DOS=HIGH must be included in CONFIG.SYS after the line that loads HIMEM.SYS.

> *Note:* If the DOS=HIGH command is included in CONFIG.SYS but the system does not have the HMA available, the DOS=HIGH command is ignored and COMMAND.COM is loaded into low memory. If this occurs, DOS supplies the following error message:
>
> ```
> HMA not available : Loading DOS low
> ```

Benefits for 80386 Systems

How much extra conventional memory becomes available when you load DOS high depends, in part, on what programs you need and how you use them. This section gives an example of the memory savings when DOS and a typical system's device drivers are moved from low to high memory. The system described uses a typical DOS 5 system configuration, which has HIMEM.SYS, SMARTDRV.SYS, MOUSE.COM, and DOSKEY.COM loaded. The following screen display uses the MEM program, a new part of DOS, to show the results when DOS is placed in low memory (as in past DOS versions):

```
655360 bytes total conventional memory
655360 bytes available to MS-DOS
537056 largest executable program size
```

As you can see, 118,304 bytes of conventional memory are used before any applications programs are loaded. Of the original 640K (655,360 bytes), only 524K is available.

Now add the following lines to CONFIG.SYS:

DEVICE=C:\DOS\HIMEM.SYS
DEVICE=C:\DOS\EMM386.EXE RAM
DOS=HIGH,UMB

Next, add the command LOADHIGH to the AUTOEXEC.BAT lines that load MOUSE.COM and DOSKEY (LOADHIGH is discussed later in the section "LOADHIGH for TSRs".) Change the following lines:

MOUSE /S100
DOSKEY DEL=DEL $1 /P

to:

LOADHIGH MOUSE /S100
LOADHIGH DOSKEY DEL=DEL $1 /P

After you make these changes and reboot your system, MEM shows results of DOS placed in high memory similar to the following screen display:

```
655360 bytes total conventional memory
655360 bytes available to MS-DOS
632896 largest executable program size
```

Instead of using 118,304 bytes of conventional memory, DOS, the device drivers, and the TSR programs use only 22,464 bytes; 632,896 bytes (618K) still remain available. In other words, loading DOS high has freed up 96K of conventional memory. This extra space enables you to process larger documents, load accessories such as spell checkers, or handle larger databases and spreadsheets.

Benefits for 80286 Systems with Extended Memory

If your system has an 80286 processor and you have extended memory, you load DOS into the HMA differently than as described in the previous section.

Instead of the directives used on an 80386-based PC, add the following lines to CONFIG.SYS:

DEVICE=C:\DOS\HIMEM.SYS
DOS=HIGH

You cannot use the command LOADHIGH to load MOUSE.COM and DOSKEY because no UMBs are available to 80286 systems. (UMBs are described in the section "Using Upper Memory Blocks.") After you make the changes above and reboot your system, MEM shows results similar to the following listing:

```
655360 bytes total conventional memory
655360 bytes available to MS-DOS
610176 largest executable program size
```

595K of conventional memory is still available, which is quite a bit more than when DOS is loaded low, in conventional memory. Exact figures will differ, depending on many factors, including which device drivers and TSR programs you normally use. Even so, placing DOS into the HMA saves considerable conventional memory.

To make even more conventional memory available, you may consider using a product like QRAM, which provides UMBs on 80286-based PCs. (QRAM was discussed earlier in this chapter.)

Benefits for 8086 and 8088 Systems

Because of the memory-addressing limitations of the 8086 and 8088 processors, PCs using those chips cannot place DOS into high memory. However, even with all its new features, DOS 5 uses slightly less memory than DOS 4. Even without placing DOS in high memory, PC users save about 4K of conventional memory. Products like QRAM can be used to place device drivers and TSR programs into LIM 4.0 expanded memory on these systems, freeing up even more conventional memory for users of 8086 and 8088 PCs.

Regardless of your choice of device drivers, TSR programs, and applications, taking advantage of DOS 5's ability to place many elements in high memory results in your having more conventional memory available.

Using Upper Memory Blocks

In addition to placing COMMAND.COM in the HMA, DOS 5 also enables you to load device drivers and TSR programs in reserved memory into Upper Memory Blocks (UMBs). UMBs are blocks of memory in the address range between 640K and 1M. UMBs are managed by HIMEM.SYS and are considered XMS memory. (XMS memory is memory above the 640K address limit, which is controlled by the extended memory manager—in this case HIMEM.SYS.)

> *Note:* Although DOS 5 provides support for UMBs only on 80386 and 80486 PCs, UMBs can be provided on any PC that has memory in the address range between 640K and 1M. The earlier section entitled "UMBs on 8086, 8088, and 80286 PCs" discussed one method of doing this.

UMBs are not always a single, contiguous block of memory. Often several small blocks can be used to load a number of device drivers and programs.

To make UMBs available for device drivers and programs, include the following lines in your CONFIG.SYS file:

DEVICE=C:\DOS\HIMEM.SYS

DEVICE=C:\DOS\EMM386.EXE RAM

DOS=HIGH,UMB

These commands load DOS into high memory and make UMBs available. To load DOS in low memory (as in previous versions of DOS), but still provide UMBs, include the following command instead:

DOS=LOW,UMB

You can specify NOUMB if you don't want UMBs available. Because this is the default setting, however, you are not likely to use this command.

> ***Note:*** Enabling UMBs is a three-fold process. First, HIMEM.SYS must be loaded to manage extended memory and provide DOS access to XMS memory. EMM386.EXE is a device driver that provides expanded memory on a 386 or a 486, but also manages the upper memory area. DOS=UMB creates and maintains the link between DOS and the upper memory area.

DEVICEHIGH for Device Drivers

With UMBs available, you can load many device drivers into high memory instead of into conventional memory. This makes more memory available for your applications programs.

> ***Note:*** Some device drivers may not work properly when loaded into UMBs. Most drivers supplied with DOS 5 should work; but others, especially older drivers supplied by a disk drive manufacturer, may not. Because device drivers are loaded when CONFIG.SYS is read during booting, one device driver that malfunctions when in HMA can cause your entire system to lock up. This is one reason that you should create a backup system disk when experimenting with device drivers and UMBs.

Suppose that you want to load DRIVER.SYS into conventional memory. You use the following syntax of the CONFIG.SYS command line:

> **DEVICE=***C:***DOS****DRIVER.SYS** */D:00* */F:01*

Loading this command line into UMBs instead, however, will save conventional memory. To do so, replace the preceding command line with the following:

> **DEVICEHIGH=***C:***DOS****DRIVER.SYS** */D:00* */F:01*

The only difference in the two commands is that in the second command, DEVICEHIGH= is used instead of DEVICE=. You may want to load several other device drivers into UMBs instead of into conventional memory. Depending on your needs, you also may want to consider PRINTER.SYS, SMARTDRV.SYS, and any other device drivers you normally use (such as a VGA BIOS driver, for example).

LOADHIGH for TSRs

TSR programs load into memory and then return the DOS prompt. Typically, a TSR program ties into one of the DOS interrupt vectors (such as the keyboard or printer controller) and performs its tasks in the background. One common TSR program is MOUSE.COM, the Microsoft mouse driver. Depending on the version of MOUSE.COM you use, between 4K and 18K of memory may be needed to load the program. Because MOUSE.COM also works just as well when loaded into high memory, you may want to consider placing it in UMBs.

Entering the following AUTOEXEC.BAT or DOS command line loads MOUSE.COM in conventional memory and sets the mouse sensitivity to the maximum:

MOUSE /S100

To load MOUSE.COM in a UMB instead, add the command LOADHIGH:

LOADHIGH MOUSE /S100

Many TSR programs, including DOSKEY (see Chapter 6), can be loaded into UMBs. Some programs, however, do not work properly when loaded high. While you experiment, issue the LOADHIGH command from the DOS prompt instead of adding the command to AUTOEXEC.BAT. Then, if the program you're trying to load into high memory crashes your system, you can reboot without problems.

Deciding What To Load High

As you change CONFIG.SYS and AUTOEXEC.BAT to add device drivers and TSR programs to UMBs, you may find that the MEM /CLASSIFY report shows that some of the programs have been loaded into conventional memory instead. If this happens, you may need to reconsider which device drivers and TSRs to place in UMBs.

Suppose that you have several device drivers and TSR programs to load into UMBs, but you find that the last one you tried to load ended up in conventional memory. The first step you should take is to find out how much room each program requires and compare this to the amount of UMB space available. You can use the MEM /CLASSIFY report to determine these sizes.

Suppose that before loading any device drivers and TSR programs, MEM /CLASSIFY shows a free block with a size of 65504 bytes. You want to load the following device drivers and TSR programs in UMBs:

RAMBIOS.SYS	10008
MOUSE	18368
CAPTURE	23600
DOSKEY	4032
MYCALC	37032

	93040

As you can see, the device drivers and TSR programs cannot all fit in the 65504 bytes available. You may decide that MYCALC will not fit, but then you will not be getting the best use of your UMBs. If you total up various byte combinations, you find that RAMBIOS, MOUSE, and MYCALC total 65408 bytes. Loading these three into UMBs, and loading CAPTURE and DOSKEY in conventional memory saves nearly 10K of conventional memory—a better solution than simply loading MYCALC in conventional memory.

Another problem you may encounter is that EMM386.EXE may provide two or more UMB areas of different size. If this happens, you may find that the order in which you load different device drivers and TSR programs affects UMB use. This is because device drivers and TSR programs must be loaded into a single block; they cannot span two noncontiguous blocks. You may have enough UMB space, but unless you load your device drivers and TSR programs in the proper order, the space may be wasted.

Suppose that using MEM /PROGRAM, the report shows two UMB areas, each containing 48,000 bytes. The 96,000 byte total is enough to load all of the device drivers and TSR programs in the above example. If you try to load them in the order listed, RAMBIOS and MOUSE load into the first block, CAPTURE and DOSKEY load into the second, and MYCALC loads into conventional memory. This happens because loading RAMBIOS and MOUSE does not leave enough space for CAPTURE in the first block. If you change the loading order so that MYCALC is loaded before MOUSE, however, all five device drivers and TSR programs can fit in the two blocks.

Because of the many differences in device drivers, TSR programs, and memory configurations, providing exact rules for the best possible UMB use in every case is impossible. These examples, however, give you general guidelines for decisions you need to make if you plan to place programs in UMBs.

> ***Note:*** Because DOS 5 can place device drivers into UMB, lower addresses of conventional memory are made available. If you are loading a "packed," or compressed, program and you receive the message `Packed File Corrupt`, your program cannot be loaded successfully into the first 64K of conventional memory. This error occurs if you load device drivers into reserved memory, therefore freeing up more low conventional memory.
>
> DOS 5 provides the LOADFIX command, which ensures that a program is loaded above the first 64K of conventional memory. If this message occurs, precede your program command with LOADFIX:
>
> **LOADFIX** *command*

Important Options for EMM386.EXE

The DOS 5 UMB provider, EMM386.EXE, requires you to supply one of the following arguments.

If you use the RAM argument (shown earlier in this chapter), EMM386.EXE sets aside a portion of reserved memory for the LIM 4.0 EMS page frame. This means that programs needing expanded memory will be able to use expanded memory; but less space will be available for UMBs.

If you use the NOEMS argument, no EMS page frame is reserved and more space is available for UMBs. Expanded memory, however, will not be available to your programs.

You must supply one of the two arguments; otherwise, EMM386.EXE defaults to provide expanded memory management only and no UMBs will be available.

Includes LIM 4.0 EMS Driver

For systems using 80386 and 80486 processors, EMM386.EXE also acts as a device driver and a controller for the device driver. When you load EMM386.EXE by issuing a CONFIG.SYS command line, you can use EMM386.EXE as a control program to set the status of the driver.

In the earlier section explaining expanded memory (or EMS), you learned that EMS memory is paged memory that is made available through device drivers. Often, the device driver is provided with an expanded memory board that you install in your PC. Systems using 80386 and 80486 processors, however, have special capabilities that enable them to emulate expanded memory by using any extended memory they may have. This capability makes it possible for DOS 5 to provide expanded memory support on these systems.

Supports Programs Using Expanded Memory

Suppose that you have an 80386 PC with extended memory and you sometimes use Symphony, a program that uses expanded but not extended memory. At other times you use AutoCAD 386, which requires extended but not expanded memory. With DOS 5, you can easily accommodate both types of programs.

To provide LIM 4.0 EMS support, you first must add the following line to CONFIG.SYS. (Note: This line must come later than the one that loads HIMEM.SYS):

DEVICE=C:\DOS\EMM386.EXE

This command loads EMM386.EXE as a device driver using the default parameters. Because none of the optional parameters are specified, the expanded memory manager goes to its default settings—AUTO mode and no Weitek math coprocessor support.

AUTO mode means that expanded memory is provided when applications request it, but are not in effect otherwise. You also can specify ON or OFF.

Weitek math coprocessor support applies only to systems containing a special math coprocessor—not the Intel 80387. If you attempt to use the W=ON switch and do not have a Weitek math coprocessor installed, you receive an error message.

When loaded in AUTO mode, EMM386.EXE determines when a program needs expanded memory. Programs that don't use expanded memory can use extended memory instead.

Other parameters are available when you load EMM386.EXE as a device driver. See the Command Reference for additional parameters.

Supports VCPI

Expanded memory managers use a DOS interrupt to access expanded memory. Several DOS extenders, such as those from Phar Lap, use the *Virtual Control Program Interface* (VCPI) specification to access extended memory by using the same DOS interrupt. The VCPI is a software specification for programs running in systems with 80286 or 80386 processors that use protected mode, or on 80386 systems that use virtual 8086 mode. Although Microsoft has developed its own method of accessing extended memory, called *DOS Protected Mode Interface* (DPMI), EMM386.EXE cooperates with programs that use VCPI.

You may be interested in the VCPI and DPMI if you use software that relies upon a DOS extender to address more than 640K of memory. Examples of these programs are AutoCAD 386 and Lotus 1-2-3 Release 3.0.

Summary

This chapter described the many options DOS 5 provides for customizing your PC's memory usage. The chapter reviewed the different types of memory available on today's PCs, and showed how you can use new features of DOS 5 to provide the best mix of conventional, expanded, and extended memory to your programs. You learned how to place DOS, device drivers, and TSR programs into the High Memory Area and Upper Memory Blocks.

For more detailed information on using DOS 5's new memory features, you may want to refer to the following Que titles: *Using MS-DOS 5* and *Que's MS-DOS 5 User's Guide, Special Edition*.

Configuring DOS 5

In earlier chapters, you looked at DOS commands that you can use during daily operation of your PC. Chapter 4 covers commands that, in most cases, are less familiar to the average PC user. The configuration commands are important to how your system functions, but are not the types of commands that you probably spend much time thinking about. Take the time, though, to read through this chapter. You may find ways to improve how your PC works.

Using CONFIG.SYS or AUTOEXEC.BAT

Configuration commands are used most commonly in your CONFIG.SYS or AUTOEXEC.BAT file to customize the basic setup of your PC. These files have a direct affect on how software functions, your screen's appearance, foreign language support, how your disk drives appear to the system, whether extended or expanded memory is available, and how fast commands can be executed.

Some common configuration options that you already may be familiar with are the BUFFERS and FILES commands used in CONFIG.SYS, and the PATH and PROMPT commands often seen in AUTOEXEC.BAT. These commands, along with a number of other commands, directly affect your day-to-day system use. Knowing how to use these commands properly can result in considerable improvement in your efficiency and enjoyment of your PC.

This book, of course, is intended to introduce the new features available in DOS 5. This book does not cover the use of the configuration commands and options available in previous releases of DOS (although some commands and options also available in DOS 4 are covered for those readers who still are using earlier DOS versions). If you need more information on using configuration commands and options from earlier DOS versions, Que has several books that can help you: *MS-DOS User's Guide*, Special Edition; *Using DOS*; *MS-DOS QuickStart*; and *MS-DOS Quick Reference*.

Using the INSTALL Directive *(also DOS V4)*

INSTALL often is called a directive instead of a command. The difference is minor. INSTALL is used exclusively as a command (or directive, if you prefer) in CONFIG.SYS.

> *Note:* CONFIG.SYS and AUTOEXEC.BAT are special files on a PC. When you load DOS, either by turning on your system's power or by pressing Ctrl-Alt-Del to reboot, your system looks for these two files in the root directory of the disk from which you're loading DOS. If either or both files exist, the commands they contain are read and executed automatically. You don't need to have either file, but they are quite useful in customizing the PC's operation.

Don't confuse the CONFIG.SYS INSTALL command with the installation programs used by many software packages. When the directions for installing a program instruct you to type the command **INSTALL** at the DOS prompt, you're using an installation program. In this section, however, we're dealing only with the INSTALL command used in CONFIG.SYS.

INSTALL was designed to load any of four different driver programs. These programs, supplied as part of DOS, are intended to be loaded once during a DOS session and cannot be unloaded except by rebooting your system. The four programs are as follows:

```
FASTOPEN.EXE
KEYB.COM
NLSFUNC.EXE
SHARE.EXE
```

You may wonder why you load these driver programs in CONFIG.SYS using the INSTALL command instead of loading them when you need them or in AUTOEXEC.BAT. The primary reason is that by loading a driver in CONFIG.SYS, you can be certain that the driver will not be loaded more than one time per DOS session—CONFIG.SYS commands are executed only when the system boots.

The INSTALL command is very easy to use because it has no options. The following syntax for INSTALL is quite simple:

INSTALL=*drive:path***filename.ext** *parameters*

In this syntax, *drive* is the disk drive letter where the program you're installing is located. The drive designator normally is optional because it usually is the same as the drive from which you boot.

path is the name of the directory where the program is located. If the program is in the root directory, path also is optional. Note, however, that because the directives in CONFIG.SYS are executed before those in AUTOEXEC.BAT, any PATH command contained in AUTOEXEC.BAT will not yet be in effect when the INSTALL command is executed.

filename.ext is the complete file name of the program being loaded. The file extension is not optional. To load SHARE, for example, you must specify the file name as SHARE.EXE.

parameters are optional arguments that are passed to the program being installed. Parameters are not evaluated or acted upon in any way by the INSTALL command.

Suppose, for example, that you want to use the INSTALL command to load a screen-capture program called CAPTURE.EXE. The program is located on drive C: in a directory called GRABIT and requires a parameter advising the display type—/VGA, for example. A typical CONFIG.SYS command line may look like the following:

INSTALL=C:\GRABIT\CAPTURE.EXE /VGA

If your system boots from drive C:, you can eliminate the C:\ from the INSTALL line. You can leave C:\ in the command line if you want, however—CONFIG.SYS is a little easier to understand if documented by using complete commands.

You now will take a brief look at the four INSTALL drivers that accompany DOS 5.

Using NLSFUNC

NLSFUNC.EXE (for National Language Support FUNCtion) is a DOS program that hooks into DOS and provides programs with extended information about a specified country. NLSFUNC also enables you to use the CHCP (change code page) command. If you will be switching code pages for any device except the keyboard, you need the NLSFUNC command. Code pages are discussed in the next section, "Understanding Code Pages."

Certain applications programs may require that you run NLSFUNC. These programs use the new extended country information provided by DOS. Your program's documentation should state whether the program requires NLSFUNC.

Because NLSFUNC becomes part of DOS, using NLSFUNC increases DOS's use of RAM by almost 2,700 bytes. NLSFUNC remains in memory until you turn off the computer or restart DOS, so you need to run NLSFUNC only once after you have started DOS. Running NLSFUNC a second time produces an error message. To prevent this error, load NLSFUNC using the INSTALL command in CONFIG.SYS.

The single parameter to NLSFUNC is the full file name to the COUNTRY.SYS file. Assuming your NLSFUNC.EXE and COUNTRY.SYS files are located in your C:\DOS directory, you can use the following command in your CONFIG.SYS file to load national language support:

INSTALL=C:\DOS\NLSFUNC.EXE C:\DOS\COUNTRY.SYS

Understanding Code Pages

To understand how international-character support works in DOS, you first need to understand the concept of code pages. Code pages enable the computer to use, display, and print non-English language characters with minimal effort on your part.

Your computer uses ASCII to communicate to peripherals. ASCII is the standard manner of translating the numeric values 0 to 255 into letters, numbers, and symbols. The dots that form the visible characters on-screen are the graphic representations of those ASCII values.

Each video adapter displays a dot-formed representation of ASCII characters. The common name for the "shape" of characters is font. Depending on the adapter in use, the fonts may be switchable, meaning that different character sets can be displayed. Although the older MDA (Monochrome Display Adapter) and CGA (Color Graphics Adapter) cannot use code pages, newer adapters such as EGA (Enhanced Graphics Adapter) and VGA (Video Graphics Array) can.

Basically, a *code page* is a font set. You may recognize names for typewriter and typesetting faces, such as Courier, Elite, and Times Roman. Similarly, code pages enable you to use different typefaces of English and international language characters.

The five international font sets are listed in table 4.1. Depending on the code page used, you can display various language characters, as indicated in the table.

Table 4.1
Code Page Numbers

Font	Code page number
United States (English)	437
Multilingual	850
Portuguese	860
Canada (French)	863
Nordic	865

Suppose, for example, that you hold down the Alt key and enter *236*, using the numeric keypad. Each font set except the Multilingual code page displays the infinity character. The Multilingual code page displays an accented Y. Hold down Alt and enter *157* using the numeric keypad, and the United States set displays a double-bar Y. If you use the Multilingual or Nordic sets, you get a 0 (zero) with a slash through the number. The Portuguese and French Canadian sets have a back-accented U in this position. Many characters are identical in all five sets, but some are customized for various localities.

Some printers also can use code pages; what can be displayed on-screen therefore can be produced on the printed page. DOS includes code pages for IBM printers. You can expect other printer manufacturers to provide code pages for their printers in the near future. Many printers now emulate to some degree one of these IBM printers. Check your printer manual to determine the printer's code page compatibility.

Most North American users find the built-in DOS code pages adequate and probably never use code page switching. Switching code pages may be important for international users, however, including those who have files established in early versions of DOS. In addition, the ability to change fonts quickly can be valuable. International users will find that code pages provide a logical and powerful way to handle languages.

Extending a Keyboard's Code Capability with KEYB

The KEYB command is used to switch between keyboards and their associated code pages. Different languages need different character sets; the alternative sets supplied with the PC enable a variety of languages to be used. When loaded, the program alters the keyboard layout, enabling you to type in foreign-language characters. KEYB also changes the video display when the DEVICE=DISPLAY.SYS command is included in CONFIG.SYS and if you issue the appropriate MODE commands to prepare and select a code page for your display.

After a keyboard driver is loaded, DOS treats the driver as a device. As you type, DOS converts the key scan codes to the appropriate characters for the current keyboard device. Switching between keyboards causes DOS to use a different "translation table" to convert what is typed at the keyboard into characters on-screen.

When KEYB is active, it reassigns some alphanumeric characters to different keys and introduces new characters. The new layout and characters vary among the different supported languages.

Some of the new characters are symbols or punctuation marks, such as the United Kingdom's pound sterling sign or the Spanish inverted question mark. Most new characters have diacritics, such as the acute accent, grave accent, circumflex, or umlaut.

If you want to see the keyboard layouts for foreign languages, consult your computer's operating manual. For older machines that do not have this information, ask your computer dealer or supplier for a copy of the appropriate pages.

Using the /ID Switch To Identify Keyboard *(also DOS V4)*

Each keyboard has a different keyboard layout, ID, and supported code pages. The French, Italian, and British keyboard layouts, for example, are available with two different keyboards, each with its own ID. Two code pages are supported on these keyboards.

To use KEYB, you can use the following syntax:

KEYB *keycode,codepage,d:path\filename.ext /ID:code*

or

KEYB *code*

In this syntax, *keycode* is the two-character keyboard layout name and *codepage* is the three-digit code page number. *d:path\filename.ext* is the drive, path, and file name for the keyboard device driver. *code* is the keyboard identification code.

The available keyboard drivers are shown in table 4.2.

Table 4.2
Keyboard Drivers

Keyboard layout	Code pages	Keyboard ID	Country
BE	850, 437	120	Belgium
CF	863, 850	058	Canada (French-speaking)
DK	850, 865	159	Denmark
FR	437, 850	120, 189	France
GR	437, 850	129	Germany
IT	437, 850	141, 142	Italy
LA	437, 850	171	Latin America
NL	437, 850	143	Netherlands
NO	850, 865	155	Norway
PO	850, 860	163	Portugal
SF	850, 437	150	Switzerland (French-speaking)
SG	850, 437	000	Switzerland (German-speaking)
SP	437, 850	172	Spain
SU	850, 437	153	Finland
SV	437, 850	153	Sweden
UK	437, 850	168, 166	United Kingdom
US	437, 850	103	United States

Installing KEYB in CONFIG.SYS
(also DOS V4)

The INSTALL directive can be used to load KEYB from the CONFIG.SYS file instead of the command line. Although using KEYB a second time is permitted, if you need to use different code pages with your keyboard, you will want the code pages installed every time you use your PC. By using the command

> **INSTALL=C:\DOS\KEYB** *keycode,codepage*
> *d:path\filename. ext /ID:code*

in your CONFIG.SYS file, you will be certain the correct keyboard driver always is loaded when you need it.

Using the /E Switch for Enhanced Keyboards

The enhanced keyboard, which was introduced with the IBM-AT, really was not intended for use on the older 8088 and 8086 PCs. Versions of KEYB prior to DOS 5 do not, in fact, recognize the enhanced keyboard on these systems. Many PC users, however, have 8088- and 8086-based PCs with enhanced keyboards. The /E switch forces KEYB to assume that an enhanced keyboard is installed. Using the /E switch is not necessary on 80286, 80386, 80386SX, or 80486 systems because they correctly report the installed keyboard type.

Using SHARE

SHARE is the DOS program for file and record locking. You use SHARE when two or more programs or processes share a single computer's files. After SHARE is loaded, DOS checks each file for locks whenever the file is opened, read, or written. If a file has been opened for exclusive use, an error message results from any subsequent attempt to open the file. If one program locks a portion of a file, an error message results if another program attempts to read or write the locked portion.

As mentioned in Chapter 1, DOS 5 no longer requires that SHARE be loaded for hard disks larger than 32M. DOS 4, however, requires SHARE if your hard disk is partitioned with a portion larger than 32M.

If you need the file and record locking provided by SHARE, you can use INSTALL in the CONFIG.SYS file to load SHARE.EXE. In the CONFIG.SYS file, for example, the line

INSTALL=C:\DOS\SHARE.EXE

loads SHARE if SHARE.EXE is found in the \DOS subdirectory on drive C:.

As with NLSFUNC.EXE, your applications software manual probably will tell you if you need to install SHARE.EXE on your system. SHARE was not designed to work on a network in which two or more computers may attempt to access the same files at the same time. SHARE was designed to control access to files by two or more programs running at the same time on a single PC. Multitasking or task-switching control programs are examples of programs that may require SHARE.EXE.

If your software doesn't require SHARE.EXE, you can save a small amount of memory by not loading the program. Depending on your DOS version and the method you use to load SHARE.EXE, the memory saved may vary from about 4900 bytes to 6400 bytes. If you must load SHARE.EXE, using the INSTALL directive in CONFIG.SYS saves about 50 bytes of memory, compared to loading SHARE in AUTOEXEC.BAT.

SHARE.EXE may be loaded automatically into your system's memory even if the program isn't included in either CONFIG.SYS or AUTOEXEC.BAT. If the SHARE.EXE program file is in the root directory of the disk you boot from or is found in a directory included in the PATH command, DOS 4.0 and DOS 4.01 automatically load SHARE if you have a hard disk that is greater than 32M in a single partition. WINDOWS/286 Versions 2.03, 2.10, and 2.11 also load SHARE.EXE if the programs can find SHARE—regardless of your hardware configuration.

Before DOS 5, hard disks larger than 32M required SHARE.EXE because a very old and no longer recommended method of accessing files, using File Control Blocks (FCBs), assumed that all disks were smaller than 32M. SHARE.EXE changed FCB file accesses into the preferred File Handle method of accessing files. If you didn't load SHARE.EXE and an old program tried to access the files on the hard disk using FCBs, the access would fail. With the introduction of DOS 5, however, the task of translating FCB file accesses into File Handle accesses is performed automatically by the DOS kernel program itself, and SHARE.EXE no longer is necessary.

Using FASTOPEN To Track Files and Directories

FASTOPEN, which was introduced originally with DOS 3.3, allocates memory to store directory information. FASTOPEN partially solves a performance problem not resolved by the CONFIG.SYS BUFFERS directive. Although BUFFERS helps when your computer reads or writes information to several files, BUFFERS is not of much help if you use many of the same files during the day. The time DOS spends traversing the subdirectory system and opening the files may take more time than actually reading or writing the files.

FASTOPEN caches (or buffers) directory information, holding in memory the locations of frequently used files and directories.

FASTOPEN's syntax is as follows:

INSTALL=*d:path***FASTOPEN.EXE d:=***nnn* . . . */X*

or

d:path**FASTOPEN d:=***nnn* . . . */X*

> *Note:* You use INSTALL and the EXE extension only if you use this line in CONFIG.SYS.

The *d:path*\ parameter is the disk drive and path to the FASTOPEN.EXE file. The **d:** following the file name is the name of the hard drive you want FASTOPEN to act on and is a mandatory part of the command. The *nnn* parameter is the number of directory entries that FASTOPEN should cache. Each file or subdirectory requires one directory entry, and you can enter a value from 10 to 999. If you do not specify a value for *nnn*, DOS defaults to 10.

Using the /X Switch To Place Name Cache in Expanded Memory

Although FASTOPEN can speed up the opening of files, the memory requirements can be considerable. Each directory entry stored in memory takes approximately 48 bytes. If you were to track the maximum of 999 files, FASTOPEN's cache buffer would use almost 48K of conventional memory. You again are faced with the problem of choosing between using software that can improve your system's performance and saving memory for applications programs.

Fortunately, FASTOPEN has been enhanced with the addition of the /X switch, which enables you to place the cache entries in expanded memory.

> *Note:* FASTOPEN's /X switch uses expanded, not extended memory. Expanded memory is a special type of memory provided by an expanded memory driver program such as EMM386.EXE (which is part of DOS 5). Expanded memory must conform to the LIM (Lotus-Intel-Microsoft) 4.0 specification. In addition to EMM386.EXE for 80386, 80386SX, and 80486 systems, expanded memory software is provided by manufacturers of expanded memory boards for 80286 and 8088 PCs.

Because FASTOPEN's /X switch uses expanded memory instead of extended memory, the /X switch can be used on any PC that has an expanded memory driver. This enables you to place the cache entries in expanded memory even on older PCs that do not support extended memory.

If you want to install FASTOPEN on a PC that doesn't have expanded or extended memory, you can use the following command in your CONFIG.SYS file:

INSTALL=C:\DOS\FASTOPEN.EXE C:=100

This command line makes the assumption that your FASTOPEN.EXE program file is in the C:\DOS directory and that you want to cache 100 directory entries for your hard disk, drive C:.

Suppose, however, that you have an expanded memory board with software supporting the LIM 4.0 specification on your PC. Instead of placing FASTOPEN's name cache in conventional memory, you can place it in expanded memory by adding the /X switch in the following command:

INSTALL=C:\DOS\FASTOPEN.EXE C:=100 /X

By making this change, FASTOPEN uses approximately 1.3K of conventional memory instead of the nearly 8K when the /X switch is not used.

Because DOS 5 does not provide a LIM 4.0 driver for 8088 and 80286 PCs, you may not be able to place FASTOPEN's name cache into expanded memory even if you have an expanded memory board in your system. Many of the expanded memory boards installed in older systems support LIM 3.2 (or even earlier versions) but do not include LIM 4.0 support. If your PC's expanded memory board doesn't support LIM 4.0, you may want to contact the expanded memory board's manufacturer to see if a newer version of the expanded memory manager software is available. Alternatively, PC Magazine has a LIM 4.0 driver, EMS40.SYS, available on CompuServe. This device driver, which works only on 80286 PCs, converts extended memory into LIM 4.0 expanded memory.

If you have an 80386, 80386SX, or 80486 PC, DOS 5 includes a LIM 4.0 expanded memory manager called EMM386.EXE, which works just fine with FASTOPEN. The next example uses HIMEM.SYS and EMM386.EXE to provide FASTOPEN.EXE with expanded memory.

Using HIMEM.SYS and EMM386.EXE To Provide Expanded Memory

Suppose that you have an 80386-based PC, you want to cache 100 directory entries for drive C:, and your DOS files are in C:\DOS. You first have to check your CONFIG.SYS file to ensure that both HIMEM.SYS and EMM386.EXE are loaded. Your entries may look like the following:

```
DEVICE=C:\DOS\HIMEM.SYS
DEVICE=C:\DOS\EMM386.EXE 640
```

The first line loads HIMEM.SYS and the second line loads EMM386.EXE, which provides 640K of expanded memory. Be sure HIMEM.SYS appears before EMM386.EXE, or no extended memory will be available for EMM386.EXE to convert to expanded memory.

Next, you need to add the line for FASTOPEN to CONFIG.SYS. (Although FASTOPEN can be loaded from the DOS prompt or in AUTOEXEC.BAT, it can be loaded only once per DOS session—loading FASTOPEN in CONFIG.SYS is safer.) The following CONFIG.SYS line adds FASTOPEN using the settings discussed earlier:

INSTALL=C:\DOS\FASTOPEN.EXE C:=100 /X

If you have additional hard disks that you want FASTOPEN to track, add their entry on the same line—you cannot install FASTOPEN more than once per session.

You should observe two restrictions when using FASTOPEN. First, the disk drive that you name cannot be one on which you use JOIN, SUBST, or ASSIGN, because these commands do not create "real" drives. Second, if you load a disk drive device driver through AUTOEXEC.BAT rather than through CONFIG.SYS (some manufacturers provide a driver that must be started from a batch file or from the DOS prompt rather than from CONFIG.SYS), you must use FASTOPEN after you define all disk drives. FASTOPEN can become confused if you add additional disk drives after you invoke FASTOPEN.

Using INSTALL To Load Other Programs in CONFIG.SYS

Although the CONFIG.SYS INSTALL command is intended for loading FASTOPEN.EXE, KEYB.COM, NLSFUNC.EXE, and SHARE.EXE, INSTALL also can be used to load some other TSR (terminate-and-stay-resident) programs, such as MOUSE.COM. Although INSTALL cannot be used for all programs, INSTALL will work for many of them. You must, however, follow these rules:

1. The program you want to load must have a COM or EXE file extension.

2. Any program loaded by INSTALL must be a TSR type of program.

3. You must provide the complete file name, including any necessary path name. For example, to use INSTALL to load MOUSE.COM from the C:\DOS directory, you use the following CONFIG.SYS command:

   INSTALL=C:\DOS\MOUSE.COM

   You also can include any necessary parameters for the TSR program on the same line. Suppose you want faster response from your mouse. You can modify the above command to read:

INSTALL=C:\DOS\MOUSE.COM /S100

In this command, **/S100** is a parameter passed to MOUSE.COM setting the sensitivity to the maximum value of 100. Any parameters following the command to install the TSR program (on the same line) are passed to the TSR program as if you were loading the program at the DOS prompt.

Note: The preceding example uses INSTALL to load MOUSE.COM instead of MOUSE.SYS. (Microsoft provides both versions of the mouse driver.) MOUSE.COM, however, offers two advantages over the MOUSE.SYS driver.

First, if you type the command **MOUSE OFF** at the DOS command line, the mouse driver is disabled. If MOUSE.SYS is used, this is all that happens. If MOUSE.COM is used, however, the memory which the driver was using is deallocated, therefore freeing up that memory for other applications.

Second, MOUSE.COM uses approximately 10K less memory than MOUSE.SYS. These two advantages make MOUSE.COM a better choice than MOUSE.SYS.

As you see, the CONFIG.SYS INSTALL command can be used to load both DOS driver programs and other TSR programs when you want to be sure those programs are loaded only once during a DOS session.

Using the BUFFERS Command

Buffers are used to increase disk performance. Before the introduction of disk-caching programs (which also keep disk information in memory), the BUFFERS command had the potential for great impact on disk performance.

Accessing information that's already in memory instead of reading information from a hard disk is much faster. Clearly, whenever you can fetch data from RAM instead of from the disk, you are way ahead.

A *buffer* is a reserved area of RAM set up by DOS to store information read from disk. If you configure your system with enough buffers, DOS frequently finds the information it needs in buffered memory. Instead of idling during a disk access, your microprocessor may be able to go back to work much sooner if the information is in a buffer.

Understanding How DOS Uses Disk Buffers

When DOS gets data from a disk, DOS reads the data in increments of whole sectors (512 bytes). Excess data not required from that sector simply is left in the buffer along with the data which was used. If this data is needed later, DOS doesn't have to do another disk access to retrieve the data.

Similarly, DOS reduces disk activity when it writes to the disk. If less than a full sector is to be written to the disk, DOS accumulates the information in a disk buffer. When the buffer is full or when a file is closed, DOS writes the information to the disk. This action is called *flushing* the buffer.

The net effect of DOS's use of buffers is a reduction in the number of disk accesses DOS performs, because DOS reads and writes only full sectors. Your programs and DOS therefore run faster.

Placing Buffers in the High Memory Area

A single buffer is 512 bytes long (plus about 20 bytes for overhead). The BUFFERS directive controls how many disk buffers your computer uses.

The number of disk buffers you should have depends on the programs you run on your computer and how much memory you have. If you use database software, for example, increasing the number of buffers may improve your system's performance.

Because each disk buffer takes about 532 bytes of memory, earlier versions of DOS sometimes required you to use a minimal number of buffers simply to preserve precious RAM.

DOS 5 has added a feature that places buffers in a previously, mostly unused area—the High Memory Area (HMA)—thereby saving conventional memory for your applications programs. (See Chapter 3 for more information on the types of memory used by DOS 5.) In DOS 5, buffers are placed automatically in the HMA if CONFIG.SYS includes the following command before the BUFFERS command and if high memory is available on your PC (HMA is available only on 8026, 8036, 80386SX, and 8046 PCs with extended memory):

DOS=HIGH

> *Note:* The BUFFERS command in DOS 4 includes the /X switch to instruct DOS to place the buffers in expanded memory. This switch has been dropped in DOS 5 because the buffers are placed automatically in the HMA if the DOS=HIGH command is issued. When upgrading from DOS 4 to DOS 5, consider the smaller size of the HMA and adjust excessively high numbers of buffers to a more reasonable number. You may, in fact, want to consider using the SMARTDRV.SYS disk cache program provided with DOS 5 instead of using a high BUFFERS number—use a BUFFERS=3 directive in CONFIG.SYS and let SMARTDRV.SYS handle the disk caching.

If the buffers are placed in the HMA, only a small amount of conventional memory is used, resulting in a considerable savings over the approximately 10K of conventional memory used by a typical BUFFERS=20 command. With applications programs growing larger every day, this extra memory can really help.

Using the MODE Command *(also DOS V4)*

MODE is a versatile command that has been around since the early versions of DOS. The most common uses for MODE have been to set the configuration of a serial port, redirect printer output from a parallel port to a serial port, and change the display mode. In a sense, MODE enables you to control some of the very basic elements of your PC.

Using the MODE Command To Set the Keyboard Typematic Rate

When you press a key on the PC keyboard, the character appears on the display. If you hold the same key down for a short period of time, nothing more happens. If you continue to hold the key down, the character pressed is repeated on-screen. The number of times a second the key is repeated is known as the *typematic rate*.

With earlier versions of DOS, you needed an add-on utility program to alter the keyboard typematic rate. You now can change this setting from DOS using the MODE CON command.

The syntax for the external MODE command that changes the typematic rate is as follows:

MODE CON *RATE=xx DELAY=yy*

The *RATE* is the number of repetitions per second; *DELAY* is the time delay before DOS starts repeating a key. Two adjustments are possible: how long you have to hold the key down before it starts repeating (the delay), and the number of times per second the character is generated (the rate).

The delay is specified in 1/4-second intervals. The range for the delay is 1 through 4, making a total possible delay of 1 second.

The rate range goes from 1 to 32. Table 4.2 shows the correlation between the rate value and the typematic rate.

Table 4.2
Typematic Rates

Rate	Typematic Rate
1	2.0
2	2.1
3	2.3
4	2.5
5	2.7
6	3.0
7	3.3
8	3.7

Rate	Typematic Rate
9	4.0
10	4.3
11	4.6
12	5.0
13	5.5
14	6.0
15	6.7
16	7.5
17	8.0
18	8.6
19	9.2
20	10.0
21	10.9
22	12.0
23	13.3
24	15.0
25	16.0
26	17.1
27	18.5
28	20.0
29	21.8
30	24.0
31	26.7
32	30.0

Notice that the increase in typematic rate is not linear. As the value for rate becomes larger, the typematic rate becomes significantly larger. Remember, the higher the typematic rate, the more times the keys are repeated in a given period.

Using MODE To Set a Delay

To set the keyboard so that the delay before the key starts repeating is 1/4 seconds, and the typematic rate is 30, type the following:

MODE CON RATE=32 DELAY=1

Try this example and see how quickly keys repeat. You'll find that the wide range of values for rate allow for fine tuning—you should be able to find the perfect delay and rate settings to suit your style of typing.

Note: You must set both the typematic rate and the delay. If you attempt to set just one, DOS informs you that both must be set.

Setting Screen Display to 25, 43, or 50 Lines

The DOS MODE command includes two additional features that are used to alter the display modes. If you have installed the ANSI.SYS device driver, you now can adjust the number of columns or the number of lines displayed on-screen.

Actually, because MODE always has been able to adjust the number of columns, only the ability to set the number of screen lines is really new. One advantage of being able to adjust the number of lines using the MODE command is that other DOS commands such as DIR and MORE now recognize the number of lines set by MODE. If, you set your VGA display to use 50 screen lines, for example, the DIR /P command will use the new 50-line setting instead of the old 25-line setting for page size.

Many of DOS 5's enhancements are intended to support the newer classes of PCs. Just as using the High Memory Area requires an 80286 or later processor and 1M or more of memory, using the MODE CON LINES= command requires at least an EGA or VGA display. The older monochrome and CGA equipped systems cannot set the number of screen lines.

Valid settings for a VGA display are 25, 43, or 50 lines. An EGA, however, can use only 25 or 43 lines. To set the number of lines, first make sure the ANSI.SYS driver is loaded in CONFIG.SYS. Look for a line such as the following in CONFIG.SYS:

DEVICE=C:\DOS\ANSI.SYS

(Note: This assumes that your ANSI.SYS file is located on drive C: in your \DOS directory). If you don't find the line, edit CONFIG.SYS to add the line and then reboot your system to load the driver.

> *Note:* The ANSI.SYS driver must be loaded before you can set the number of screen lines. If the ANSI.SYS driver is not installed, the following error message is displayed:
>
> ```
> ANSI.SYS must be installed to perform requested function
> ```

After ANSI.SYS is loaded, you can set the number of screen lines. The proper syntax to display 43 lines, for example, is as follows:

MODE CON LINES=43

After you set the display mode, you then can start your application program. The display mode, unless reset by the application, will remain. Using the preceding MODE example on an EGA- or VGA-based computer enables you to use WordPerfect in 43-line mode without adjusting the settings in WordPerfect.

Not all applications will sense the extra lines available. Symphony and 1-2-3, for example, reset the number of screen lines according to the display driver installed for them. You will have to try some MODE CON commands to see whether you can use the extra lines. Using MODE CON to set 43 or 50 lines makes viewing long DIR listings more convenient than using the standard 25 lines.

Summary

In Chapter 4, you examined some of the commands improved in DOS 5 that you can use to enhance your PC's configuration. You learned how using these commands can improve your system's performance and also how to configure your PC for foreign language use. Although the configuration commands may not be at the top of your list of interesting PC subjects, learning to take advantage of them can make your PC easier to use. Chapter 5 discusses your options for interfacing with DOS 5.

Interfacing with the DOS 5 Shell

Chapter 5 looks at your options for using DOS 5's two separate but completely compatible environments—the command line and the DOS 5 Shell. You see how you can retain the command line appearance you're familiar with from earlier releases or change to the more modern and intuitive Shell.

Using the Command Line or the DOS 5 Shell

The *command line* has been around since computers first acquired terminals. Since the early days of PCs, the default command line has consisted of the drive letter and a greater than symbol such as:

```
C>
```

When your computer uses a command line prompt, you enter commands by typing them on the computer's keyboard. To see a listing of files in a directory, for example, you type the following:

DIR

Your PC's command interpreter understands this command as "show me a directory listing." The one big problem with the DOS command line, however, is that you have to remember each command or take the time to look up the commands before you can use them. A good example of this can be seen in the many variations different operating systems have for the same command. The DIR command may be LISTCAT, LC, LS, L * *, LS, or even CAT in some other operating systems. This doesn't even take the command variations (like obtaining a wide or maybe a paged directory listing) into consideration. With all these confusing possiblities, it's no wonder PCs seem difficult to understand for many people.

The DOS 5 Shell, however, represents a new way of looking at the programs and files on your PC. Whereas the command line prompt displayed as little information as possible, the Shell shows much more. In figure 5.1, you can see an example of just some of the information the DOS 5 Shell provides. As you can see, not only does the DOS 5 Shell show a disk's directory structure in a graphic, easy-to-understand manner, the Shell also shows the file listing without requiring any sort of special command. As you examine the Shell more closely, you will see many more benefits.

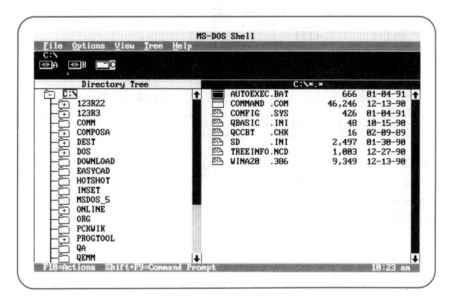

Fig. 5.1. *A typical MS-DOS Shell screen.*

Using the Familiar DOS Command Line

To some PC users, the idea of using any sort of DOS 5 Shell is frightening. They don't want anything extra between their keyboard and the heart of the machine. If you fit in this category, rest assured you won't be forced to use the DOS 5 Shell if you upgrade to DOS 5. You still can gain most of DOS 5's improvements without using the DOS 5 Shell. Don't totally dismiss the Shell, however. You may find some interesting tools in the DOS 5 Shell that you won't find elsewhere. With the Shell, for example, you now can move (not copy) a file from a directory on one disk—either floppy disk or hard disk—to a directory on another disk in one step.

Some PC users treat their PC as a single-purpose machine such as a word processor. For these people, the DOS 5 Shell may be a complication. Instead of loading their word processing software in AUTOEXEC.BAT, they would have to select the program from a menu.

Many users also need every free byte of memory possible because of the large applications programs they often run. For these users, the command line may be a better choice than the DOS 5 Shell. Keep in mind, however, that with DOS 5's memory usage enhancements, you may be able to use the DOS 5 Shell and still have more available memory than you had in earlier versions of DOS without a Shell.

Another point you should consider is that you can have both the command line and the DOS 5 Shell. If you include a line in your AUTOEXEC.BAT file to automatically load DOSSHELL (the name of DOS 5's Shell program), the DOS command line prompt is as close as pressing Shift-F9. You can issue your old familiar DOS commands and then type **EXIT** to return to the Shell.

If you want to keep the DOS command line prompt as the default, however, you can alternate between the DOS 5 Shell and the command prompt by loading the DOS 5 Shell from the command line. Simply type **DOSSHELL** and press Enter. When you're ready to return to the command line, press F3 or Alt-F4 to exit the DOS 5 Shell (or press Shift-F9 to issue a command and then type **EXIT** to return to the DOS 5 Shell).

Remember, you don't lose your command prompt just because you use the DOS 5 Shell. Even if you've never wanted to try a different type of environment on your PC before, you should at least give the DOS 5 Shell a try. You may find you like it.

Comparing the DOS 5 Shell to Windows 3.0

The DOS 5 Shell was designed with many of the same features as Windows 3.0. The Shell offers a Graphical User Interface (GUI), a task-swapping Program Manager, a File Manager, mouse support, and also uses many of the same keyboard commands. The Shell and Windows also provide some level of user customization so that you can control their appearance. In fact, if you compare figures 5.1 and 5.2, you see how similar their File Manager components are.

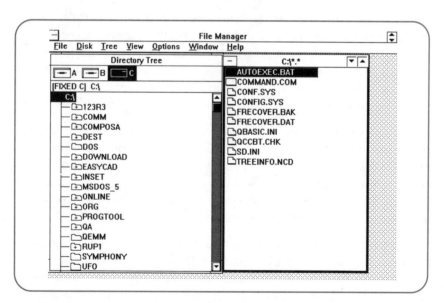

Fig. 5.2. The Windows 3.0 File Manager.

The DOS 5 Shell and Windows 3.0 use similar icons, menus, scroll bars, and commands, but also have many differences. Although the Shell provides task-swapping, it does not support multitasking. Additionally, although programs such as PageMaker require Windows, the DOS 5 Shell runs standard DOS programs.

Note: With task-swapping, DOS 5's Shell suspends a program when you switch to another program. Multitasking, as performed by Windows 3.0, however, enables two or more programs to actually continue running at the same time as you switch between them. Because of this difference, task-swapping environments such as the DOS 5 Shell do not allow background communications. You cannot, for example, transfer a file to someone while you're using your word processing software to work on another document.

A Graphical User Interface

The DOS 5 Shell and Windows 3.0 are examples of *Graphical User Interfaces* or GUIs (often pronounced "gooey"). Instead of a blank command line, a GUI presents the user with considerable information and menus of command options. Figures 5.1 and 5.2 show how a GUI presents much more information than a command line prompt such as C>.

Note: Although the DOS 5 Shell is called a Graphical User Interface, the Shell was designed to work also on systems without sophisticated graphics capabilities. The DOS 5 Shell can provide slightly more information when using graphics mode, but the Shell also runs perfectly in text mode.

Looking at the DOS 5 Shell Screen

When you load the DOS 5 Shell, the program displays an information box informing you that the program is reading the disk information. If you have many directories and files, you can watch as the number of files and directories read increases. After the disk information is read, the default DOS 5 Shell screen appears (see fig. 5.3). As you learn later, the default screen is one of the display options available on the View menu and is called Program/File Lists.

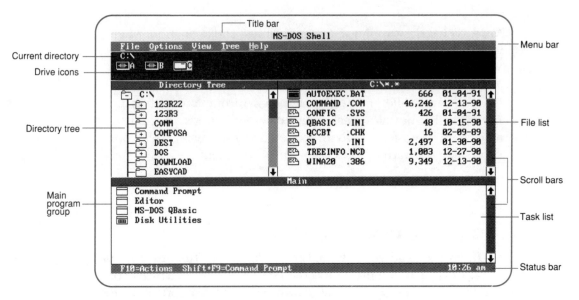

Fig. 5.3. The default MS-DOS Shell screen.

Understanding the Menu Bar

Notice the bar that goes across the screen just above the menu selections. This bar displays the program name, MS-DOS Shell, and is called the title bar. As you can see in figure 5.3, the DOS 5 Shell screen is divided into sections, and each section of the screen also has a title bar to indicate the purpose of that section. If you have a color monitor, the title bar of the currently active section is displayed in a contrasting color so that you can determine which section is active.

The menu bar area includes the main menu, the current directory indicator, and the available disk drives. As you can see, the currently active drive is highlighted.

The menu bar itself contains five main options. (Note: The Tree option disappears when a program group or the task list is active.) The method you use to access the menu depends on whether you are using the keyboard or a mouse. For now, assume that you don't have a mouse and will use either the F10 function key or the Alt key to activate the menu.

The DOS 5 Shell menu is a *drop down* menu. First, you press Alt or F10 to activate the menu bar. You then select an option by moving the cursor to the option and pressing Enter, or you press the key that corresponds to the underlined letter in the menu option. The menu then drops down and displays a series of additional options.

> ***Note:*** Early versions of Windows had "pull down" menus, which did not remain down if you released the Alt key or the mouse button that was used to activate the menu. The effect was similar to a window shade that popped back up as soon as you let go of the handle. The DOS 5 Shell, however, follows the Windows 3.0 standard of leaving the menu open until you make a selection or press the Esc key to close the menu.

The File Menu

After you press Alt, you can select a menu by typing the underlined letter in that menu heading. If you press Alt (or F10) and the letter F, for example, the File menu shown in figure 5.4 is displayed.

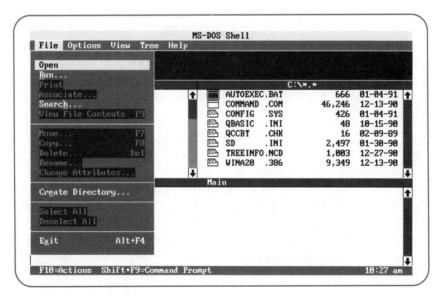

Fig. 5.4. *The File menu with no file selected.*

Looking at figure 5.4, you can see that many of the choices are shown in reverse video. Figure 5.5 shows you how the reverse video affects a selected file.

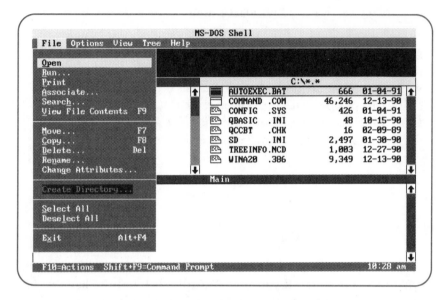

Fig. 5.5. The File menu with a file selected.

In figure 5.4, no files have been selected. In figure 5.5, however, you can see that the file AUTOEXEC.BAT in the directory listing is highlighted in reverse video. Most of the menu choices now appear in normal print. Items that are shown in reverse or, depending on the type of monitor you have and your color selection choice, in a different color are not currently available.

> *Note:* The first menu choice, Open, also is highlighted in reverse video because the cursor is shown on that choice. Notice, however, that when the cursor is shown highlighting a menu selection, the cursor starts to the left of the first letter of the menu selection and extends nearly to the right border of the menu box. Unavailable items are shown with the reverse video highlight extending only as far as the text of the item itself.

Many of the File menu selections are followed by three periods (also known as an ellipsis). When the ellipsis follows a command, this indicates that a dialog box appears if the command is selected. The *dialog box* prompts you for additional input or information necessary to execute the command. Figure 5.6, for example, shows the Move File dialog box that appears when you select Move from the File menu. In this dialog box, you must enter the destination to which the selected file, AUTOEXEC.BAT in this example, should be moved.

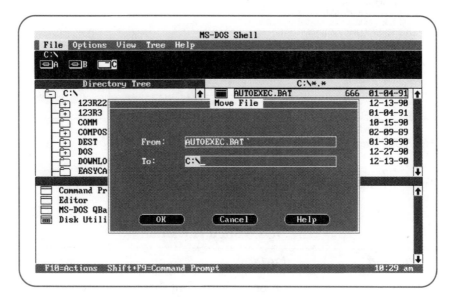

Fig. 5.6. *The Move File dialog box.*

Some File menu selections, such as View File Contents, are followed by a keyboard shortcut for selecting the command (refer to fig. 5.5). The View File Contents selection is followed by F9, which indicates that pressing the F9 key is a shortcut you can use instead of pressing Alt (or F10), F, and then V. Figure 5.7 shows what happens when the F9 key is pressed while AUTOEXEC.BAT is selected.

Fig. 5.7. *Viewing the AUTOEXEC.BAT file with the MS-DOS Shell.*

Table 5.1 describes the File menu choices.

Table 5.1
The DOS 5 Shell File Menu

Selection	Purpose
Open	Opens a document that has been associated with a program using the Associate command, or starts a program
Run	Enables you to enter the commands needed to run a program by providing a dialog box for your entries
Print	Prints the selected file or files if you installed the DOS print spooler using the PRINT command at the DOS prompt
Associate	Associates a program, such as a word processor or spreadsheet program, with a specified type of file. When you open a file of the specified type, the associated program is run automatically.

Selection	Purpose
Search	Searches for specified files after providing a dialog box for you to specify which files to search for
View File Contents	Displays the contents of the currently selected file in either a text or binary display, depending on the file. This option also may be selected using the F9 function key as a shortcut.
Move	Moves the selected file or files to another disk and/or directory. You also may use the F7 function key as a shortcut.
Copy	Copies the selected file or files to another disk and/or directory. You also may use the F8 function key as a shortcut.
Delete	Deletes the selected file, files, or directory. Unless the Options Confirmation Delete option has been changed, this option requires confirmation before deletion. The Del key serves as a shortcut for this command.
Rename	Enables you to rename the selected file. Unlike the DOS REN command, also enables you to rename directories.
Change Attributes	Displays and enables you to change a file's Hidden, System, Archive, or Read-Only attributes
Create Directory	Creates a new directory as a subdirectory of the currently selected directory. If no directory other than the root directory is currently selected, creates a new directory immediately under the root directory.

continues

Table 5.1 *(Continued)*

Selection	*Purpose*
Select All	Selects all files in the currently selected directory. You also may use the Ctrl and / (slash) keys (hold down Ctrl and press /) as a shortcut method of selecting all files.
Deselect All	Removes the selection of any files in the current directory. The Ctrl \ (backslash) key combination is a shortcut to this command.
Exit	Leaves the DOS Shell and removes it from memory. To return to the Shell, you must enter DOSSHELL at the DOS prompt. You may use the Alt-F4 key combination as a shortcut to exit the Shell quickly.

The File menu options are slightly different if a program group is selected, in which case the following options will be displayed:

Selection	*Purpose*
New...	Enables you to add new items to a program group or to create new program groups
Open	Selects and executes the currently highlighted program group item. The Enter key is the shortcut for this selection.
Copy	Enables you to copy a program item to another program group
Delete	Deletes the currently selected item. The Del key is the shortcut for this option.
Properties	Enables you to edit the commands used to activate the selected items, enter help text, and assign a "hot key" combination
Reorder	Enables you to change the display order of items in the program group window

Selection	Purpose
Run	Enables you to enter the commands needed to run a program item by providing a dialog box for your entries
Exit	Leaves the DOS Shell. Alt-F4 is a shortcut to exit quickly.

The Options Menu

The next main menu selection is Options. While the File menu includes actions relating to selected files, the Options menu selections deal with how the Shell itself functions. As you see later in the sections on customizing the DOS 5 Shell, you have many choices. Depending on your equipment, you may be able to select from several screen resolutions and color combinations. Figure 5.8 shows the Options menu.

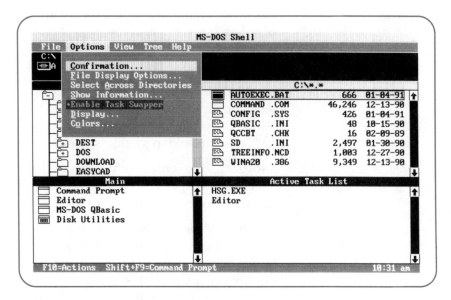

Fig. 5.8. *The Shell Options menu.*

Notice the Enable Task Swapper option in figure 5.8. (You learn about this option later, in the section "Understanding the Task List.") The diamond preceding this option shows that it is selected. Several of the menus include options that can be toggled on or off. The diamond is used in front of toggle options to show that the option is selected. Table 5.2 explains the Options menu selections.

Table 5.2
The Options Menu

Selection	Purpose
Confirmation	Provides a dialog box in which you may select if you want to confirm when files are being deleted or replaced and if you want to confirm mouse actions.
File Display Options	Enables you to select which types of files will be displayed. Also enables you to specify the sort order of displayed files and if hidden and system files should be displayed.
Select Across Directories	Enables you to specify if identically named files in different directories can be selected at the same time. This choice is a toggle and displays a diamond in front of the choice if it is selected.
Show Information	Displays information about the currently selected file, directory, and disk drive. Shows the number of files, their total size, and available space on the disk.
Enable Task Swapper	A toggle used to enable or disable DOS 5 Shell task swapping. A diamond appears before this selection when it is enabled.
Display	Enables selection of the screen mode used to display the DOS 5 Shell. Depending on the adaptor and monitor, this option may present several modes to choose from. In some cases, Display may allow between 25 and 60 lines of text.
Colors	Displays a selection box in which you may select from several different color combinations for the display.

The View Menu

The View menu includes several options that change the way the DOS 5 Shell appears (see fig. 5.9). Depending on your needs, you may want to view directories, files, program groups, and active tasks in different combinations. Table 5.3 shows the options available on the View menu.

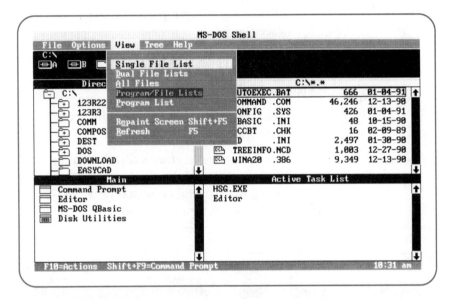

Fig. 5.9. The View menu.

Table 5.3
The View Menu

Selection	Purpose
Single File List	Displays only the current drive's directory tree and files (see fig. 5.10)
Dual File Lists	Displays two directory trees and file lists at the same time (such as the directories and files from two drives at the same time) (see fig. 5.11)

continues

Table 5.3 (*Continued*)

Selection	Purpose
All Files	Displays all of the files on the current drive regardless of location (see fig. 5.12)
Program/File Lists	Displays the default listing of directories, files, program groups, and active tasks (see fig. 5.13)
Program List	Displays program groups and active tasks only (see fig. 5.14)
Repaint Screen	Redraws the screen using the currently selected view. Shift-F5 is the shortcut for this option.
Refresh	Re-reads the directories and files on the current disk and then redraws the screen using the currently selected view. F5 is the shortcut for this option.

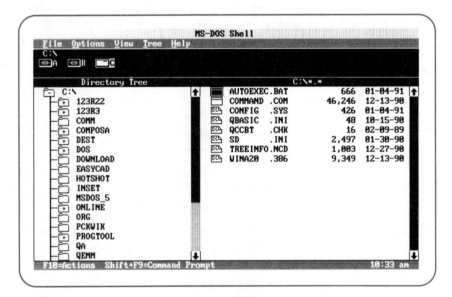

Fig. 5.10. The View Single File List option.

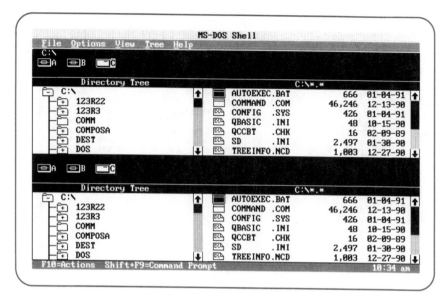

Fig. 5.11. *The View Dual File Lists option.*

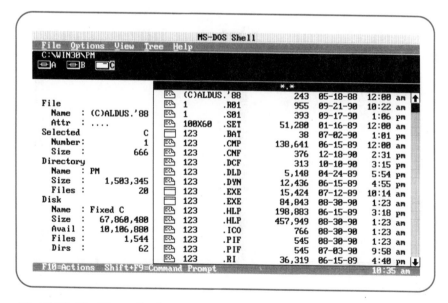

Fig. 5.12. *The View All Files option.*

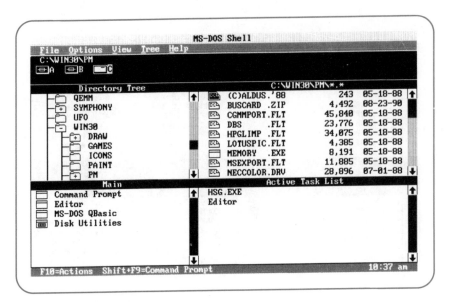

Fig. 5.13. *The View Program/File Lists option.*

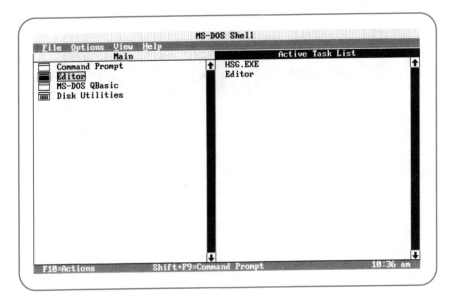

Fig. 5.14. *The View Program List option.*

The Tree Menu

The DOS 5 Shell Tree menu, as shown in figure 5.15, affects how the directory tree is displayed on-screen. If your system has a complex directory structure, the commands available on this menu and their shortcut keys can make it considerably easier for you to make your way around the directories.

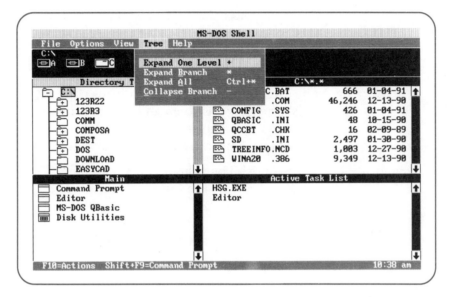

Fig. 5.15. The MS-DOS Shell Tree menu.

Note: If you select graphics mode, the directory tree shows directories as file folders. If the folder is empty, the directory does not have any subdirectories. If a directory's folder contains a minus sign (–), the subdirectories below the directory have been expanded at least one level. If the folder contains a plus sign (+), there are subdirectories below the directory that currently are not shown.

Table 5.4 shows the Tree menu options. Figure 5.16 shows the default directory tree.

Table 5.4
The Tree Menu

Selection	Purpose
Expand One Level	Shows the directory tree with the current branch expanded to show one additional level. The plus (+) key is a shortcut for this command. Figure 5.17 shows the result of issuing this command when the C:\SYMPHONY directory is current.
Expand Branch	Expands the entire branch of the directory as far as subdirectories exist under the current directory. The asterisk key (*) is a shortcut for this command. Figure 5.18 shows the same directory as figure 5.17 with the branch completely expanded.
Expand All	Expands all branches of the entire directory tree. The Ctrl-plus-asterisk (Ctrl- + - *)=key combination is the shortcut for Expand All. Figure 5.19 shows the result of this command.
Collapse Branch	Collapses all of the subdirectories below the current branch of the directory tree but does not affect any other parts of the tree. The minus key (–) is the shortcut key. Figure 5.20 shows the directory tree after using Collapse Branch to collapse the subdirectories of the C:\SYMPHONY directory.

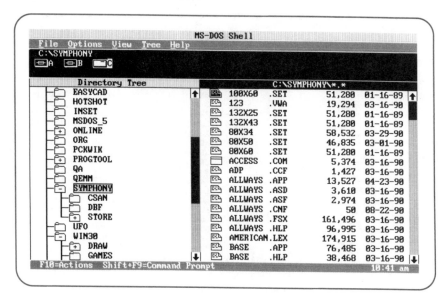

Fig. 5.16. *The Tree default display.*

Fig. 5.17. *The Tree Expand One Level option.*

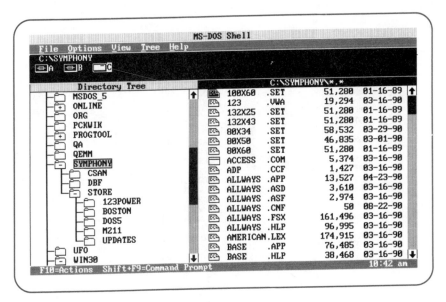

Fig. 5.18. *The Tree Expand Branch option.*

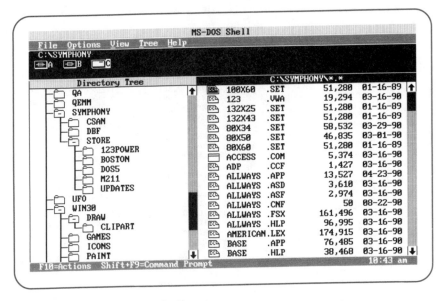

Fig. 5.19. *The Tree Expand All option.*

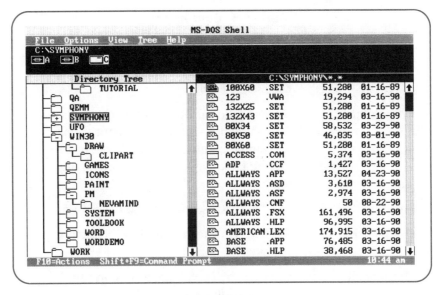

Fig. 5.20. *The Tree Collapse Branch option.*

The Help Menu

The final menu, the Help menu, is shown in figure 5.21. In the DOS 5 Shell, you can press the F1 key to receive context-sensitive help whenever one of the menu choices is highlighted. You also can access the help menu for specific information if you're not sure which of the menu options applies. Table 5.5 lists the Help menu options.

Table 5.5
The Help Menu

Selection	Purpose
Index	Enables you to select any help topic from an alphabetical listing
Keyboard	Provides a listing of the keyboard short cuts you can use to perform Shell operations

continues

Table 5.5 *(Continued)*

Selection	Purpose
Shell Basics	Provides basic information about using the DOS 5 Shell
Commands	Explains the various menu commands. This same help information (but specific to a single command) is available by pressing the F1 key when a command is highlighted.
Procedures	The "how-to" section of the Help menu
Using Help	Explains how to use the DOS 5 Shell help system
About Shell	Displays the DOS 5 Shell version number and copyright notice

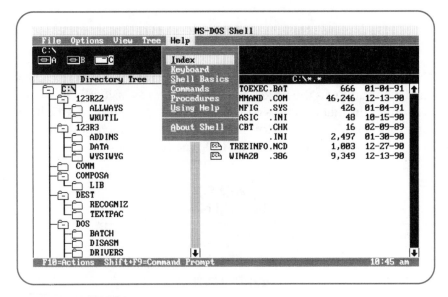

Fig. 5.21. The MS-DOS Shell Help menu.

Understanding the Directory Tree

The DOS 5 Shell was designed to make working with complex directory structures very easy. The directory tree window is an important part of this ease of use. Figure 5.22 shows a typical directory layout you may have on your hard disk.

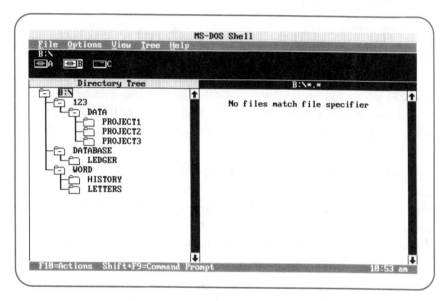

Fig. 5.22. *The MS-DOS Shell directory tree.*

In this figure, separate directories were established for Lotus 1-2-3, a database program, and a word processing program. Each of these program directories has one or more subdirectories used to store data files for different projects. Because you can easily see the layout of the directories with the DOS 5 Shell, you can easily visualize their structure. Understanding a disk's directory structure without this kind of visual clue, however, is not so easy.

Suppose, for example, that you want to see what files are in the B:\DATABASE\LEDGER directory while you are working with files in the

B:\123\DATA\PROJECT2 directory. To move from your current directory to the LEDGER directory, you type the following command and then press the Enter key:

CD \DATABASE\LEDGER

After you finish working in that directory, you enter:

CD \123\DATA\PROJECT2

and press Enter to return. Suppose, however, that you forget the exact name of the \123\DATA\PROJECT2 directory and you type the following:

CD \123\DATA\PROJECTB

Instead of changing directories, DOS displays the message `Invalid directory` and you remain in the \DATABASE\LEDGER directory. You then have to try and determine the correct name and issue the corrected command.

Using the DOS 5 Shell directory tree, however, moving from directory to directory is as simple as moving the cursor. In fact, if you have a mouse, you can simply place the mouse pointer on the directory and click the mouse button. As you move the cursor to different directories, the file window to the right of the directory tree window automatically displays the files in the highlighted directory.

Although the directory tree shown in figure 5.22 shows the disk's complete directory structure fully expanded, you can use the Tree menu commands or the equivalent shortcut keys to control the display. Suppose that you want to see the complete DATABASE branch and the complete WORD branch, but you don't want to see the subdirectories under the 123 branch. If your tree is fully expanded, as in figure 5.22, place the cursor on the 123 directory and press the minus (–) key. The 123 branch collapses and the 123 folder now contains a plus (+) to show that it has hidden subdirectories. To expand a branch one level, highlight the branch and press the plus key. To completely expand a branch, highlight the branch and press the asterisk (*) key. You also can use the mouse to click the folder to expand or collapse.

The DOS 5 Shell directory tree provides an easy, intuitive means of both visualizing and moving through a disk's directory structure. The Shell greatly simplifies the task of managing your files (as you see later in the section "Easier Control of Your Files").

Understanding the Directory Listing

The DOS 5 Shell directory listing appears much like the standard DOS directory listing that you see when you enter the **DIR** command at the DOS prompt. The following differences, however, make the DOS 5 Shell listing an improvement over the standard listing:

- The DOS 5 Shell directory listing is presented automatically in sorted order. As shown in figure 5.23, you can select the sort order (which can include DiskOrder, the DOS command line default) using the File Display Options selection on the Options menu.

- You can execute a program in the directory listing by highlighting the program and pressing Enter, or double-clicking the program with the mouse.

- If the listing is too large to fit on a single screen, you can scroll forward or backward in the listing using the cursor keys or the mouse.

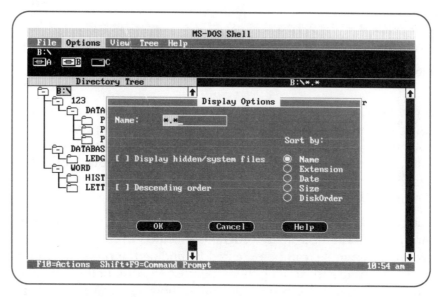

Fig. 5.23. *The File Display Options.*

Understanding the Program Group

A *program group* consists of one or more files organized so that you can work easily with the files. The Main program group, shown in figure 5.24, includes a group called Disk Utilities.

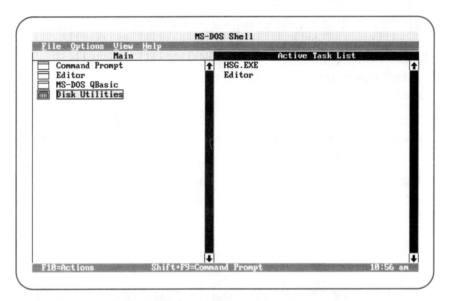

Fig. 5.24. The MS-DOS Shell Main program group.

If you highlight the Disk Utilities group and press Enter (or, if you're using a mouse, double-click the left button), you see the programs that you need to copy a disk, back up or restore your hard disk, and format a disk. Figure 5.25 shows the Disk Utilities group. Notice that the title bar above the programs has changed from Main to Disk Utilities to indicate the currently active program group.

You can find and execute programs easier by organizing your programs into groups. The disk utility programs included in the Disk Utilities group, for example, can be executed by finding the programs in the directory listing and running them. Because the disk utility programs require parameters for proper operation, however, you first have to select the program and press Alt or F10 for the menu, choose File and then Run, and finally enter the parameters.

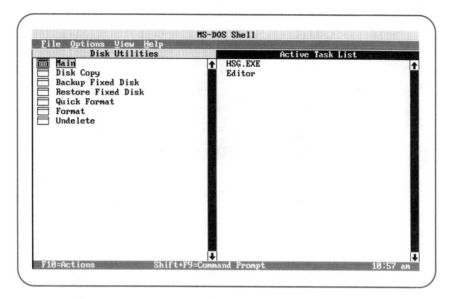

Fig. 5.25. The Disk Utilities program group.

By placing these same programs in a program group, you can specify that these programs require parameters before being executed. To format a floppy disk, for example, you select the Disk Utilities program group, select Format, and then a dialog box requesting parameters pops up (see fig. 5.26).

You can add or delete programs from program groups, and you can create new program groups. You can even require that the users provide a password before they can use a particular program group.

Adding programs to program groups does not create an extra copy of the program on your disk. You can, therefore, include the same program in several program groups without wasting disk space. In the same manner, deleting a program from a program group does not delete that program from the disk—the program is removed only from the group.

Understanding the Active Task List

The Active Task List portion of the DOS 5 Shell screen shows programs that were executing, but currently are suspended. For example, suppose that you are using a word processing program and you decide you need

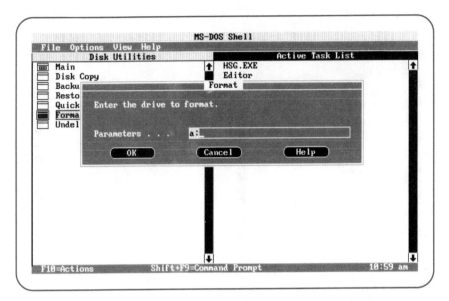

Fig. 5.26. *Formatting a disk with the Disk Utilities program group.*

to run 1-2-3 to calculate some information for your document. Instead of leaving the word processor, loading 1-2-3, doing the calculations, leaving 1-2-3, and reloading your word processor, you can use the task swapper to suspend one task and execute another. The task list then shows which tasks (such as your word processor) are suspended currently. When you return to a suspended task, you're returned to the same point where you left the task. In a later section, "Task Swapping with the Shell," you examine how to use the task swapper.

Easier Control of Your Files

With the DOS 5 Shell, you can control your files more easily because you can perform many functions in a simplified manner. If you have a mouse, you can even select and move files without typing any commands. Figure 5.27 shows how easily you can copy a file using a mouse.

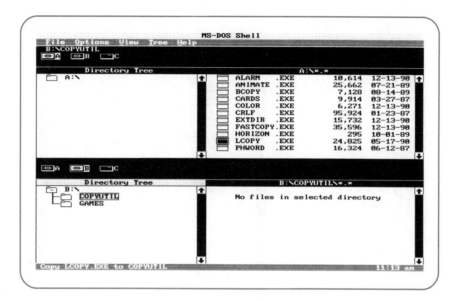

Fig. 5.27. *Copying a file with the MS-DOS Shell.*

In this figure, the view is set to dual file lists with the top list showing drive A: and the bottom list showing drive B:. The file LCOPY.EXE is selected on drive A: and the mouse pointer is used to select the \COPYUTIL directory on drive B: by holding down the mouse button as the pointer is moved from A:\LCOPY.EXE to B:\COPYUTIL. As this is done, the DOS 5 Shell displays the message Copy LCOPY.EXE to COPYUTIL at the bottom of the screen. When the mouse button is released, the file is copied. Figure 5.28 shows that LCOPY.EXE now appears in the B:\COPYUTIL directory listing.

Next, you are going to copy some game programs from drive A: to the B:\GAMES directory by following these steps:

1. Select each of the game programs using either the keyboard or the mouse.

    To select the game programs with the keyboard, move the cursor to the first program, ANIMATE.EXE, press Shift-F8, press the space bar, then move the cursor down and select each game by pressing the space bar until all five games are selected.

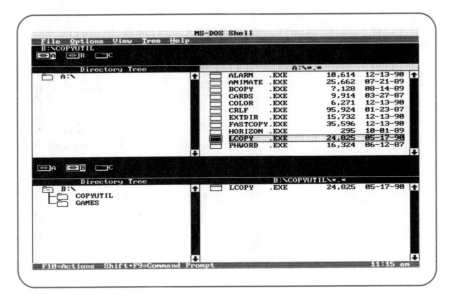

Fig. 5.28. The results of copying a file.

To select the game programs with the mouse, hold down the Ctrl key while you click the pointer on each game program's folder.

2. To copy the programs, press the F8 shortcut key, or press Alt (or F10) for the menu and select File and Copy.

    The Copy File dialog box appears with as many of the selected files displayed as will fit in the From: box.

3. Enter **B:\GAMES** in the To: box, and your screen should look like figure 5.29.

4. Press Enter to copy the files.

You also have the option of moving the mouse cursor to the destination directory, while you continue to hold down the left mouse button, and then releasing the mouse button.

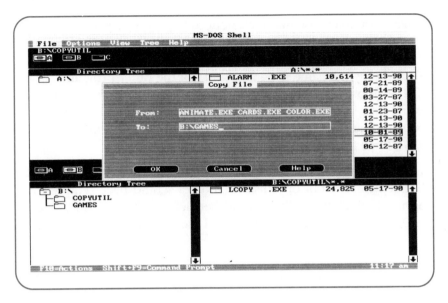

Fig. 5.29. *Copying a group of files.*

The files are copied from A:\ to B:\GAMES. To confirm that the files have been copied, select the GAMES directory in the lower file list. Your screen should look like figure 5.30.

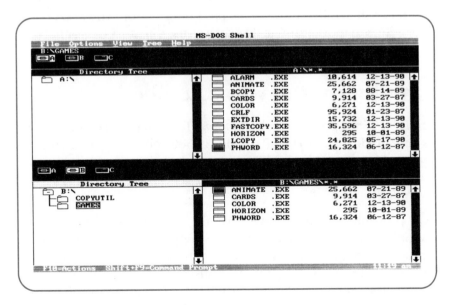

Fig. 5.30. *The results of copying a group of files.*

In these examples, you may have noticed how easily you can select files to copy or move with the DOS 5 Shell. The game programs were mixed in with a number of other programs, and no DOS wild card could have selected only the game programs and not the other programs. At the DOS prompt, therefore, you would have been required to perform several copy operations or use the /P parameter with the XCOPY command, and then verify each file before it was copied. Using the DOS 5 Shell is much easier.

The DOS command line does not have a MOVE command. To move the file LCOPY.EXE from one disk to another would have required first copying the file to B:\COPYUTIL, and then deleting the file from A:\. Again, the DOS 5 Shell provides a much easier method of managing your files.

Using the Keyboard or a Mouse

You can see that the DOS 5 Shell works quite well with the keyboard or a mouse. Like Windows 3.0, however, the Shell really was designed so that many operations are quite easier with a mouse. Using a mouse, you can make selections anywhere on the screen by simply moving the mouse pointer and clicking the button. To move to different screen areas using the keyboard, you have to use the Tab key to move to the next section or Shift-Tab to move to the preceding section. You also use the cursor keys to move through lists such as the directory tree or file lists.

Task Swapping with the Shell

The DOS 5 Shell provides *task swapping*. Task swapping is not the same as multitasking. Windows 3.0 running in 386 enhanced mode provides multitasking of standard DOS programs, but requires a much higher level of hardware power and memory than does the DOS 5 Shell's task swapping.

You probably are wondering what the difference is between task swapping and multitasking. With task swapping, you can load and run a program, and without exiting the program, return to the DOS 5 Shell. When you do this, your program is suspended, which means that it pauses. The program isn't running, but you can return to it and pick up right where you left the program. Multitasking, on the other hand, enables a program to continue running when you place the program in the background. For example, you can start to download a large file from another computer and, while the file is being transfered, switch to your word processor to work on another document. Because the communications program is still executing, your PC is performing multiple tasks at the same time—multitasking.

Loading Several Programs Simultaneously

Suppose that you are doing a report that requires you to examine database records and analyze trends. You can try to determine beforehand all the information you will need from the database, run your database manager program and obtain the results, exit, and load your word processor to begin the report. As you work on the report, however, you find that you need some additional information. To take another look at the database, you have to save your work, exit, load the database manager, get the new information, exit, load your word processor again, and then continue.

Using Shell's task swapping, however, makes your job much easier. Instead of exiting the database manager, you just hold down the Alt key, press the Tab key, and the database manager is suspended while you return to the Shell. Select and run your word processor as you would normally. When you need more database information, hold down the Alt key and press the Tab key until the name of the database manager appears at the top of the screen. Release the Alt key and your word processor is suspended as you switch back to the database manager.

Task swapping is much faster than loading, saving, exiting, and running another application.

> *Tip:* Many game programs have a "boss key" that places a fake spreadsheet on the screen to hide the fact that you're really playing a game. With the Shell's task swapping, you actually can have a real spreadsheet, word processor, or other application ready to pop up and hide the game you're really playing.

Custom Screen Combinations

The DOS 5 Shell enables you to make maximum use of the display adapter and monitor on your PC by supporting everything from 25-line text displays to 60-line graphics mode displays. In addition to text and graphics display modes, the DOS 5 Shell supports a full range of color choices.

If you have a graphics capable monitor, especially a higher resolution EGA or VGA color monitor, the DOS 5 Shell offers quite a few opportunities for customization. The following sections look at the choices available on systems that use today's standard VGA color monitor. Depending on your hardware configuration, you may not have as large a selection of choices, but most systems will have some range to choose from.

Colors

When you first load the Shell, the program uses the default color combination called Basic Blue. In this selection, the screen background is bright white, some of the screen elements are bright blue or bright cyan, and bright red is used for warning messages. If you wish to try another color combination, the Options Colors menu offers the following choices:

Color	Description
Basic Blue	The standard color combination
Ocean	An alternate color selection
Monochrome - 2 colors	A black and white selection
Monochrome - 4 colors	A black and white selection
Reverse	A reverse video black and white selection
Hot Pink	An alternate color selection
Emerald City	An alternate color selection
Turquoise	An alternate color selection

To select any of these combinations, press the Alt or F10 key, select Options, Color, highlight your choice, and press Enter. The DOS 5 Shell then displays the selected color choice, and you may choose to keep the color or cancel your selection. If you select one of the alternate choices, that color will be used when you start the Shell (until you make another selection).

None of the standard color selections uses the full range of available colors. You can, however, create your own color setting using any combination of the following colors:

```
Black
Blue
Green
Cyan
Red
Magenta
Brown
White
Brightblack
Brightblue
Brightgreen
Brightcyan
Brightred
Brightmagenta
Brightyellow
Brightwhite
```

Creating a new color selection is easy. You can choose to add a new selection to the four standard colors, or you can change one of the color selections to suit your preferences. The color selections are contained in a file called DOSSHELL.INI, which is located in the same directory as your DOS files.

To create a new color selection, follow these steps:

1. Make a copy of DOSSHELL.INI so that you can go back to that file if you make an error.

2. Change to the directory containing DOSSHELL.INI and load the file into the DOS editor using the following command:

   EDIT DOSSHELL.INI

3. Move down through the file until you find the section that begins `color =`. All of the color selections follow this prompt.

4. Move the cursor down two lines to the beginning of the line that says `selection =`.

5. Select that line and the lines below by holding down the shift key and pressing the down-arrow key. Continue selecting lines until you have selected all lines down to and including the line just above the next `selection = line`.

6. Hold down the Ctrl key and press the Ins key to copy the selected lines to the buffer.

7. Move the cursor to the beginning of the next `selection =` line, hold down the Shift key, and press the Ins key to paste in a new section of color selection lines.

8. Move the cursor down to the line `title = basic blue`, and enter a new name such as **My Colors**.

Your new color selection now should look like the following:

```
selection =
{
    title = My Colors
    foreground =
    {
        base = black
        highlight = brightwhite
        selection = brightwhite
        alert = brightred
        menubar = black
        menu = black
        disabled = white
        accelerator = cyan
        dialog = black
        button = black
        elevator = white
        titlebar = black
        scrollbar = brightwhite
        borders = black
        drivebox = black
        driveicon = black
        cursor = black
    }
    background =
    {
```

```
        base = brightwhite
        highlight = blue
        selection = black
        alert = brightwhite
        menubar = brightwhite
        menu = brightwhite
        disabled = brightwhite
        accelerator = brightwhite
        dialog = brightwhite
        button = white
        elevator = white
        titlebar = white
        scrollbar = black
        borders = brightwhite
        drivebox = brightwhite
        driveicon = brightwhite
        cursor = brightcyan
    }
}
```

Be sure that the section contains the same number of curly brackets shown here. You now can edit the color choices for any section of the DOS 5 Shell screen using the color names listed earlier. Notice that each item, such as the highlight (cursor), has both a foreground and background setting. Make sure that your choices enable you to see text (usually the foreground setting) over the background color. For a very colorful screen, you may want to try the following:

```
selection =
{
    title = My Colors
    foreground =
    {
        base = black
        highlight = blue
        selection = green
        alert = cyan
        menubar = red
        menu = magenta
        disabled = brown
        accelerator = white
```

continues

```
        dialog = brightblack
        button = brightblue
        elevator = brightgreen
        titlebar = brightcyan
        scrollbar = brightred
        borders = brightmagenta
        drivebox = brightyellow
        driveicon = brightwhite
        cursor = blue
    }
background =
    {
        base = green
        highlight = cyan
        selection = red
        alert = magenta
        menubar = brown
        menu = white
        disabled = brightblack
        accelerator = brightblue
        dialog = brightgreen
        button = brightcyan
        elevator = brightred
        titlebar = brightmagenta
        scrollbar = brightyellow
        borders = brightwhite
        drivebox = black
        driveicon = blue
        cursor = brightred
    }
    }
```

After you make your changes, select File Save, and then exit from the editor. Restart the DOS 5 Shell, select Options, Colors, and choose My Colors. Your DOS 5 Shell should be quite colorful, and certainly different from anyone else's copy. Remember, you always can re-edit DOSSHELL.INI to modify your color choices.

Note: The file DOSSHELL.INI can contain lines exceeding 256 characters. Some text-editing programs will truncate lines that are longer than 256 characters and can damage DOSSHELL.INI. The DOS 5 editor, EDIT, is safe to use when editing DOSSHELL.INI because the program will not truncate long lines.

Number of Lines

On a system with a VGA monitor, the DOS 5 Shell gives you eight different options on the display resolution. In text mode, you can have 25, 43, or 50 lines on the screen. In graphics mode, you can have 25, 30, 34, 43, or 60 lines on the screen. To select the number of lines on the display, press Alt (or F10), select Options, Display, and make your choice from the selections listed. The following screens show the different resolutions (figs. 5.31 through 5.38).

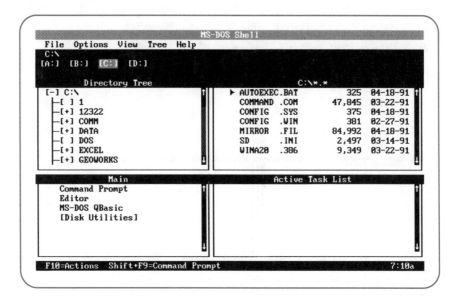

Fig. 5.31. The 25-line text mode display.

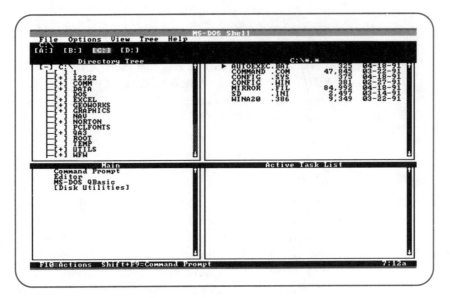

Fig. 5.32. *The 43-line text mode display.*

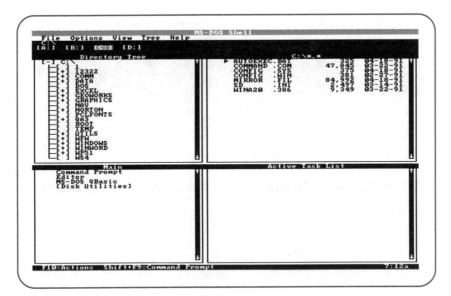

Fig. 5.33. *The 50-line text mode display.*

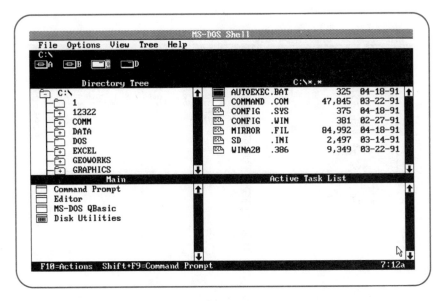

Fig. 5.34. *The 25-line graphics mode display.*

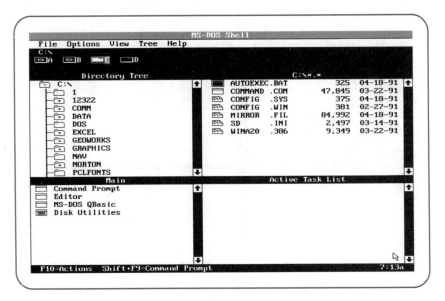

Fig. 5.35. *The 30-line graphics mode display.*

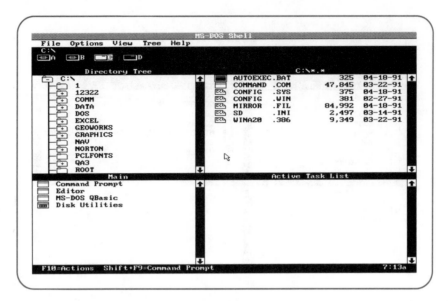

Fig. 5.36. *The 34-line graphics mode display.*

Fig. 5.37. *The 43-line graphics mode display.*

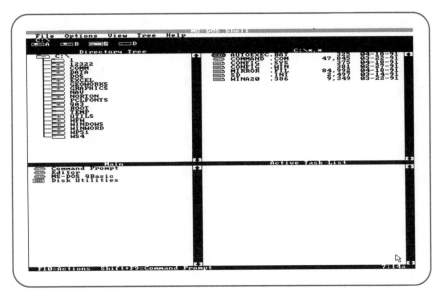

Fig. 5.38. *The 60-line graphics mode display.*

Graphics or Text Mode

Although 25- and 43-line displays are available in both text and graphics mode, graphics mode usually is a better choice if supported by your system. The graphics mode display uses more sophisticated symbols to represent files and directories and has a much more polished appearance. Text mode, however, may provide slightly higher performance. Whichever mode you choose, the DOS 5 Shell provides a whole new way of viewing and managing the files on your system.

Summary

Chapter 5 provided you with an introduction to the DOS 5 Shell and gave you information on using and customizing the Shell. You learned how you can use the Shell to be more efficient in managing your files. Even if you normally prefer the command line, you have seen examples of how the DOS 5 Shell can be easier to use. In the next chapter, you look at how macros also can help you use your PC.

Using DOS Macros

6

C hapter 6 introduces a DOS 5 feature that makes DOS commands easier to use. The DOSKEY program enables you to create macros and keeps a list of commands available for reuse. DOSKEY macros are powerful tools for customizing DOS 5 commands.

Using the New DOSKEY Program

DOSKEY is included for the first time in DOS 5. DOSKEY offers several options that enable you to reuse DOS commands more easily and provide you with the tools to customize all DOS commands to suit the way you work. With DOSKEY macros, you also can create new, shorthand DOS commands.

DOSKEY, like most DOS 5 command additions and enhancements, works on all PCs, regardless of the processor that is used. You don't need an advanced PC system to take advantage of DOSKEY.

Note: Because DOSKEY is a separate program and not actually a part of COMMAND.COM, DOSKEY must be loaded into memory before you can use all of its features. The most direct way to load DOSKEY is to add it as a line in AUTOEXEC.BAT. You also may want to use some of DOSKEY's optional parameters to increase the DOSKEY buffer size and to load DOS macros. Table 6.1 shows the DOSKEY optional parameters.

Table 6.1
DOSKEY Optional Parameters

Parameter	Function
/INSERT	Forces insert mode as default
/OVERSTRIKE	Forces overstrike mode as default
/REINSTALL	Installs a new copy of DOSKEY
/BUFSIZE=	Specifies the size of the command buffer
/MACROS or /M	Displays all macros and enables you to redirect them to a file
/HISTORY or /H	Displays all command lines stored in memory
macro=text	Creates a DOSKEY macro of up to 127 characters

Recalling DOS Commands

Previous DOS versions enabled you to use the function and cursor keys to recall, edit, and reuse the last DOS command. The F3 key, for example, retypes the last command exactly as you entered it. Although this is often handy, the F3 function is useless when you need to reissue a series of commands. Suppose that you decide to clear some space on your hard disk. You probably would perform the following steps:

1. Change to a directory to check the existing files and how much room currently is available.

2. Copy old, seldom used files to a disk.

3. Delete the copied files from your hard disk.

4. Return to step 1, select another directory for cleanup, and continue to copy and delete files until you clear enough room.

Because this entire process requires several different DOS commands, at each step you are forced to retype the command from a preceding step. DOSKEY, however, remembers several earlier commands and enables you to select one of these commands to edit and reuse. Table 6.2 shows how, through DOSKEY, you can recall several previous commands for reuse (the number of stored commands depends on the buffer size specified when you first load DOSKEY).

Table 6.2
DOSKEY Command Recall Keys

Key	Function
F7	Displays the list of commands recorded by DOSKEY
Alt-F7	Clears the list of commands
↑	Displays the previous recorded command
↓	Displays the next recorded command
F8	Searches the list for a command that starts with text you provide
F9	Selects a command from the list by number
PgUp	Displays the oldest recorded command
PgDn	Displays the newest recorded command
Esc	Erases the displayed command
Alt-F10	Clears all macro definitions

Editing Command Lines

DOSKEY enhances DOS's use of function and arrow keys to recall and edit previous commands. Table 6.2 explains the new keys DOSKEY uses to recall previous commands. Table 6.3 shows the DOS editing keys that still can be used with DOSKEY.

> *Note:* DOS stores the last typed command in a small memory buffer, which is referred to as the *template* because the last existing command can be recalled and used as a pattern, or template (often after editing), for the next DOS command. When DOSKEY is loaded, you have the option to select from several previously issued commands for template editing.

Table 6.3
Command Template Editing in DOS

Key	Function
F1 or →	Copies the next character in the template to the command line
F2	Copies characters from the template until the next character you type is reached
F3	Copies the remaining characters in the template
F4	Moves the cursor forward in the template until the next character you type is reached, but without copying characters from the template
Backspace	Deletes the character to the left of the cursor and restores it in the template
Del	Deletes the character at the cursor position and removes it from the template
Ins	Inserts new characters starting at the cursor position without affecting the template

Note: The DOSKEY /INSERT and /OVERSTRIKE switches modify the method DOS uses when you edit existing commands. The /OVERSTRIKE switch causes editing to function as if DOSKEY isn't loaded (any key you type replaces a character in the template). The /INSERT switch, however, causes any key typed to be inserted before existing characters from the template.

If you use the combination of function and arrow keys already existing in DOS and the new keys provided by DOSKEY, you can recall, select, edit, and reissue DOS commands several levels back. Instead of retyping long command lines, just recall them with DOSKEY for edit and reuse. When you consider the previous example—copying files from your hard disk directories to floppy disks—you can see how DOSKEY can make this task more manageable. Figure 6.1 demonstrates how DOSKEY displays a listing of the previous commands and enables you to select from the list.

```
C:\MSDOS_5>
1: C:
2: CD \MSDOS_5
3: DIR *.COM
4: CD MSDOS_5
5: DIR *.COM
6: COPY *.COM A:
7: DIR
8: ERASE *.COM
9: DIR
10: CLS
C:\MSDOS_5>
```

Fig. 6.1. Using More Than One DOS Command Per Line.

MS-DOS requires that you type each command on its own line. When DOSKEY is loaded, however, you can issue a series of related commands if you type them on the same command line and separate each command with a Ctrl-T. Suppose that you want a directory listing of the current directory, but you first want to clear the screen of existing information. You normally type **CLS** and press Enter, and then type **DIR** and press Enter to execute the commands. If you use DOSKEY, however, you can type **CLS**, then hold the Ctrl key while you press **T**, and then type **DIR** and press Enter to execute both commands.

> ***Tip:*** Although most PC screens display only 80 characters per line, the DOS command line is actually 128 characters long. You can string together multiple DOS commands by using DOSKEY, as long as the commands don't exceed 127 total characters (the Enter key counts as a character). Be careful, however, when you string together commands. The failure of one command in the string can cause problems when subsequent commands are executed. You probably don't want to follow a COPY command with a DEL command in case the COPY operation isn't successful.

Creating Macros with DOSKEY

DOSKEY's macro creation capabilities enable you to completely customize DOS by altering the default parameters for any of the commands or by creating new commands. In this section, you look at how the macro feature works and examine some examples that you may want to use. As you read later about other new and enhanced DOS commands, consider the examples of how DOSKEY macros are used to make DOS commands work the way you want.

Comparing Macros and Batch Programs

In many ways, macros function like batch programs. You can use macros or batch programs to create new commands that consist of DOS commands executed in a specific order and, in some cases, with a predetermined group of switches and parameters.

Macros are limited to 127 characters on a single command line (although, as mentioned earlier, you can include multiple commands as long as they fit into the 127 character limit). Batch files, however, have no practical size limit. Macros are loaded into RAM and must be reloaded whenever you reboot. Batch files are stored on disk and must be in the current directory, in a directory included in your PATH environment variable, or you must specify the batch file's complete path name if you want to execute the batch file.

One of the most important differences between macros and batch files, however, is based in part on the way MS-DOS selects the order in which program files execute, depending upon the file extension. The only file extensions DOS allows for program files are COM, EXE, and BAT. When you issue a command to run a program such as FORMAT, for example, DOS first tries to find and run FORMAT.COM. If FORMAT.COM doesn't exist, DOS next looks for FORMAT.EXE, and finally for FORMAT.BAT. This means that your carefully prepared FORMAT.BAT file containing the parameters you prefer will not run if DOS finds FORMAT.COM or FORMAT.EXE first.

Macros, on the other hand, are executed before DOS looks for a COM, EXE, or BAT file. In fact, macros are executed before DOS internal commands (such as DIR, COPY, and so on). Because macros execute first, you can name a macro with a DOS command name and customize that command's execution.

> *Note:* Although the terms "internal" and "external" often are used with DOS commands, it's seldom clearly explained how they actually differ. *Internal* commands are those contained inside COMMAND.COM, such as DIR and COPY. *External* commands are separate programs such as FORMAT.COM. External programs can be renamed easily, which enables them to be customized with batch programs. However, internal commands like DIR and COPY are more difficult to change. DOSKEY's macros can substitute for both internal and external DOS commands.

Consider the previous FORMAT example. Assume that you normally use 360K disks in your 1.2M A: drive and you want to use the new DOS 5 /Q switch for a "quick" format (the /Q switch is discussed in FORMAT's new options in Chapter 7). You would type the following command:

FORMAT A: /4 /Q

Rather than type the A:, /4, and /Q parameters every time you need to format a disk, you now can use a DOSKEY macro to make those parameters the defaults. You then can simply type **FORMAT** to accomplish the same task.

To load DOSKEY and create the FORMAT macro at the same time, enter the following at the DOS prompt:

DOSKEY FORMAT=FORMAT A: /4 /Q

The first time you load DOSKEY after you turn the power on or reboot your system, you see the message `DOSKey installed`. If DOSKEY is already loaded and you are just adding a new macro, no message appears.

To test your macro, place a previously formatted 360K disk in drive A: and enter the FORMAT command. The disk formats quickly, and you don't waste time by entering parameters. If you encounter a problem, use the DOSKEY /MACROS switch (which also can be typed as /M) to make sure you didn't make a typing error and to check that the disk is formatted at the same 360K size.

Using a DOS Command with the Same Name as a Macro

Although the sample FORMAT macro works well, consider what happens if you want to format a new disk, or perhaps a 1.44M disk, in drive B:. The /Q switch isn't allowed unless a disk already is formatted, and specifying A: and /4 as defaults appears to lock your system into formatting only 360K disks on drive A:. Fortunately, an easy solution is available.

Recall from the preceding discussion that, when you type a program's name at the DOS prompt, DOS tries to run program files in the COM, EXE, and then BAT order. To override this order, you can type the entire program name, including the extension. To run a batch file called FORMAT.BAT instead of the FORMAT.COM program, for example, type **FORMAT.BAT** at the DOS prompt. DOSKEY macros use a similar "back door" method that enables you to load an unaltered version of a DOS command instead of the macro—simply type a space before the command name. In fact, although DOS ignores extra spaces typed before a command name, DOSKEY macros do not. Macros simply do not execute if a space is entered before the macro name is typed. If a macro is called FORMAT and a command is called FORMAT, typing a space before FORMAT causes the command rather than the macro to work.

Going back to the previous example, to format a new 1.44M disk in drive B:, press the space bar before you type **FORMAT B:**. Because of the extra space, the DOSKEY macro is ignored and FORMAT.COM is executed using B: as the only parameter. Because no size parameter is included, the disk is formatted with the default size for the drive—in this case 1.44M.

Tip: Although the example used a macro name that matched an existing DOS command, you also can name your macros with other names. You may consider creating a macro called FORMATB by issuing the following DOSKEY command:

DOSKEY FORMATB=FORMAT B: /U /F:720

This macro name prevents an override of your existing FORMAT macro. Always keep your macro names descriptive and easy to remember.

Saving Your Macros

As you learn more about DOS 5 and decide on your own DOSKEY macro-customized versions of DOS commands, you should save your macros in a batch file so that you can reload them automatically. If you typed the macros recently enough so that they still reside in DOSKEY's command buffer, you can use the /HISTORY switch and DOSKEY to display, print, or save the macro definition steps in a file. You also can use the /MACROS switch to save the current macros by redirecting DOSKEY's output to a file using the greater than (>) redirection operator. Edit your AUTOEXEC.BAT file to incorporate your macro definitions or to run another batch file containing the definitions, and DOS will work the way you want.

Saving DOSKEY Macros in a Batch File for Later Recall

After you create a number of macros that you want to save, you can create a batch file that will re-create the macros. Although you have several optional methods of creating this batch file, the following steps are straightforward and quite easy.

1. Enter the following command to place all current macro definitions in a file called MACROS.TXT:

   DOSKEY /M >MACROS.TXT

2. Load the MACROS.TXT file into the DOS editor by issuing the following command:

   EDIT MACROS.TXT

3. Edit each line in the file by adding the word DOSKEY and a space to the beginning of the line. For example, change the following line:

   FORMATB=FORMAT B: /U /F:720

   to

   DOSKEY FORMATB=FORMAT B: /U /F:720

4. Press the Alt key and select the File menu by pressing the letter F.

5. Select Save As by pressing the A key.

6. Save the file as MACROS.BAT.

7. Exit from the editor by pressing the Alt key, selecting the File menu, and pressing X.

The file you just created, MACROS.BAT, will re-create all of your DOSKEY macros. You easily can add the commands to your AUTOEXEC.BAT file to create these macros. Your macros then will always be available whenever you use your PC. To add the commands to your AUTOEXEC.BAT file, follow these steps:

1. Rename your AUTOEXEC.BAT file by entering the following command:

   REN AUTOEXEC.BAT AUTOEXEC.ORG

2. Combine your AUTOEXEC.ORG file and the MACROS.BAT into a new AUTOEXEC.BAT file using the following command:

    COPY AUTOEXEC.ORG+MACROS.BAT AUTOEXEC.BAT

3. Reboot by pressing the Ctrl, Alt, and Del keys.

Note: Although you can use either the /HISTORY or /MACROS switch to save macro definitions in a file, the two methods differ in what is saved. The /HISTORY switch produces a list of the steps that you used to type the macro definitions. This list also may contain several DOS commands (not related to creating the macros) that you must delete from the file. The /MACROS switch, however, produces a list of only the macro definitions, as the following example shows:

FORMATB=FORMAT B: /U /F:720

Before you use this list in a batch file, you may need to type **DOSKEY** before each line of macro definitions, as in the following example:

DOSKEY FORMATB=FORMAT B: /U /F:720

Increasing the DOSKEY Buffer Size

The DOSKEY command history buffer and the DOSKEY macros share the same memory buffer area. Unless you specify a larger size using the /BUFSIZE= switch, 512 bytes are made available as the default. Although the command buffer and the macros share this memory, running out of room has little effect on the command buffer because the oldest commands are discarded to make room for new ones. You can soon run out of room, however, if you try to define too many macros. DOSKEY displays the message Macro storage depleted. If this happens, save your macros as mentioned previously, and then type the following command:

DOSKEY /REINSTALL /BUFSIZE=1024

Note that in this example, the buffer is set to 1024 bytes.

The /BUFSIZE parameter can be specified only when you first load DOSKEY or when the command is combined with the /REINSTALL switch. The /REINSTALL switch also removes any existing command history buffer and macros from memory. Be sure to save your macros before increasing the buffer size.

> *Note:* Using the DOSKEY /REINSTALL command adds a second copy of DOSKEY to memory and reduces the available conventional memory, unless you use the techniques discussed in Chapter 3 to place DOSKEY into upper memory. If your system has UMBs available, you can replace the following command:
>
> **DOSKEY /REINSTALL /BUFSIZE=1024**
>
> with
>
> **LOADHIGH DOSKEY /REINSTALL /BUFSIZE=1024**
>
> This loads the new copy of DOSKEY into UMBs and does not use any additional conventional memory.

Creating Sample DOSKEY Macros

You can enter and use the following DOSKEY macros without changes. You also can modify the macros to suit your special needs. After all, the purpose of DOSKEY is to enable you to modify DOS 5 to your requirements. Keep in mind, however, that you may have to increase DOSKEY's buffer size, as mentioned in the previous section, if you create a number of macros.

HIDE and UNHIDE

You can use the following HIDE macro to apply the "hidden" file attribute to a single file or a group of files.

    DOSKEY HIDE=ATTRIB +H $1

The UNHIDE macro removes the hidden file attribute.

    DOSKEY UNHIDE=ATTRIB -H $1

You also can create DOSKEY macros that affect the other file attributes. (See Chapter 9 for more information on the ATTRIB command.)

BACK2A

The BACK2A macro backs up all files modified since the last backup from drive C: to disks in drive A:.

    DOSKEY BACKC2A=BACKUP C:*.* A: /S /M

A useful variation of BACKC2A is to add the /F:size argument if you normally use backup disks that have a smaller capacity than the drive's default. For example, if you use 360K disks to back up your files, and drive A: is a 1.2M drive, BACKC2A may be modified as follows:

    DOSKEY BACKC2A=BACKUP C:*.* A: /S /M /F:360

Chapter 9 covers the BACKUP command in greater detail.

GODATA

The GODATA macro is quite specialized and is used to change easily to a specific directory. In this case, you set up the macro to change to the \SYMPHONY\DATA directory. You may want to modify this macro so that you can change easily to a directory that you use often.

    DOSKEY GODATA=CD \SYMPHONY\DATA

CLEAN

The CLEAN macro executes the CHKDSK command by using the /F switch to clean up any lost clusters on your hard disk. You may find this macro especially useful if you often experience problems with power failures, or if you occasionally need to reboot your PC because a program locks up your system.

    DOSKEY CLEAN=CHKDSK C: /F

DEL and ERASE

The DEL and ERASE macros are two examples of how you can use DOSKEY to modify the defaults for internal DOS commands. These macros take advantage of the option to have DOS request verification before you delete files.

> DOSKEY DEL=DEL $1 /P DOSKEY ERASE=ERASE $1 /P

DEL and ERASE are covered more fully in Chapter 8.

FORMAT3, FORMATQ, and FORMATS

These three macros enable you to format disks easily by using the options that are most useful to you. FORMAT3 formats a 360K disk in a high-density drive, FORMATQ applies DOS 5's new quick format to a disk, and FORMATS creates a system disk.

> DOSKEY FORMAT3=FORMAT A: /F:360
> DOSKEY FORMATQ=FORMAT A: /Q
> DOSKEY FORMATS=FORMAT A: /S

Disk-formatting macros offer many customization possibilities. Chapter 7 examines the options offered by the FORMAT command in DOS 5.

TYPEM and TYPEP

The TYPEM and TYPEP macros were designed to help you examine text files. TYPEM displays the file a page at a time, and TYPEP types a file on your printer.

> DOSKEY TYPEM=TYPE $1 $BMORE
> DOSKEY TYPEP=TYPE $1 $GPRN

DIRW

The DIRW macro can be used when you want a 5-column directory listing, as in the following example:

DOSKEY DIRW=DIR $1 /W

If you want to start with a clean screen before the directory listing is displayed, you can modify the DIRW macro to use DOSKEY's ability to include more than one command on a command line. Just remember to separate multiple commands using $T.

DOSKEY DIRW=CLS $T DIR $1 /W

In Chapter 8, you learn how the DIR command gains many new features in DOS 5. In addition to creating DOSKEY macros for the DIR command, you also can use the new DIRCMD environment variable to modify this command's defaults.

XCOPYP

The XCOPYP macro causes XCOPY to ask you for verification before it copies each file. If you prefer to have this the XCOPY default, just name this macro XCOPY instead of XCOPYP.

DOSKEY XCOPYP=XCOPY $1 $2 /P

Creating Your Own DOSKEY Macros

These few examples of DOSKEY macros should start you thinking about even more macro possibilities as you learn about the new features added to DOS 5's commands. Consider which DOS commands don't seem to have the right defaults, and correct them using DOSKEY macros. Remember, DOSKEY macros not only execute faster than batch files, they also make modifying internal DOS commands easier. You also can partially disable DOS commands by creating DOSKEY macros with the same names.

Summary

In this chapter, you learned how to use DOSKEY to recall and edit several
levels of DOS commands. You learned how DOSKEY's macro facility
enables you to customize DOS functions. You examined methods of
saving macros and adjusting DOSKEY's buffer to allow more extensive
macro creation. Finally, you created some sample DOSKEY macros to
start you thinking about macro possibilities. In Chapter 7, you see the
new and enhanced disk commands.

Preparing, Protecting, and Repairing Disks

This chapter examines the new and enhanced disk commands that make DOS 5 easier or safer to use. One command, FORMAT, is enhanced in DOS 5. The MIRROR and UNFORMAT commands are new additions to DOS 5. These two commands add some of the features that, prior to DOS 5, required special disk utilities.

Understanding How Disk Commands Work

Disk commands are DOS commands that prepare disks for use. Disk commands also apply to an entire disk rather than a single file or group of files. One example of a disk command is the FORMAT command, which places magnetic marks on a disk that enables DOS to save and retrieve files from the disk's magnetic surface. These magnetic marks perform a function similar to the lines on a piece of paper. Imagine what happens when you give several young children a sheet of blank paper and instruct them to print their names on the sheet. Without lines to guide them, the printing probably wanders. Add lines, however, and the results improve.

If you give a computer an unprepared, unformatted disk, the computer cannot decipher the disk and displays the message `General failure reading drive x.`

Using the Enhanced FORMAT Command

One of the most destructive errors you can make is to accidentally FORMAT your hard disk. If you have ever done this or if you have seen it happen, you know how quickly the FORMAT command destroys the data on a disk. Ignore the warnings that DOS provides, press Enter, and your data disappears.

The DOS 5 FORMAT command is modified to provide you with a *Safe Format* method to format disks. The original method of formatting disks was to overwrite the root directory area, the File Allocation Table (FAT), and all of the data areas on a disk. Doing this destroys all existing data. In contrast, the Safe Format method writes over the root directory area and the FAT, but not the data area. The data remains, but is not accessible in the normal fashion. In the section "Using UNFORMAT To Recover Information from Accidentally Formatted Disks" later in this chapter, you see how data often can be recovered from a "safe formatted" disk.

The FORMAT command first checks a disk for an existing format. If FORMAT detects a new, unformatted disk, a complete format is performed. If a disk has already been formatted, however, the root directory and FAT are first saved, then overwritten after the disk is checked for bad sectors. An interesting and useful benefit of the Safe Format mode is that previously formatted disks are reformatted faster than earlier DOS versions.

Selecting FORMAT Modes

You can select three different formatting modes with DOS 5's FORMAT command. These commands have both advantages and limitations that you should understand to select the correct command for different situations.

Safe Format

The Safe Format mode is the default mode, if you do not specify format options (except /B, /S, or /V). This mode clears the FAT (File Allocation Table) and the root directory and then checks the entire disk for bad sectors. If bad sectors are found, they are marked so that DOS will not use this bad disk space to save files.

You may wonder why the /B, /S, and /V switches do not override the Safe Format mode as the other switches can. The Safe Format and Quick Format modes can be used only if the disk's capacity is not being changed. These three switches don't cause the disk's overall capacity to change (although /B and /S may reduce the available capacity if the disk was not already a system disk). The balance of FORMAT's switches can result in a change in the disk's formatted capacity. If the capacity is changed, an unconditional format is performed.

The Safe Format mode is a new option in DOS 5, but several utility programs have offered similar formatting modes for years.

Safe Format mode doesn't actually erase the data on the disk. Information about the root directory and the FAT are saved on the disk. You don't see the information, but the UNFORMAT program described later in this chapter uses the information to recover the other files on the disk.

Clearing the FAT and the root directory makes the entire disk (except for those sectors marked as bad) available for use.

You cannot use the Safe Format mode to change the formatted capacity of a disk. Because Safe Format doesn't overwrite existing information, this mode is a poor formatting choice if a disk contains confidential information that should be destroyed.

Quick Format

The Quick Format mode is similar to the Safe Format mode. Quick Format does not actually overwrite files; only the FAT and the root directory are cleared. Unlike Safe Format, however, Quick Format does not check the disk for bad sectors.

Quick Format also saves the information that UNFORMAT can use to recover the files if you accidentally formatted the disk.

Quick Format has the same limitations as Safe Format, plus an additional limitation. Because this mode doesn't check for bad sectors, DOS possibly may try to use a bad sector to store data. Never use Quick Format on a disk you suspect has bad sectors.

The main advantage of Quick Format is the speed at which it formats a disk. As you learn later, performing a Quick Format is extremely fast.

Unconditional Format

The final mode, Unconditional Format, is the familiar FORMAT mode that previous DOS versions use. In this mode, the entire disk is overwritten, and all existing information is destroyed.

You use Unconditional Format mode when you add any FORMAT switches that alter the storage capacity of the disk. Also, Unconditional Format prepares new, unformatted disks for use.

Comparing Speed of Operation

In normal daily operation, the biggest difference between the three format modes is the amount of time each command requires to format a disk. Many factors affect the length of time required to format a disk: system clock speed, disk seek times, and disk capacity. Table 7.1 compares the average time required to format a 360K disk on one system.

Table 7.1
DOS 5 360K Disk Format Times

Mode	Time (in seconds)
Unconditional Format (also DOS 3.x and DOS 4)	45
Safe Format	35
Quick Format	10

Syntax of the FORMAT Command

The FORMAT command is used to prepare a disk for use by DOS. Several options are available, and you often may need to combine several of these options.

The following syntax is used for the FORMAT command:

FORMAT drive: */Q /V:label /S /B*

FORMAT drive: *F:size /U /V:label /S /B*

FORMAT drive: */1 /4 /U /V:label /S /B*

FORMAT drive: */8 /U /S /B*

FORMAT drive: */N:sectors /T:tracks /U /V:label /S /B*

The following list explains the switches available with the FORMAT command.

Switch	Action
/Q	Performs a quick format
/U	Performs an unconditional format
/V:label	Labels the disk as specified
/S	Copies operating system files to the formatted disk
/B	Allocates space on the formatted disk for operating system
/F:size	Formats specified floppy disk size (for example, 360, 720, 1.2, 1.44, 2.88)
/N:sectors	Formats specified number of sectors per track
/T:tracks	Formats specified number of tracks per disk side
/1	Formats a single side of a floppy disk
/4	Formats a 360K floppy disk in a high-capacity drive
/8	Formats eight sectors per track (DOS 1.x compatible)

Understanding the /B Switch

The /B switch allocates space on the formatted disk for the operating system. This means the switch places two hidden system files—IO.SYS and MSDOS.SYS—on the disk after the disk is formatted. Although the file names may lead you to believe the files actually are copies of IO.SYS and MSDOS.SYS taken from your hard disk, they are not. The two files are dummy files that serve only one purpose: to reserve space for the real IO.SYS and MSDOS.SYS files.

The SYS command can convert disks created with the FORMAT /B option to boot disks. Note, however, that although the /B switch reserves space for IO.SYS and MSDOS.SYS, the switch does not reserve space for COMMAND.COM, which also must be present on a bootable disk.

Using the /U Switch for Unconditional Format

Although you may want to use the new, faster Safe Format mode, the FORMAT command now offers the /U switch to perform an old-fashioned, unconditional full format. Suppose that you stored sensitive information on a stack of floppy disks and you want to ensure that no one else can access that information. Simply erasing the files won't do. "Unerase" programs have been around for years, and now even DOS 5 includes an UNDELETE command.

If you specify the /U switch, you instruct FORMAT to overwrite everything on the disk. Although the Unconditional Format mode takes longer, when files must be destroyed, the extra time is worthwhile.

You also must use the Unconditional Format if you format a new disk (FORMAT.COM performs an unconditional format on a new disk even if you do not specify /U) or if you change the capacity of a disk. The Safe Format and Quick Format modes do not perform actual disk formats— they only mark the disk space as available for file storage.

As you upgrade to DOS 5, you should remember that the Unconditional Format mode is identical to the Format mode that DOS 3.x and DOS 4 uses. Although the Safe Format and Quick Format modes are faster, Unconditional Format takes no longer than a DOS 3 or DOS 4 disk-formatting operation.

In choosing which format mode to use, consider the following points:

- New, unformatted disks and disks that are being changed in capacity automatically use the Unconditional Format mode.

- Using the Unconditional Format mode prevents the use of the UNFORMAT command to recover files contained on the disk before the format was performed. Only the Safe Format and Quick Format modes allow the use of UNFORMAT. The Unconditional Format mode, therefore, should be used when you need to ensure the destruction of sensitive files. The other two modes, however, give you the chance to recover accidentally formatted disks.

- The Quick Format mode does not check for bad sectors on the disk. You never should use this mode if you suspect problems with a disk. This mode is, however, the fastest method of reformatting disks.

- The Safe Format mode is slower than the Quick Format mode, but faster than the Unconditional Format mode. Safe Format checks for bad sectors.

Identifying Bad Sectors

Bad sectors are areas on a disk that cannot be used reliably because of problems found on the magnetic surface of the disk. Nearly all hard disks have some bad sectors, but the hard disk isn't considered defective unless the percentage of defective disk space is quite high, or if more sectors fail during use. In fact, a low number of sectors marked as bad is an acceptable condition on a large hard disk.

Floppy disks, however, generally should not be used if they have bad sectors. Unlike hard disks, which run in sealed containers, floppy disks are exposed to dust, smoke, and other airborne particles. If floppy disk sectors start to fail, make a copy of all files contained on the floppy and then throw out the old disk.

If you choose to ignore this advice, remember that the Quick Format mode does not check for sectors that may have failed since the disk was last formatted. Both Safe Format and Unconditional Format modes detect bad sectors and therefore offer more safety if you plan to store valuable information on these disks. This added safety is particularly important if your workspace is dusty, smoky, or visited by pets.

Using the New /Q Switch for Quick Format

Although the new Safe Format mode is fast, you can specify the /Q switch when you reformat a previously formatted disk for even faster operation. When you use this switch, FORMAT simply erases the FAT and the root directory.

The effect of a quick format is similar to simply erasing all of the files on a disk. If you format a floppy disk that lacks subdirectories, read-only, hidden, or system files, both methods take about the same length of time. If your disk has subdirectories, read-only, hidden, or system files, however, the Quick Format method is much faster because FORMAT ignores these files, but DEL does not.

Suppose that you want to remove the system files from a floppy disk to use the disk's capacity for data files. Before you can delete IO.SYS and MSDOS.SYS, you first must use the ATTRIB command with both the -S and -H parameters to change these two files from hidden, system files to normal files. You then can delete any existing files, and your disk will be ready to use.

Using the Quick Format mode to prepare the disk is much faster in the preceding example because a single command performs the operation. Quick Format also removes all subdirectories even when they still contain files—unlike the RD (Remove Directory) command, which requires that you empty a directory before you delete it.

Using the /F:x Switch To Specify Disk Capacity *(also DOS 4)*

With the ever-expanding capacity of floppy disks, Microsoft found it necessary to add a simple switch that specifies the capacity FORMAT is supposed to use. The /F:x switch, although offered as an addition to the existing switches, really can be thought of as a replacement for the confusing set of size switches, which include /1, /4, /8, /N:x, and /T:x.

Using the /F:x switch is simple. Just replace the x with the size of disk you want to format. For example, suppose that you want to format a 360K disk in your 1.2M A: drive. Type the following command:

FORMAT A: /F:360

You also can combine the /F switch with the /Q, /S, /B, /U, and /V switches. Note, however, that the /F and /Q switches are compatible only if you don't change capacity.

The /F:x switch now also supports the new 2.88M disk drives. As this book goes to press, 2.88M disks aren't yet common, but it is nice to know that DOS will be ready when the drives arrive.

The /F:x switch currently supports the following disk sizes and capacities:

> 160K, single-sided, 5 1/4-inch
> 180K, single-sided, 5 1/4-inch
> 320K, double-sided, 5 1/4- inch
> 360K, double-sided, 5 1/4-inch
> 720K, double-sided, 3 1/2-inch
> 1.2M, double-sided, 5 1/4-inch
> 1.44M, double-sided, 3 1/2-inch
> 2.88M, double-sided, 3 1/2-inch

The suffix K or M is optional—FORMAT accepts all of the size designations shown, with or without the suffix. You also can specify the 1M-plus disk sizes in K by moving the decimal point three places to the right. For example, a 2.88M disk can be specified as 2880, 2880K, 2880KB, 2.88, 2.88M, or 2.88MB. The following command lines have the same effect:

> FORMAT A: /F:2880
> FORMAT A: /F:2880K
> FORMAT A: /F:2880KB
> FORMAT A: /F:2.88
> FORMAT A: /F:2.88M
> FORMAT A: /F:2.88MB

Using MIRROR To Create a Delete Tracking File

MIRROR is an optional enhancement to the UNDELETE and UNFORMAT programs (UNDELETE is covered in Chapter 8, UNFORMAT is covered later in this chapter). You can use MIRROR to create a *Delete Tracking File*, which records File Allocation Table (FAT) information about each deleted file.

Syntax for the MIRROR Command

You can use the following syntax for the MIRROR Command:

MIRROR *drive: .../1 /Td -nnn /U /PARTN*

The syntax elements for the MIRROR command are listed as follows:

Parameter	Action
drive:	Saves copy of root directory & FAT for specified drive(s)
/1	Keeps only the latest root & FAT information (no BAK)
/Td[-nnn]	Installs resident Delete Tracking for drive d. The optional -nnn can be used to specify the tracker file limit (-999 is the default).
/U	Attempts to unload Delete Tracking software from memory
/PARTN	Saves hard disk partition tables onto a floppy disk

Using MIRROR To Track Deleted Files

Erased files aren't really removed from the disk—they are marked as erased in the directory listing and their FAT entries are released so that the disk space they occupy can be reused. If your files are contiguous—that is, they occupy only one continuous space on the disk—you can unerase the files fairly easily. The files' directory entry, although marked as erased, still contains the last recorded file information, including the file's size and its starting location in the FAT. An unerase program such as UNDELETE, therefore, can simply assume that the file itself occupies enough disk space, starting at the point indicated in the FAT, to include the entire file.

Because the space occupied previously by erased files is marked as available, however, DOS overwrites that space when you save more files. The available space usually is broken into many small pieces and your files are, as a result, saved in many small chunks spread around the disk. This fragmentation makes use of the UNDELETE program more difficult because you cannot assume that an erased file will stay in one contiguous piece. If the file is no longer in one piece and the FAT entries that provide the map to the pieces are gone, how do you recover the file?

Creating the Delete Tracking File

You can use MIRROR to create the Delete Tracking File, a record of the FAT entries for erased files. By using MIRROR to record this information, even badly fragmented files can be recovered if new files haven't taken the original files' space.

When you load MIRROR, the program creates either two or three files on a disk. The read-only, hidden, system file MIRORSAV.FIL, and the read-only file MIRROR.FIL always are created. These two files contain a record of the disk's root directory and FAT as they existed when the program was loaded. Both the UNDELETE and UNFORMAT programs use this information to restore the disk to the same condition—if you haven't written too much data since the two files were created or updated.

If you specify the /T switch, MIRROR also creates a system file called PCTRACKR.DEL, which is updated whenever a file is deleted. The PCTRACKR.DEL file also records directory and FAT information, but on a continuous basis. PCTRACKR.DEL, therefore, logs a more current record of the files on your disk. This enables the UNDELETE program to recover files that were created and deleted after MIRORSAV.FIL and MIRROR.FIL were last updated.

Using the /T Switch

If you specify the /T switch when you load MIRROR, the program tracks files as you delete them by loading a small TSR program (6560 bytes) that records information on deleted files in PCTRACKR.DEL. The PCTRACKR.DEL file's default size and the number of files that can be tracked will vary according to the size of the disk. Table 7.2 shows the default number of files and the approximate size of the file for different disk sizes.

Table 7.2
Disk Formats and File Capacities

Disk capacity	Files tracked	Approximate size of PCTRACKR.DEL
360K	25	5K
720K	50	9K
1.2M	75	14K
1.44M	75	15K
20M	101	18K
32M	202	36K
Over 32M	303	55K

Note: Although the 2.88M capacity disk is not specified, it seems that MIRROR's default for this disk is in the 75 to 100 range with a tracking file of 15K to 18K.

Removing MIRROR from Memory

Because MIRROR installs itself as a terminate-and-stay-resident (TSR) program when you use the /T switch to enable Delete Tracking, you probably should include a MIRROR/T command in your AUTOEXEC.BAT file. The TSR program doesn't use much memory, and you probably will not notice the slight delay as PCTRACKR.DEL updates the list when you delete files. MIRROR's TSR portion also can be loaded into reserved memory on an 80386 system, using the LOADHIGH command (see Chapter 3).

You may want to consider removing MIRROR from memory to speed up file operations while you use programs that create and delete large numbers of temporary files. Certain operations of database programs (sorting records, for example) may fall into this category. By removing the MIRROR TSR before loading the database program application, you stop PCTRACKR.DEL from filling up with information about the temporary files.

If the MIRROR TSR program was the last TSR loaded into memory, you can remove the program by typing the following command:

MIRROR /U

If MIRROR successfully removes itself from memory, it responds with `Delete Tracking removed from memory`. If the removal is unsuccessful, the screen shows one of the following two messages:

```
Cannot unload resident Delete Tracking. Vectors or
memory have been altered.
```

```
Cannot unload. Delete-Tracking is not resident or is a
different version.
```

If you see the first message, another TSR program probably was loaded after MIRROR. Because TSR programs can be removed from memory only in the reverse order in which they are loaded, you need to remove the other TSR (or TSRs) before you can remove MIRROR.

The second `Cannot unload` message probably indicates that the MIRROR TSR program was not in memory. If you have PC Tools installed on your system, you may have accidentally loaded that version of MIRROR. (Microsoft is licensing the MIRROR, UNDELETE, and UNFORMAT programs from Central Point Software, Inc. You can find these programs in PC Tools 6.0.)

Using the /PARTN Switch

MIRROR also has another function. Although you may never use the information the MIRROR /PARTN switch records, the switch can be invaluable if you ever do need it. This switch records hard disk partition table information on a disk. Unlike the Delete Tracking File, which MIRROR creates and is used by the UNDELETE command, the partition table information is used by the UNFORMAT command.

The partition table is a reserved area located at the beginning of a hard disk's physical sectors. The partition table tells DOS (and all other operating systems that may be installed on the disk) which disk cylinders the system can access. The partition table normally is inaccessible to DOS programs. Even so, your hard disk can be damaged in this area, thus preventing you from accessing data. The MIRROR /PARTN switch's design provides a means to recover disk file data if this damage occurs.

Using MIRROR To Save Partition Information

You need to use the MIRROR /PARTN switch only once to save your hard disk's partition table information. The partition table information never changes unless you change the hard disk partitions—in which case you should use the MIRROR /PARTN switch again.

If you ever need to restore your hard disk's partition table, however, you will be glad you were prepared. To save your hard disk's partition table information, follow these steps:

1. Format a disk in your A: drive by typing the following command:

   FORMAT A: /S

2. To save the partition table information file on the disk, type the following command:

   MIRROR /PARTN

   MIRROR then offers to save the partition table information on drive A:.

3. Press Enter to accept drive A:.

Figure 7.1 shows the messages that appear on-screen.

4. Copy UNFORMAT.COM to the disk. This is the program that uses the PARTNSAV.FIL file to restore your hard disk's partition table.

   If you have room, you may want to copy additional DOS files to the disk. In an emergency such as a corrupted hard disk partition table, you should have as many of DOS 5's commands available as possible. Exactly which files you want to copy can be based on several factors (disk capacity is a major factor). EDIT.COM and QBASIC.EXE are good choices for editing files, although EDLIN.EXE is probably a better choice if you use a 360K disk.

5. Label the disk to indicate that it holds your hard disk's partition table information, and then store the disk in a safe place. In fact, you may even want to DISKCOPY this important recovery disk.

```
C:\>MIRROR /PARTN
MIRROR, UNDELETE, and UNFORMAT (C) 1987-1991 Central Point Software Inc.

Disk Partition Table saver.

The partition information from your hard drive(s) has been read.

Next, the file PARTNSAV.FIL will be written to a floppy disk.  Please
insert a formatted diskette and enter the name of the diskette drive.
What drive? A

Successful.

C:\>
```

Fig. 7.1. Using MIRROR to save hard disk partition table information.

Remember to update the PARTNSAV.FIL file if you ever change the hard disk's partition structure. Unless you make this type of change, however, you have no reason to use the MIRROR /PARTN switch again.

Recovering Information with UNFORMAT

Although the FORMAT command includes warnings and requires verification before the command begins formatting a hard disk, you still may format your hard disk in error. In the past, this type of accident meant the immediate loss of everything on your hard disk.

Accidentally formatting a floppy disk, of course, is even easier and does not come with a warning. You may forget to change from an important data disk to a blank disk before you issue a command to format a new disk.

New to DOS 5, and used in combination with the Safe and Quick modes of DOS 5's FORMAT command, the UNFORMAT command offers a chance to recover from such errors. UNFORMAT, which is licensed from Central Point Software, was originally a part of the disk utility program PC Tools.

Syntax of the UNFORMAT Command

The syntax for the UNFORMAT command is as follows:

> **UNFORMAT** *drive: /J /L /P /TEST /U*
>
> **UNFORMAT** */PARTN /L /P*

The syntax elements of the UNFORMAT command are listed as follows:

Parameter	Action
drive:	Drive to unformat
/PARTN	Restore disk partition table
/J	Verify that the Mirror files agree with information on the disk
/L	List all file and directory names found, or display current partition table, when used with /PARTN
/P	Echo messages to print on LPT1
/TEST	Do not write changes to disk
/U	Unformat without using Mirror file

Using UNFORMAT To Recover Disks

The UNFORMAT command works in cooperation with two other DOS 5 enhancements, the FORMAT command's Safe Format and Quick Format modes and the MIRROR command, both discussed earlier in this chapter.

Note: UNFORMAT cannot recover a disk formatted with an earlier version of the DOS FORMAT command, or a disk formatted with the DOS 5 FORMAT /U Unconditional Format mode. These formatting modes actually overwrite all of the information on a disk, therefore destroying all existing data.

Using the MIRROR Files with UNFORMAT

UNFORMAT can recover data from an accidentally formatted disk because, as mentioned previously, the Safe Format and Quick Format modes don't write over a disk's data. Existing files stay on the disk, but FORMAT makes them inaccessible by creating a new, blank root directory and a FAT with every good sector marked as available. A blank root directory and a FAT that provides no help are major obstacles when you want to recover data lost by the FORMAT command. The MIRROR files can help in this situation.

As discussed earlier, MIRROR creates a file on your disk that tracks the locations of all files. UNFORMAT, like the UNDELETE command covered in Chapter 8, can use this file to find your data.

If you didn't use MIRROR to track your files, you still may be able to recover them. The Safe Format and Quick Format modes of the FORMAT command also store the MIRROR files on a disk as they format the disk.

Note: The MIRROR files—MIRORSAV.FIL and MIRROR.FIL—will not appear to be on a disk after you format it with the Safe Format or the Quick Format mode. Both files are placed on the disk, however, and marked as deleted as part of the formatting process. If you don't need to UNFORMAT the disk, neither of these files will use disk space.

The MIRROR files, however, can be too outdated to use or may be missing if you saved a number of files since you formatted the disk. As you add more files to the disk, the space previously used by the MIRROR files—as well as the files tracked by the MIRROR files—is likely to be used by new files. Even so, as you see in later sections on the UNFORMAT switches, you sometimes can recover files even when the MIRROR files are missing or invalid.

A Sample UNFORMAT Session

The UNFORMAT command normally is easy to use. You simply enter the command, followed by the drive that contains the disk you want to unformat. In this sample session, you see how UNFORMAT functions in this case.

Figure 7.2 shows the directory listing of a high-density 5 1/4-inch disk. As you can see, the root directory contains a subdirectory called DATA, but no other files. Because the disk's capacity is 1.2M, we can tell that the DATA directory must contain some files because only 839,680 bytes are free.

```
C:\MSDOS_5>DIR A:

 Volume in drive A is a test disk
 Volume Serial Number is 1540-10D9
 Directory of A:\

DATA        <DIR>      01-16-91   9:46a
        1 file(s)          0 bytes
                      839680 bytes free
C:\MSDOS_5>
```

Fig. 7.2. A typical directory listing.

Suppose that after examining the directory listing in figure 7.2, you assume that the disk contains no useful files (because you didn't see any in the listing). Rather than checking the DATA directory, you then issue a FORMAT command to prepare the disk for reuse. Figure 7.3 shows the result.

Figure 7.4 shows that the disk is indeed formatted and that the DATA directory is gone. Also notice that the volume label is changed from a test disk (refer to fig. 7.2) to LOST DATA, the name you used when you reformatted the disk.

```
C:\MSDOS_5>FORMAT A:
Insert new diskette for drive A:
and press ENTER when ready...

Checking existing disk format
Saving UNFORMAT information
Verifying 1.2M
Format complete

Volume label (11 characters, ENTER for none)? LOST DATA

   1213952 bytes total disk space
   1213952 bytes available on disk

       512 bytes in each allocation unit
      2371 allocation units available on disk

Volume Serial Number is 1666-10FA

Format another (Y/N)?N

C:\MSDOS_5>
```

Fig. 7.3. Formatting the disk.

```
C:\MSDOS_5>DIR A:

 Volume in drive A is LOST DATA
 Volume Serial Number is 1666-10FA
 Directory of A:\

File not found

C:\MSDOS_5>
```

Fig. 7.4. The disk after formatting.

You suddenly realize your error—the disk you formatted contained valuable data files. Fortunately, you haven't yet saved new files on the disk, so you needn't worry about the MIRROR files or data files being overwritten. Figure 7.5 shows how the UNFORMAT command works.

Notice that UNFORMAT warns you that files modified since the last time MIRROR was used may be lost. This warning is slightly vague and definitely misleading. If you proceed with UNFORMAT, all files modified or added since the MIRROR files were created *are* lost. Because both FORMAT and MIRROR create MIRROR files, running the MIRROR program at this point can prevent you from unformatting the disk. The reason is that MIRROR makes a backup copy of all existing MIRROR files and, if you ran MIRROR since the disk was formatted, the backup MIRROR files are replaced by the last files created by MIRROR rather than the files created by FORMAT.

```
C:\MSDOS_5>UNFORMAT A:
Insert diskette to rebuild in drive A:
and press ENTER when ready.

Restores the system area of your disk with
the image file created by MIRROR.
     WARNING !!          WARNING !!
This should be used ONLY to recover from the inadvertent use
of the DOS FORMAT command or the DOS RECOVER command.
Any other use of UNFORMAT may cause you to lose data!  Files modified
since the last use of MIRROR may be lost.

The LAST time MIRROR was used was at 10:25 on 01-16-91.

The MIRROR image file has been validated.

Are you SURE you want to update the SYSTEM area
of your drive A (Y/N)?Y

The system area of drive A has been rebuilt.
  You may need to reboot the system.
C:\MSDOS_5>
```

Fig. 7.5. UNFORMAT can recover an accidentally formatted disk.

If you saved any files on your disk since you formatted it, copy the files to another disk before using the UNFORMAT command. By doing this, you can allow UNFORMAT to proceed without destroying your data.

Figure 7.6 shows the results of the UNFORMAT command. Notice that the volume label is restored to a test disk and the volume serial number also is restored to its original value. Additionally, because you used the /S switch with the DIR command (see Chapter 8), you can see that the files in the DATA directory also are restored. The UNFORMAT command returns the disk to the condition it was in prior to reformatting.

Using the /TEST, /U, /P, and /L Switches

Although UNFORMAT usually works best if you use the MIRROR files, those files can be invalid or missing. If so, you need to determine if the files on the reformatted disk are fragmented and, therefore, not recoverable.

```
C:\MSDOS_5>DIR A: /S

 Volume in drive A is a test disk
 Volume Serial Number is 1540-10D9

 Directory of A:\

DATA          <DIR>      01-16-91   9:46a
        1 file(s)           0 bytes

 Directory of A:\DATA

 .            <DIR>      01-16-91   9:46a
 ..           <DIR>      01-16-91   9:46a
LS0816   WR1      3909 08-16-90   2:10p
NEW701   PIX      1915 01-11-91  12:14p
OUTLINE2 WR1    367319 01-11-91   9:40a
        5 file(s)      373143 bytes

 Total files listed:
        6 file(s)      373143 bytes
                       839680 bytes free
C:\MSDOS_5>
```

Fig. 7.6. *The disk after using UNFORMAT.*

Note: Without the MIRROR files, UNFORMAT cannot recover fragmented files because it is able to locate only the first pieces of a file. With the exception of simple text files, your chances of finding usable partial files is highly unlikely.

Figures 7.7 and 7.8 show how the UNFORMAT /TEST switch works. Despite the warnings, /TEST does not actually change information on the disk—/TEST simply shows you what the /U switch does. Notice that Simulation only is displayed twice to inform you that no actual changes are taking place.

If you use the /L, /P, or /U switch instead of the /TEST switch, UNFORMAT unformats the disk without using the MIRROR files. These three switches vary only slightly. /L and /P are identical except that /P directs its output to your printer so that you can have a printed record of the UNFORMAT process. You cannot use /U with the /PARTN switch, but you can use the other two switches.

```
C:\MSDOS_5>UNFORMAT A:/TEST

Insert diskette to rebuild in drive A:
and press ENTER when ready.


   CAUTION !!
This attempts to recover all the files lost after a
FORMAT, assuming you've NOT been using MIRROR.  This
method cannot guarantee complete recovery of your files.

The search-phase is safe: nothing is altered on the disk.
You'll be prompted again before changes are written to the disk.

Using drive A:

Are you SURE you want to do this?
If so, type in 'Y'; anything else cancels.
? Y

Simulation only.

Searching disk...
10% searched, 1 subdir found.
```

Fig. 7.7. *The first half of the UNFORMAT /TEST display.*

Using the /J Switch

The UNFORMAT /J switch checks to see that the MIRROR files contain the same information as the system area (root directory and FAT) on the disk. You may, however, find its messages slightly confusing. Figure 7.9 shows an example of using the /J switch on a disk that recently had its MIRROR files updated. Notice that UNFORMAT /J specifies that The system area of drive A has been verified to agree with the image file. **If the disk is reformatted, the message says** The system area does NOT agree with the image file.

```
Files found in the root: 0
Subdirectories found in root: 1

Walking the directory tree to locate all files...
Path=A:\
Path=A:\SUBDIR.1\
Path=A:\

Files found: 3
Simulation only.

Are you SURE you want to do this?
If so, type in 'Y'; anything else cancels.
? Y

Checking for file fragmentation...
Path=A:\
Path=A:\SUBDIR.1\
Path=A:\
3 files recovered.

Operation completed.

C:\MSDOS_5>
```

Fig. 7.8. The second half of the UNFORMAT /TEST display.

```
C:\MSDOS_5>UNFORMAT A: /J

Insert diskette to rebuild in drive A:
and press ENTER when ready.

Restores the system area of your disk with
the image file created by MIRROR.
      WARNING !!          WARNING !!
This should be used ONLY to recover from the inadvertent use
of the DOS FORMAT command or the DOS RECOVER command.
Any other use of UNFORMAT may cause you to lose data!  Files modified
since the last use of MIRROR may be lost.

Just checking this time.

The LAST time MIRROR was used was at 10:25 on 01-16-91.

The MIRROR image file has been validated.


The system area of drive A has been verified
to agree with the image file.

C:\MSDOS_5>
```

Fig. 7.9. Using the UNFORMAT /J switch.

These messages are intended to inform you whether the MIRROR files match the current information in the root directory and FAT. When you reformat the disk, the MIRROR files saved on the disk don't match the root directory and FAT. The MIRROR files instead contain the previous root directory and FAT information.

UNFORMAT /J is most useful as a tool to determine whether the MIRROR command should be issued to update the MIRROR files. If the system area and image file agree, no changes were made. If they do not agree, changes occurred. Finally, if the MIRROR files are missing, the disk space they occupied was overwritten and you should run MIRROR to rebuild the files.

Using the /PARTN Switch with UNFORMAT

UNFORMAT has one feature that you may never need. By using the /PARTN switch, you can instruct the program to recover a hard disk that suffers from a corrupted partition table. Using a special file, also created by the MIRROR command, UNFORMAT enables you to correct problems that otherwise make a hard disk totally inaccessible. Under normal conditions, you will never use the /PARTN switch, but a poorly designed program, the careless use of utility programs that write directly to the disk, or a computer virus someday may make this switch a lifesaver.

If you are interested in seeing your hard disk's partition information, you can combine the /PARTN switch with either the /L or /P switch to show the information on the screen (/L) or to send the data to the printer (/P). Figure 7.10 shows a typical example of using UNFORMAT /PARTN /L.

You won't need to use the hard disk's partition information very often, but like the MIRROR /PARTN option, this information someday may save your hard disk data if you develop a serious problem. Of course, the technique involved in using this information goes well beyond the scope of this book. Even so, you should print out and file a copy of that information for future reference. (If you want more information on using partition table information, you can refer to *Que's MS-DOS 5 User's Guide,* Special Edition.)

```
C:\MSDOS_5>UNFORMAT /PARTN /L
Hard Disk Partition Table display.

Drive # 80h has 1022 cylinders, 5 heads, 26 sectors (from Bios).

The following table is from cylinder 0, head 0, sector 1:

                 Total_size      Start_partition   End_partition
                 Bytes   Sectors  Cyl Head Sector   Cyl Head Sector    Rel#
     Type        -----   -------  ---------------   ---------------    -----
     --------
HUGE  Boot       65M     132834    0    1    1      1021   4    26       26

C:\MSDOS_5>
```

Fig. 7.10. Using UNFORMAT /PARTN /L to display partition information.

Summary

In Chapter 7, you learned how the FORMAT command is enhanced in DOS 5. You also looked at how the new MIRROR and UNFORMAT commands can prevent disk disaster. You examined ways that these commands make using disks safer. In the next chapter, you look at some enhancements to file-related commands in DOS 5.

Managing Directories and Files

8

In Chapter 8, you examine four new and enhanced commands—DIR, TREE, DEL and UNDELETE. As each command is covered, customizing suggestions—using DOSKEY macros (if appropriate)—are presented. Although this chapter focuses on the new and enhanced features of each command, the DOSKEY macro examples may, as in other chapters, suggest better ways to use the existing features as well.

Using DIR's New Features

You should be pleased with the new features DOS 5 has added to the DIR command. DIR probably is the most often-used DOS command, and the improvements add features previously available only in such stand-alone utilities as Norton's Filefind program.

The syntax for the DIR command is as follows:

DIR *pathname* /P /W /A:*attributes* /O:*sortorder* /S /B /L

The switches used in the syntax are described in the following list:

Switch	Action
/P	Pauses after each screen page of display
/W	Lists files in columns with up to five file names on each line
/A:attributes	Displays only files with the attributes you specify
/O:sortorder	Displays files sorted in the specified order
/S	Displays files in the specified directory and all subdirectories
/B	Lists file names, one per line, without file information
/L	Uses lowercase

DOS 5 has five new switches you can use with the DIR command. In the following sections, you look at each switch and consider their options. You learn how you can use these new options to your benefit.

Using the /S Switch To Search Subdirectories

On a higher-capacity hard disk, you may have difficulty finding a particular file. You know that the file is there, but the file is not in the directory where you expected to find it. By using the /S switch, DIR now can locate every file that matches a file-name template. You also can use the new DIR /S switch to produce complete listings of all files on a disk. The following examples show why the new DIR /S switch is important.

Using DIR /S To Find Copies of the Same File

Suppose that when you upgrade to DOS 5, you want to find all old copies of your Microsoft mouse drivers. Figure 8.1 shows what you may see if you type the following command in the C:\ directory:

DIR MOUSE.* /S

```
C:\>DIR MOUSE.* /S

 Volume in drive C is Fixed C
 Volume Serial Number is 1594-6E14

Directory of C:\DOS

MOUSE    COM     31833 06-07-90   2:24a
         1 file(s)      31833 bytes

Directory of C:\WIN30\SYSTEM

MOUSE    COM      4896 05-01-90   3:00a
         1 file(s)       4896 bytes

Total files listed:
         2 file(s)       36729 bytes
                       9695232 bytes free

C:\>
```

Fig. 8.1. Using DIR /S to find files in subdirectories.

The program finds two copies of MOUSE.COM—one in the C:\DOS directory and one in the C:\WIN30\SYSTEM directory. From the listing, you can tell easily that the file in the C:\DOS directory is the newer version. Because you should use the latest available release of drivers, such as the mouse driver, you can use the DIR /S switch to find old copies that you want to delete.

When you use the new DIR /S switch and a file name, or a wild card that displays a selected group of file names, you can find all copies of a single file or a group of files. You can use this listing to ensure that you always work with the latest copy of a worksheet, letter, or database file. You also can use the DIR /S switch, along with the new /A switch, before performing a backup to determine which files you want to back up.

Using DIR /S To Find All Files

The /S switch also can be used without specifying a particular file name. In this case, DIR /S lists all the files on the disk. Of course, your hard disk probably contains too many files for this to be useful—unless you redirect the output to a file or to your printer. To obtain a printed listing of all the files on your hard disk, type the following command:

DIR C:\ /S >PRN

A printed listing is handy to keep with the backup disks when you perform a complete backup of your hard disk. You then can examine the printed listing to check the date and size of the backup files. If you rely on the log file produced by BACKUP /L:logfile, you can tell which files are on which disk. The log file, however, doesn't include each file's size or date.

Comparing DIR /S with Other DOS Commands

DOS 5 provides several methods to determine which files are contained on a disk. Each method, however, provides slightly different information.

First, use DIR/S to look at a typical disk. The result of using this command should look like the following:

```
Volume in drive B is TYPICAL

Directory of B:\

DOS            <DIR>         12-05-90      8:56a
PROGRAM        <DIR>         12-05-90      8:57a
COMMAND  COM        41765    08-15-90      3:33a
        3 file(s)           41765 bytes

Directory of B:\DOS

.              <DIR>         12-05-90      8:56a
..             <DIR>         12-05-90      8:56a
ASSIGN   COM         6169    08-15-90      3:33a
ATTRIB   EXE        16223    08-15-90      3:33a
BACKUP   EXE        35911    08-15-90      3:33a
CHKDSK   EXE        17952    08-15-90      3:33a
        6 file(s)           76255 bytes

Directory of B:\PROGRAM

.              <DIR>         12-05-90      8:57a
..             <DIR>         12-05-90      8:57a
DATA           <DIR>         12-05-90      8:57a
LOOKUP   COM         3560    03-24-86     12:00p
SPELL    COM        18614    03-24-86     12:00p
```

```
WORD      COM       44498   02-01-88    9:33a
WORDFIND  COM        2844   03-24-86   12:00p
         7 file(s)             69516 bytes

Directory of B:\PROGRAM\DATA

   .             <DIR>        12-05-90    8:57a
   ..            <DIR>        12-05-90    8:57a
CONTRACTDOC       11726       09-14-90    9:39a
LETR      DOC      7001       09-14-90    9:39a
MEMO      DOC      8555       09-14-90    9:39a
REPORT    DOC     13356       09-14-90    9:39a
         6 file(s)             40638 bytes

Total files listed:
        22 file(s)          228174 bytes
                            491520 bytes free
```

Next, look at the same disk, this time using the command TREE /F.

```
Directory PATH listing for Volume TYPICAL
```

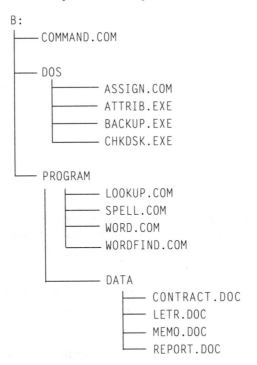

```
B:
├── COMMAND.COM
│
├── DOS
│       ├── ASSIGN.COM
│       ├── ATTRIB.EXE
│       ├── BACKUP.EXE
│       └── CHKDSK.EXE
│
└── PROGRAM
        ├── LOOKUP.COM
        ├── SPELL.COM
        ├── WORD.COM
        └── WORDFIND.COM
        │
        └── DATA
                ├── CONTRACT.DOC
                ├── LETR.DOC
                ├── MEMO.DOC
                └── REPORT.DOC
```

Finally, the following shows the result when you use the CHKDSK /V command.

```
Volume TYPICAL    created 12-05-1990 8:56a
Directory B:\
Directory B:\DOS
B:\DOS\ASSIGN.COM
B:\DOS\ATTRIB.EXE
B:\DOS\BACKUP.EXE
B:\DOS\CHKDSK.EXE
Directory B:\PROGRAM
Directory B:\PROGRAM\DATA
B:\PROGRAM\DATA\CONTRACT.DOC
B:\PROGRAM\DATA\LETR.DOC
B:\PROGRAM\DATA\MEMO.DOC
B:\PROGRAM\DATA\REPORT.DOC
B:\PROGRAM\LOOKUP.COM
B:\PROGRAM\SPELL.COM
B:\PROGRAM\WORD.COM
B:\PROGRAM\WORDFIND.COM
B:\COMMAND.COM

    730112 bytes total disk space
      3072 bytes in 3 directories
    235520 bytes in 13 user files
    491520 bytes available on disk

      1024 bytes in each allocation unit
       713 total allocation units on disk
       480 available allocation units on disk

    655344 total bytes memory
    635264 bytes free
```

All three commands—DIR /S, TREE /F, and CHKDSK /V—display all the file names on the disk. Only DIR /S shows the file information (size, date, and time). DIR /S also displays the total size of the files in each directory, as well as the total of all files.

TREE /F displays a graphical representation of the disk's structure and locates each file in that structure, but provides no further information about individual files.

CHKDSK /V shows more information concerning the overall disk space but, like the TREE /F command, shows little information about the individual files.

As mentioned earlier, you also can use the log file, produced by the BACKUP /L:logfile command, to determine where erased files existed previously on a disk. This log file does not contain file information, either.

The new DIR/S switch provides new, useful information that was difficult to obtain in previous DOS releases without a separate utility program, such as the Norton Utilities.

Using the /O Switch To Specify Sort Order

The DIR command normally displays file names in the order in which the files are listed in the directory. As you add new files to a directory, the new files are placed at the end of the listing, unless a file entry has been deleted. In this case, DOS replaces the deleted entry with the new file and DIR shows the new file at the same place the deleted file was listed originally.

This somewhat random placement of files within a directory listing often makes locating particular files difficult, especially when the directory contains a large number of files.

In previous DOS versions, you used the DOS SORT filter to produce a sorted directory listing. With DOS 5, however, the DOS SORT filter no longer is necessary. You now can use the /O:sortorder switch to specify the sort order. Table 8.1 shows the values that you can substitute for sortorder, to sort the directory in the order you desire.

These sortorder switches also can be combined. Combined switches are evaluated from left to right. For example, if you type the following command:

DIR /O:NG

the directory listing is sorted by name only. To produce a listing sorted with the directories listed first and the files listed and sorted by name, the following command is correct:

DIR /O:GN

Table 8.1
DIR /O:sortorder Switches

Switch	Action
N	Sorts by name
–N	Sorts by name in reverse order (B before A)
E	Sorts by extension
–E	Sorts by extension in reverse order (B before A)
D	Sorts by time and date, earliest first
–D	Sorts by time and date, latest first
S	Sorts by size, smallest first
–S	Sorts by size, largest first
G	Sorts with directories grouped before other files
–G	Sorts with directories grouped after other files

You may want to display directory listings in a specified sort order for several reasons. Finding a particular file is easier if the directory is sorted by name. Finding groups of files of a particular type may be easier if the listing is sorted by file extension and then by name. Sorting by date enables you to more easily identify old data files that are no longer used. A sort by size may be useful if you run short of disk space and need to make room for more files. Finally, sorting the listing with all of the subdirectories grouped together makes it easier to find data directories.

Note: The /O:sortorder switch changes the order in which files are displayed, but does not physically change the files' position in the directory on the disk.

Therefore, DOS operations that use the directory, such as DEL, COPY, and XCOPY, may not present the files in the same order as a DIR command using the /O:sortorder switch.

Using the /A Switch To Specify File Attributes

The DIR /A:attribute switch enables you to specify which files are displayed, based on each file's attributes (see ATTRIB in Chapter 9 for a more complete explanation of file attributes).

In previous versions of DOS, for example, the DIR command doesn't show hidden or system files. You also have no way to tell which files are marked read-only or which files were modified since the last backup and therefore have their archive attribute set. Table 8.2 shows the /A:attributes that you can use to determine which files are displayed by DIR.

Table 8.2
DIR /A:attribute Switches

Switch	Action
H	Displays all hidden files
–H	Displays all files that are not hidden
S	Displays all system files
–S	Displays all files other than system files
D	Displays directories only
–D	Displays all files other than directories
A	Displays all files ready for archiving (backup)
–A	Displays files that have been archived
R	Displays all read-only files
–R	Displays only files that are not read-only

As with the /O:sortorder switches, you can combine the /A:attribute switches to customize the DIR listing. If you want to see all of the files that are hidden and marked read-only, you can use the following command line:

DIR /A:HR

You can use the DIR /A:A switch, for example, to determine in advance which files would be affected by a BACKUP /M, XCOPY /A, or XCOPY /M command. Because the directory would show all files that had their archive bit set (meaning they had been modified since the last backup), these files would be backed up or copied by one of the above commands.

If you installed copy-protected software on your hard disk and later you want to remove that software, you may find the DIR /A:H switch quite useful. Copy-protection schemes often place hidden files and, in some cases, hidden directories on a hard disk. In the root directory (for example, C:\) of your hard disk, any hidden files and directories are displayed if you type the following command (see fig. 8.2):

DIR /S /A:H

```
C:\>DIR /S /A:H

 Volume in drive C is Fixed C
 Volume Serial Number is 1594-6E14

Directory of C:\

IO       SYS      33044 12-13-90    4:09a
MSDOS    SYS      37506 12-13-90    4:09a
         2 file(s)        70550 bytes

Total files listed:
         2 file(s)          70550 bytes
                          9693184 bytes free

C:\>
```

Fig. 8.2. Using DIR /S /A:H to find hidden files.

If you normally boot from your hard disk, two files—IO.SYS and MSDOS.SYS—always appear. These two files are used by DOS, and are not part of any copy-protection scheme. Any other hidden files or directories, however, may be left over from your old copy-protected software and, therefore, wasting disk space. If you're not sure, however, call the customer support department of the software manufacturer before removing these files.

Using the /B Switch To List Only File Names

The DIR command has another new switch, /B, for a bare file-name listing. When you use the /B switch, only the file names are displayed; file size, date, and time are not included (see fig. 8.3). This switch may be handy if you need a file listing to use in a batch file—you wouldn't have to edit the listing to remove unnecessary information. You also can use the DIR /B switch to redirect output of DIR to another command because most DOS commands use file names only.

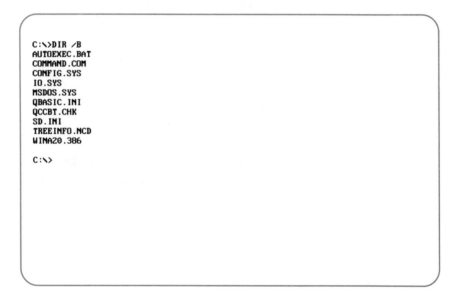

```
C:\>DIR /B
AUTOEXEC.BAT
COMMAND.COM
CONFIG.SYS
IO.SYS
MSDOS.SYS
QBASIC.INI
QCCBT.CHK
SD.INI
TREEINFO.NCD
WINA20.386

C:\>
```

Fig. 8.3. *Using DIR /B to see only the file names.*

Using the /L Switch To List File Names in Lowercase

The final new DIR switch, /L, is used to list file names in lowercase instead of uppercase. Figure 8.4 shows an example of using the /L switch.

```
C:\>DIR /L

 Volume in drive C is Fixed C
 Volume Serial Number is 1594-6E14
 Directory of C:\

autoexec bat        657 01-07-91  10:18a
command  com      46246 12-13-90   4:09a
config   sys        430 01-07-91   9:39a
io       sys      33044 12-13-90   4:09a
msdos    sys      37506 12-13-90   4:09a
qbasic   ini         48 10-15-90   3:55p
qccbt    chk         16 02-09-89   4:20p
sd       ini       2497 01-30-90   3:35p
treeinfo ncd       1019 01-13-91  10:22a
wina20   386       9349 12-13-90   4:09a
        10 file(s)      130812 bytes
                       9687040 bytes free

C:\>
```

Fig. 8.4. Using DIR /L to list file names in lowercase.

Note: The /W switch has changed slightly in the way that it displays the directory listings. When you type **DIR /W**, the file names in the directory listing are displayed in the form

```
FILENAME.EXT
```

instead of

```
FILENAME    EXT
```

Using SET DIRCMD To Customize DIR

DOS 5 includes a new environment variable—DIRCMD. *Environment variables* are used by a number of DOS programs to customize the operation of the program. PATH and PROMPT are two other environment variables that most people are familiar with and use on their computers.

Note: To see the current settings for all DOS environment variables, type the command **SET** (without any parameters) at the DOS prompt. The strings assigned to COMSPEC, PATH, PROMPT, and any other environment variables are displayed but not changed.

DIRCMD, which stands for DIRectory CoMmanD, enables you to customize the DIR command. By setting DIRCMD to contain your preferred set of switches for DIR, those switches become the default for DIR. The following examples show you how this works:

Command	Explanation
DIRCMD=/W	The default directory listing is the wide display, with all normal files and directories listed.
DIRCMD=/O:GN	The default directory listing is the full file listing, sorted with directories listed first, followed by all normal files sorted by name.
DIRCMD=/P /A:H	The default directory listing displays only hidden files and pauses after each page of files.

To set DIRCMD to a value, you can type the command **SET DIRCMD=** at the DOS prompt, or you can include the same command in a batch file like AUTOEXEC.BAT. For example, if you want DIR to pause after each page and sort the listing by name and then extension, but not display directories, add the following line to AUTOEXEC.BAT:

SET DIRCMD=/P /O:NE /A: −D

You can see that DIRCMD enables you to create exactly the kind of directory listing that suits your needs. You can use a DOSKEY macro rather than DIRCMD, however, to customize DIR. You actually can use either method, but DIRCMD works even if you don't load DOSKEY. Additionally, because DOSKEY macros first are translated into the command line they replace before being executed, using DIRCMD is slightly faster on most systems.

Overriding SET DIRCMD

One advantage DOSKEY macros have over DIRCMD is that DIRCMD is harder to override. Suppose that you include SET DIRCMD=/A:H in your AUTOEXEC.BAT file. This command would result in a DIR command showing only hidden files. To display non-hidden files, you would have to issue the following command:

DIR /A: –H

To override a default setting, you must issue the opposite command. In the preceding example, you are required to specify that you want to see files which do not match the default of being hidden files.

If you intend to use DIRCMD to set new defaults for the DIR command, be certain to plan your new defaults carefully so that you don't have to override the defaults very often. Otherwise, you will be wasting time.

Using DIRCMD with Batch Files

As mentioned previously, one advantage of DIRCMD is that you can use it to establish new defaults for the DIR command. You later may want to change the defaults. Suppose that you used the following line in your AUTOEXEC.BAT file:

SET DIRCMD=/O:NE

This command makes DIR sort first by name and then by extension. Although you may find this most convenient, you sometimes need to set the default so that the listing is sorted first by extension, and then by name. At other times, you may need to sort by size. Create the following batch file (either with EDIT, the full-screen editor discussed in Chapter 11, or with the COPY CON: filename command) and name the file DIRCHG.BAT.

```
@ECHO OFF
IF %1=="N" SET DIRCMD=/O:NE
IF %1=="E" SET DIRCMD=/O:EN
IF %1=="S" SET DIRCMD=/O:S
```

After you create this batch file, you can create a new default for the DIR command by typing **DIRCHG**, followed by a space and the letter **N**, **E**, or **S**. If you use **N**, DIR sorts first by name and then by extension. If you use **E**, DIR sorts by extension first, then name. If you use **S**, DIR sorts by ascending file size. Note that if you include a SET DIRCMD command in your AUTOEXEC.BAT file, the DIR default resets whenever you reboot.

Note: Because the check performed by the batch IF statement is case sensitive, the above batch file recognizes only uppercase letters as parameters. You can, of course, expand the batch file to also test for lowercase letters. Because of this case sensitivity, however, you may want to keep your parameters as short as possible. Testing for every variation of upper- and lowercase letters in NAME, for example, requires 16 IF tests.

Using DOSKEY Macros Instead of DIRCMD

Rather than using the SET DIRCMD command, you may want to create DOSKEY macros to customize DIR's actions. A DOSKEY macro may be a better choice than SET DIRCMD, for example, if you frequently want different types of directory listings. Suppose that you want to create DOSKEY macros to produce the same three differently sorted directory listings as the DIRCHG.BAT batch file you created earlier. Simply add the following lines to your AUTOEXEC.BAT file:

```
DOSKEY DIRN=DIR /O:NE
DOSKEY DIRE=DIR /O:EN
DOSKEY DIRS=DIR /O:S
```

To see a directory listing sorted first by name and second by extension, enter the command DIRN at the DOS prompt. Similarly, use DIRE for a listing sorted first by extension and then by name, and DIRS for a listing sorted by size.

DOSKEY macros have the additional advantage of leaving DIR's defaults untouched. Using different settings at the command line then is slightly easier. Either way, however, the enhancements to DIR in DOS 5 are quite useful.

Controlling Screen Size *(also DOS 4)*

The standard PC display normally is 80 columns by 25 lines. DOS commands that use the standard page size, such as DIR and MORE, always have used 25 lines as the size of a full page. When EGA and VGA displays made more lines possible, however, the limitations of a fixed page size became more apparent. If your VGA displays 50 lines, but the DIR /P command pauses after 25 lines, you waste half of the display. DOS 5 is adapted to the new display options. If you include a line in your CONFIG.SYS file that loads the ANSI.SYS device driver and you use the MODE command to set your screen to 43 or 50 lines, both DIR and MORE will use the new setting for page size. To set the display to 50 lines, use the following command:

```
MODE CON LINES=50
```

Note that this command works only if ANSI.SYS is loaded (by including a **DEVICE=ANSI.SYS** line in your CONFIG.SYS file) and your monitor and adapter card can display more than 25 lines.

Displaying More Information

The DIR command in DOS 5 displays more information than past versions of DOS. This additional information is quite helpful if you are working with a disk that contains many files.

Directory Name Listed on Each Screen

When you use the /P switch to pause the display after each page, a new piece of information is displayed by DIR. If the display continues over several pages, the name of the displayed directory is shown at the top of each page after the first page. In figure 8.5, you can see the message (continuing C:\SYMPHONY), which is displayed at the top of the last page.

Shows Total Size of Files

The DIR command now shows not only the remaining space available on the disk, as in previous versions, but also the total size of the displayed files. In figure 8.5, for example, you can see that the size of the 98 files totals 4,256,025 bytes.

```
SW       HLP      23690 02-03-86  12:43a
SWSETUP  COM      64162 09-22-87  12:00a
SWSYMSET EXE       2184 07-14-85  12:01a
SWSYMVID EXE       6183 11-08-85   1:49a
SYMPHONY CMP     222417 03-16-90   8:00p
Press any key to continue . . .

(continuing C:\SYMPHONY)
SYMPHONY CNF       1143 01-24-91   9:39a
SYMPHONY DYN      25675 03-16-90   8:00p
SYMPHONY EXE      49920 04-13-90  11:02a
SYMPHONY HLP     162361 03-16-90   8:00p
SYMPHONY VWA      19566 03-16-90   8:00p
TEXT     VWA       5996 03-16-90   8:00p
TIMES    AFL     289324 03-16-90   8:00p
TRIUM    AFL     284723 03-16-90   8:00p
UTIL     SET      10138 03-16-90   8:00p
VIEWER   APP      30076 03-16-90   8:00p
VIEWER   HLP        734 03-16-90   8:00p
VT100    APP      13536 03-16-90   8:00p
WR1DCA   CNF        344 03-16-90   8:00p
        98 file(s)     4256025 bytes
                       9684992 bytes free

C:\SYMPHONY>
```

Fig. 8.5. The DIR /P command shows the name of the directory on each page.

The number of bytes shown is the sum of the files that match the template you use. In this case, all files in the directory are shown because a simple DIR command with no parameters is used. Suppose, however, that you issue the following command:

DIR SY*.*

Instead of showing all files in the directory, the listing now includes only those files that start with the characters SY. Figure 8.6 shows that the total number of files shown, 6, matches the number below the listing. Also, the total bytes shown for the size of the files, 481,082 bytes, is the total of all files selected by the SY*.* template.

This information can be helpful when you are determining the number of floppy disks needed to copy or back up a series of files. If you specify that the DIR command is to display only files with the archive bit set (when you use the /A:A switch), for example, the total number of bytes for those files is displayed. Figure 8.7 shows an example of this switch.

```
C:\SYMPHONY>DIR SY*.*

 Volume in drive C is Fixed C
 Volume Serial Number is 1594-6E14
 Directory of C:\SYMPHONY

SYMPHONY CMP     222417 03-16-90   8:00p
SYMPHONY CNF       1143 01-24-91   9:39a
SYMPHONY DYN      25675 03-16-90   8:00p
SYMPHONY EXE      49920 04-13-90  11:02a
SYMPHONY HLP     162361 03-16-90   8:00p
SYMPHONY VWA      19566 03-16-90   8:00p
        6 file(s)      481082 bytes
                      9682944 bytes free

C:\SYMPHONY>
```

Fig. 8.6. *Total file size matches displayed files.*

```
C:\SYMPHONY>DIR /A:A

 Volume in drive C is Fixed C
 Volume Serial Number is 1594-6E14
 Directory of C:\SYMPHONY

3DGRAPH  APP      62982 01-07-91   9:37a
3DGRAPH  HLP      21826 09-10-87   4:57a
3DINST   EXE       8192 06-17-88   9:39a
COMPSERV CCF       1428 01-18-91   7:23a
FORECALC APP      62792 05-23-90   2:29p
FORECALC HLP      34276 09-20-90   3:49p
MAC      CCF       1428 09-19-90   8:19a
PERSONAL DCT       2955 01-22-91   9:48a
PGRAPH   CNF        297 01-07-91   9:59a
SIDEWAYS APP      37922 09-22-87  12:00a
SIDEWAYS COM      37553 12-24-90   3:11p
SIDEWAYS HLP      18029 09-22-87  12:00a
SPELLER  SCF        462 09-13-90  12:52p
SWSETUP  COM      64162 09-22-87  12:00a
SYMPHONY CNF       1143 01-24-91   9:39a
       15 file(s)      355447 bytes
                      9680896 bytes free

C:\SYMPHONY>
```

Fig. 8.7. *A directory listed by the /A:A switch.*

Remember, the BACKUP /M, XCOPY /A, and XCOPY /M commands apply only to files with the archive bit set. If you enter DIR /A:A before you use one of these commands, you can determine easily how many disks you need before you begin backup operations.

If you use the DIR /S switch, the total number of files and the files' size is shown for each directory. In addition, a grand total for all the displayed files and directories is shown.

DOS 5 adds many improvements to DIR, one of the most often-used commands. These new features include many of the functions found in utility programs such as the Norton Utilities: file find, file size, directory sort, and file attribute. Of course, these stand-alone utility programs offer features not included in DOS 5's DIR command, but many of the important and popular features are included.

Using the TREE Command *(also DOS 4)*

As the number of files on your hard disk increases, keeping track of the directory structure becomes more difficult. The TREE command was designed to assist you by showing that structure. You can use Tree, for example, to determine the proper path name when you access files in directories other than the current directory.

The syntax for the TREE command is as follows:

TREE *pathname: /f /a*

/f displays the names of the files in each directory, and /a forces TREE to use ASCII instead of extended characters.

Early versions of TREE display a text listing of the directory tree. When you use the new graphic directory tree display, however, you get a better visualization of the structure. Figure 8.8 shows an example of using the TREE command on a hard disk with a number of directories.

The TREE command also can be redirected to your printer to produce a graphic map of the structure of your hard disk.

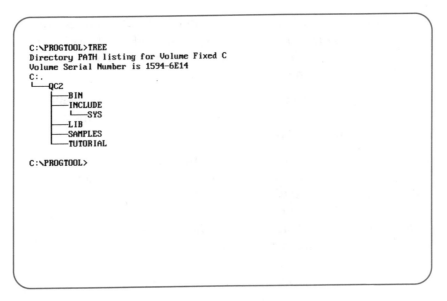

```
C:\PROGTOOL>TREE
Directory PATH listing for Volume Fixed C
Volume Serial Number is 1594-6E14
C:.
└──QC2
        ├──BIN
        ├──INCLUDE
        │   └──SYS
        ├──LIB
        ├──SAMPLES
        └──TUTORIAL

C:\PROGTOOL>
```

Fig. 8.8. An example of the TREE command.

> **Note:** Although most printers can print the TREE listing as shown in figure 8.8, the TREE command has an optional switch, /A, which forces TREE to use characters that any printer can print.

Using DEL and ERASE *(also DOS 4)*

One of the most dangerous commands in MS-DOS has always been DEL (because DEL and ERASE are the same command, you can use DEL to indicate either one). With this command, a user can quickly erase a single file, a group of files, or all the files on a disk. Using wild cards, you can easily erase many more files than you intend—just press the Enter key and your files are gone! Some warning is provided by DOS if the user enters the following command:

    DEL *.*

Depending on the version of DOS you are using, the warning can be either of the following:

```
All files in the directory will be deleted. Are you sure
(Y/N)?
```

or

```
Are you sure (Y/N)?
```

If by chance you type **DEL *.EXE**, DOS simply erases all of your EXE program files *without issuing a warning*.

With no DOS command to undo the erasure, users turned to programs like the Norton Utilities and PC Tools so that they could recover from simple mistakes. Worse, because DEL is an internal DOS command (one that is part of COMMAND.COM) DEL cannot, therefore, be replaced or renamed easily.

The /P Prompt Switch

DEL has been modified with the addition of the /P (for prompt) switch. When you add the /P switch, DEL shows each file's name before taking action. You then are prompted to press Y or N to indicate whether the file should be erased. As an additional confirmation, you also must press Enter after pressing Y or N. Figure 8.9 shows an example of the /P switch when used with the DEL command.

```
C:\MSDOS_5> DEL D*.COM /P

C:\MSDOS_5\DISKCOMP.COM,    Delete (Y/N)?N
C:\MSDOS_5\DISKCOPY.COM,    Delete (Y/N)?Y
C:\MSDOS_5\DOSKEY.COM,    Delete (Y/N)?B
C:\MSDOS_5\DOSKEY.COM,    Delete (Y/N)?N
C:\MSDOS_5\DOSSHELL.COM,    Delete (Y/N)?T
C:\MSDOS_5\DOSSHELL.COM,    Delete (Y/N)?Y

C:\MSDOS_5>
```

Fig. 8.9. The /P switch, used with the DEL command.

Figure 8.9 shows that you must press the Y or the N key. If you press any other key and then press Enter, you are prompted with the same file name again.

A DOSKEY Macro for DEL

The DEL command presents an excellent opportunity for customizing DOS with a DOSKEY macro. By defining a macro, you can make DEL use the /P switch by default, thus ensuring that DOS always prompts you before files are deleted. The suggested DOSKEY macro for the DEL command is the following:

DOSKEY DEL=DEL $1 /P

In this macro, the **$1** represents the file name(s) you type after the DEL command. To use the DEL command without the prompt, press the space bar before you type DEL, or use ERASE when you don't want the prompt.

> *Note:* DOSKEY uses the dollar sign ($) to represent replaceable parameters instead of the percent sign (%) used in batch files.

External DOS commands, such as FORMAT and BACKUP, can be renamed with the REN command. Internal DOS commands, however, are renamed only by changing an entry in the internal command table within COMMAND.COM by using DEBUG or a program like the Norton Utilities. When using commands with potential for danger, such as DEL, DOSKEY macros are even more important.

If you include this macro in your AUTOEXEC.BAT file, be sure to exercise caution when you use someone else's system. You can forget that /P isn't the default—and may not even exist on another PC—especially if the computer uses an earlier version of DOS. A good way to verify that this macro is installed is to type the following command:

DEL *.*

If the macro is installed, each file is presented in turn with the prompt for deletion. If the macro is not installed, you see the message Are you sure?. You also can use the DOSKEY /MACROS command to verify that the macro is listed. Older versions of DOS don't include DOSKEY, so you see the error message Bad command or filename. Whichever method you use, verify that the macro is installed before you start erasing files.

Using UNDELETE To Recover Erased Files

Unlike words printed on paper, erased files aren't really removed from a disk. Instead, they are marked as erased in their directory listing and the space they occupy is marked as available in the File Allocation Table (or FAT). Prior to DOS 5, however, unless you purchased one of the utility programs like PC Tools or the Norton Utilities, erased files were lost as far as the PC user was concerned.

The new UNDELETE command, however, has changed this. Now, if you accidentally erase a file, you may be able to recover it. Figure 8.10 shows an example of using the UNDELETE command to recover files.

```
C:\MSDOS_5>UNDELETE *.COM

Directory: C:\MSDOS_5
File Specs: *.COM

    Delete Tracking file not found.

    MS-DOS Directory contains    7 deleted files.
    Of those,    7 files may be recovered.

Using the MS-DOS Directory.

    ?DIR    COM    796  9-05-85  3:39p  ...A
Do you want to undelete this file? (Y/N)
```

Fig. 8.10. Using the UNDELETE command to recover erased files.

Note: Because the space an erased file was using is marked as available in the FAT, you must UNDELETE accidentally erased files as soon as possible. If you wait until more files have been saved, DOS likely will have used the space for saving another file. When this happens, the erased file cannot be recovered by any means.

The syntax for the UNDELETE command is as follows:

UNDELETE *x:\path\filespec /HELP /DT /DOS /LIST /ALL*

The UNDELETE command has several switches that you can use to control its operation, as shown in the following list:

Switch	Action
/DT	Instructs UNDELETE to use only the information in the "delete tracking" file (produced by the MIRROR command discussed in Chapter 7) to recover files. Any deleted files that are not listed in the delete tracking file are ignored. You will be prompted to confirm each file before it is recovered.
/DOS	Instructs UNDELETE to use only the information in the DOS directory listing for recovering files. The delete tracking file, if it exists, is ignored. You will be prompted to confirm each file and supply the first character of its file name before the file is recovered.
/LIST	Displays files available for recovery, but does not actually recover them. If you supply a file-name template (such as *.COM), only those files that match the template are listed.
/ALL	Attempts to recover all files that have not been overwritten. Automatically supplies a character for the first letter of the file name. The supplied character probably will not be correct, and the file will need to be renamed using the REN command.

Because of the unique nature of UNDELETE, you may not want to create a DOSKEY macro to customize this command. If you need to use UNDELETE, you probably should control its operation manually so that you can make certain the correct files are recovered and named properly.

When a file is deleted, the first character of its file name is changed to a special character (E5 in hexadecimal, which is 229 in decimal). This special character indicates an erased file to DOS. No record of the original character is retained, and this directly affects how you use the UNDELETE command.

In the MS-DOS file system, two files in the same directory cannot use the same name. You cannot, for example, have two files named REPORT.DOC in the same directory. If you use the UNDELETE command to recover erased files, this fact becomes quite important regardless of the switches you use.

Suppose that you keep all of your document files in a directory called \PROGRAM\DATA. When you issue a DIR command, you may see the following:

```
Volume in drive B is Typical
Directory of B:\PROGRAM\DATA

REPORT1   TXT      6510 12-06-90    7:35a
REPORT2   TXT      8812 12-06-90    7:36a
REPORT3   TXT     15556 12-06-90    7:36a
REPORT4   TXT     13356 09-14-90    9:39a
     4 file(s)            44234 bytes
                         468992 bytes free
```

Notice that each file has a slightly different name. If you erase REPORT1.TXT, however, you are free to save another file called REPORT1.TXT. If you save another file using the same file name and then try to use UNDELETE /DOS to recover the original REPORT1.TXT file, you see the following listing:

```
        ?EPORT1   TXT       6510 12/06/90  7:35a      ...A
Do you want to undelete this file?  (Y/N)
Y
Enter the first character of the filename.
R
A filename with that first character already exists.
Press any key to reenter the first character.
B
        ?EPORT1   TXT       6510 12/06/90  7:35a      ...A

Enter the first character of the filename.
B
File successfully undeleted.
```

The delete tracking file, produced by the MIRROR command, keeps a record of deleted files. As part of this record, the first character of the file name is saved. The same rule that allows only one file to have a particular name applies here, however. If you use the UNDELETE command with the /DT switch or with the /ALL switch, UNDELETE automatically provides a first character. To prevent duplications, the first available character of the following list is used:

% & - 0 1 2 3 4 5 6 7 8 9 and then A through Z

Therefore, if you use the /DT or the /ALL switch, the deleted version of REPORT1.TXT becomes #EPORT1.TXT. If a second deleted version of REPORT1.TXT exists, after recovery the second file is named %EPORT1.TXT.

Recovering One Type of File

You sometimes may want to recover a subset of the erased files in a directory rather than all of the files. Perhaps you had several different types of files in a directory and you erased all of the files, but later realized that you accidentally erased your program files along with the old data files. If you type the following command, UNDELETE will recover all the EXE program files, using the file information in the delete tracking file:

UNDELETE *.EXE /DT

Remember, however, that UNDELETE can recover a file only if its disk space has not been overwritten by saving another file.

Note that this example uses the /DT switch instead of the /DOS switch. Using the /DT switch is possible only with MIRROR loaded. Without MIRROR, you have no delete tracking file for the /DT switch to use.

As you learned in the discussion of MIRROR in Chapter 7, using a delete tracking file has some disadvantages. First, of course, is that the delete tracking file uses disk space to store the file information. Second, using MIRROR somewhat slows disk operations. The amount of this slow-down depends entirely on the components in your PC. On a 80386 computer equipped with a high-speed hard disk, you may not notice a difference. On a slower system with database software that creates and deletes many temporary files, you may notice a considerable difference.

Recovering Noncontiguous Files

As you use your PC, files may become fragmented (or noncontiguous) because the disk space made available when you delete files doesn't always come from the end of the total file space. Disk space becomes available in individual pieces, which may not be large enough to store an entire file. DOS then allocates disk space to a file in several noncontiguous pieces.

Recovering noncontiguous files is more difficult than recovering contiguous files, because you have to find all the pieces and splice them together in the correct order. Because the delete tracking file keeps information on the location of deleted files, you have a better chance of recovering noncontiguous files if you have a delete tracking file.

Recovery Problems

Most files are of little use unless you have the complete file. If half of a program file has been overwritten, for example, the untouched portion of the file isn't going to run. On the other hand, recovering 90% of a long document may be worthwhile. Even so, if part of an erased file's space has been overwritten, the program displays one of the following messages:

```
This file cannot be automatically recovered since not
all of the clusters are available.

Only some of the clusters for this file are available.
Do you want to recover this file with only the available
clusters? (Y/N)

None of the clusters for this file are available. The
file cannot be recovered. Press any key to continue.

Starting cluster is unavailable. This file cannot be
recovered with UNDELETE. Press any key to continue.
```

If you receive one of these messages, but still feel that part of the file would be of value, you may find that a program like the Norton Utilities or PC Tools can recover some of the data. Using one of these programs to recover partial files, however, is a complex and difficult task.

UNDELETE may find several deleted copies of files that have the same name. The first deleted file UNDELETE offers to recover may not be the file you want. You may have to recover several files, providing each with a unique name, until you find the correct file. Always keep in mind that each time a file is saved, the chances of recovering existing erased files is reduced. The sooner you use UNDELETE, the better your chance for success.

Summary

Starting with the many enhancements to DIR, Chapter 8 showed you four new and enhanced commands. Next, you learned how the TREE command helps you navigate the directories on your hard disk. Finally, you learned how the new /P switch makes the DEL command much safer to use and how UNDELETE can rescue your files if you delete them accidentally. You will use these commands often, and the improvements they gain in DOS 5 offers many benefits.

Maintaining Disk and File Integrity

Chapter 9 covers four of the DOS 5 commands that help you maintain the integrity of the files on your disks. These commands are ATTRIB, REPLACE, BACKUP, and DISKCOPY. As in previous chapters, this chapter looks primarily at the enhancements new to DOS 5.

Using the ATTRIB Command

The ATTRIB file attribute command, introduced with DOS Version 3.0, provides MS-DOS users a minimal level of file security. Until DOS 5, ATTRIB did not enable users to change several important file attributes. Many PC users, therefore, turned to utility programs such as the Norton Utilities FA program.

Note: File attributes are controlled by bits in the file attribute byte of each file's directory listing. A file may be marked as a read-only, hidden, system, volume label, subdirectory, or archive entry. The volume label and subdirectory attributes normally are not applied to files and cannot be set using ATTRIB.

The ATTRIB command in DOS 5 has the following syntax:

ATTRIB *+R|-R +A|-A +S|-S +H|-H pathname /S*

The syntax elements are described as follows:

+   Sets an attribute

-     Clears an attribute

R   Read-only file attribute

A   Archive attribute

S   System file attribute

H   Hidden file attribute

/S   Processes files in all subdirectories of the specified path

Figure 9.1 shows how the ATTRIB command displays the attributes set for each file. Notice that the display indicates A if the archive bit is set, S if the system bit is set, H if the hidden bit is set, and R if the file is marked read-only.

```
C:\>ATTRIB
  A   SH      C:\MSDOS_5\IO.SYS
  A   SH      C:\MSDOS_5\MSDOS.SYS
  A           C:\MSDOS_5\CONFIG.SYS
  A           C:\MSDOS_5\COMMAND.COM
  A           C:\MSDOS_5\DISKCOMP.COM
      S       C:\MSDOS_5\DISKCOPY.COM
  A   H       C:\MSDOS_5\DOSKEY.COM

C:\>
```

Fig. 9.1. Using ATTRIB to examine file attributes.

Using ATTRIB's New Switches

Although DOS 3.0 enabled ATTRIB to control the read-only attribute and DOS 3.2 added the archive bit, before DOS 5, ATTRIB lacked important options. With the new switches added in DOS 5, however, ATTRIB now can control all of the file-related attributes.

Using S for System Attribute

The System attribute normally is applied to very few files. When applied, this attribute hides a file and treats the file as read-only. The new ATTRIB S switch allows control of a file's system attribute bit.

To change a file called MYFILE.COM so that its system attribute is set, for example, you use the following command:

ATTRIB +S MYFILE.COM

After issuing this command, type the following command to show that the system attribute has been set:

ATTRIB MYFILE.COM

You then can remove the system attribute from MYFILE.COM by typing the following:

ATTRIB -S MYFILE.COM

Using H for Hidden Attribute

The Hidden attribute prevents files from appearing in directory listings or from being deleted. Use the ATTRIB H switch to control the hidden attribute of a file.

The hidden attribute can be set or reset in the same manner as the system attribute. To change MYFILE.COM to a hidden file, enter the following command:

ATTRIB +H MYFILE.COM

To remove the hidden attribute, type the following:

ATTRIB -H MYFILE.COM

Figure 9.2 shows how ATTRIB is used to reset file attributes. In this example, the read-only attribute of COMMAND.COM is reset, but the files marked as system or hidden (IO.SYS, MSDOS.SYS, DISKCOPY.COM and DOSKEY.COM) are not reset. ATTRIB displays a message listing the files that are not affected by the attribute reset command.

```
C:\>ATTRIB
    A   SH      C:\MSDOS_5\IO.SYS
    A   SH      C:\MSDOS_5\MSDOS.SYS
    A           C:\MSDOS_5\CONFIG.SYS
    A       R   C:\MSDOS_5\COMMAND.COM
    A           C:\MSDOS_5\DISKCOMP.COM
        S       C:\MSDOS_5\DISKCOPY.COM
    A   H       C:\MSDOS_5\DOSKEY.COM

C:\>ATTRIB -R
Not resetting hidden file C:\MSDOS_5\IO.SYS
Not resetting hidden file C:\MSDOS_5\MSDOS.SYS
Not resetting system file C:\MSDOS_5\DISKCOPY.COM
Not resetting hidden file C:\MSDOS_5\DOSKEY.COM

C:\>ATTRIB
    A   SH      C:\MSDOS_5\IO.SYS
    A   SH      C:\MSDOS_5\MSDOS.SYS
    A           C:\MSDOS_5\CONFIG.SYS
    A           C:\MSDOS_5\COMMAND.COM
    A           C:\MSDOS_5\DISKCOMP.COM
        S       C:\MSDOS_5\DISKCOPY.COM
    A   H       C:\MSDOS_5\DOSKEY.COM

C:\>
```

Fig. 9.2. *Using ATTRIB to remove the read-only file attribute.*

Using the S and H Switches Together

MS-DOS sometimes uses a combination of the system and hidden attributes to prevent certain files from being deleted accidentally. Figure 9.2 shows that IO.SYS and MSDOS.SYS have both of these file attributes set.

Note: IO.SYS and MSDOS.SYS had the hidden and the system file attributes set for a good reason. Both files must be in the root directory of any disk that you use to boot your PC. In addition, the files must be located at the proper position in the directory and physically on the disk. If you remove the hidden and system attributes from these two files, the files can be erased or moved accidentally. If this happens, you cannot start your system from the boot disk. Unless you are absolutely sure of what you are doing, do not change the file attributes of IO.SYS or MSDOS.SYS.

To reset the system or the hidden attribute, you normally issue the appropriate ATTRIB command. Because both attributes are used together to mark the special files DOS needs, however, you cannot reset just one of these two attributes if the other also is set for the file. Figure 9.3 shows the result of trying to reset the system attribute for the file IO.SYS.

```
C:\>ATTRIB -S IO.SYS
Not resetting hidden file C:\MSDOS_5\IO.SYS

C:\>ATTRIB
  A   SH      C:\MSDOS_5\IO.SYS
  A   SH      C:\MSDOS_5\MSDOS.SYS
  A           C:\MSDOS_5\CONFIG.SYS
  A           C:\MSDOS_5\COMMAND.COM
  A           C:\MSDOS_5\DISKCOMP.COM
      S       C:\MSDOS_5\DISKCOPY.COM
  A   H       C:\MSDOS_5\DOSKEY.COM

C:\>
```

Fig. 9.3. Attempting to reset the system attribute of IO.SYS.

ATTRIB does not reset the system attribute of IO.SYS, but displays the following message: `Not resetting hidden file C:\MSDOS_5\IO.SYS.` If you issue another ATTRIB *.SYS command, the result will be identical to figure 9.3. If you attempt to reset the hidden attribute instead of the system attribute, ATTRIB will display the message: `Not resetting system file C:\MSDOS_5\IO.SYS.`

When the hidden and the system attributes both have been set for a file, you must reset both attributes with a single command (see fig. 9.4).

```
C:\>ATTRIB -S -H IO.SYS

C:\>ATTRIB
   A            C:\MSDOS_5\IO.SYS
   A   SH       C:\MSDOS_5\MSDOS.SYS
   A            C:\MSDOS_5\CONFIG.SYS
   A            C:\MSDOS_5\COMMAND.COM
   A            C:\MSDOS_5\DISKCOMP.COM
       S        C:\MSDOS_5\DISKCOPY.COM
   A   H        C:\MSDOS_5\DOSKEY.COM

C:\>
```

Fig. 9.4. Resetting both the hidden and system attributes.

By combining the system and the hidden attributes in a single ATTRIB command, you can reset the file attributes for DOS's special files (refer to fig. 9.4).

> *Note:* You can use either the system or the hidden file attribute to prevent files from being deleted. This method is not recommended, however, because some programs may not function properly if their related files are hidden or system files. This problem occurs because these file attributes prevent files from appearing in a normal directory listing. Instead of using these two attributes to protect your files, use the read-only file attribute.

Using /S to Affect Subdirectories

You use the /S ATTRIB switch to apply a file attribute to the files within subdirectories, but not to the subdirectories themselves. One useful application of this switch is in conjunction with the /M switch of the BACKUP command. Suppose that you have several data subdirectories under an application program's directory. To use the BACKUP /M switch (for backing up files modified since the last backup) to make a new backup of all your data files, you can use the ATTRIB command with the /S and +A switches to make sure that all of the data files are marked for backup.

Using ATTRIB with BACKUP

Suppose that you use Lotus 1-2-3 for several different projects and keep each project's files in separate data directories in your 1-2-3 program directory. You can use the following steps to back up all of your 1-2-3 data files:

1. Change to the C:\123 directory by typing the following command:

   CD \123

2. Set the archive attribute for all of the files in the current directory and its subdirectories by issuing the following command:

   ATTRIB +A /S

3. Clear the archive attribute for the program files in the \123 directory (which you don't need to back up) by typing the following command:

   ATTRIB -A

4. Back up the data files in all of the subdirectories under the \123 directory (which have their archive attribute set) with the following command:

   BACKUP *.* A: /S /M

> ***Note:*** You may be tempted to use the system and/or hidden file attributes to prevent files from being backed up because the BACKUP command does not back up the DOS files IO.SYS, MSDOS.SYS, and COMMAND.COM. Notice, however, that COMMAND.COM is not a hidden or system file. The reason these three files are not backed up has nothing to do with their file attributes, but because the BACKUP command specifically excludes them.

Creating a DOSKEY Macro for ATTRIB

If you often back up your data files, you may want to place the steps just described into a DOSKEY macro. The following command line, which you can place in your AUTOEXEC.BAT file, creates a DOSKEY macro called BACKDATA that performs the same steps automatically:

DOSKEY BACKDATA=CD \123 $T ATTRIB +A /S $T ATTRIB -A $T BACKUP *.* A: /S /M

Using the REPLACE Command *(also DOS 4)*

The external command REPLACE was added in DOS 3.2 as a utility that enables you to use different versions of a file to update that file. REPLACE is, in most respects, a variation of the COPY command. By using switches with REPLACE, you have greater control over which files are copied. REPLACE is beneficial if you update a disk or directory from another disk or directory.

REPLACE is more versatile than COPY because REPLACE offers conditional copying of source files to the destination. Without switches, REPLACE transfers files only from the source that already exists on the destination. Using the *.* wild-card designation, COPY transfers all files from the source to the destination.

By adding appropriate switches, you can make the REPLACE command more selective, choosing among several different conditions. REPLACE also can perform an optional search of the target disk directory's subdirectory for a replaceable file.

You can use REPLACE to collect the most recent versions of common files from a group of PCs to a floppy disk, or to upgrade to a new version of a software package.

The syntax for the REPLACE command is as follows:

REPLACE sourcepathname1 *targetpathname2* /A /P /R /S /W /U

The following listing describes the switches used with the REPLACE command:

Switch	Action
/A	Adds, instead of replaces, new files in the target directory
/P	Prompts the user before replacing a file or adding a source file
/R	Replaces read-only files as well as unprotected files
/S	Searches all subdirectories of the target directory
/W	Waits for disk insertion before beginning to search for source files
/U	Replaces only those files that are older than the source directory

Using the /U Switch To Replace Older Files

With DOS 4, the /U switch was added to REPLACE to update files. The /U switch copies only those files that are newer than the files they will replace. Because REPLACE cannot change file names as it copies files, however, the newer files must have exactly the same name as the older files they're replacing.

The /U switch also cannot be used with the /A switch, which is used to add files that do not exist on the destination disk. To update and add files requires two separate executions of REPLACE.

Updating Files with REPLACE

Suppose that you have a group of data files you update frequently and copy to floppy disks. After awhile, the latest versions of different data files may be on several different floppies. To collect the latest version of each data file on a single floppy disk, follow these steps:

1. Copy any data files that exist on drive A:, but not on drive B:, by using the following command:

   REPLACE A:*.* B: /A

2. Replace any files from drive B: that are older than the same file in drive A: by issuing this command:

   REPLACE A:*.* B: /U

Creating a DOSKEY Macro for REPLACE

One disadvantage of the REPLACE command is that you cannot combine the /A (add) and /U (update) switches. Collecting the newest versions of your data files, therefore, requires two steps. A DOSKEY macro, however, can combine the two commands on a single line as follows:

   DOSKEY NEWEST=REPLACE A:*.* B: /A $T REPLACE A:*.* B: /U

To use this macro, place the source disk in drive A:, the target disk in drive B:, and enter the command **NEWEST**.

Using the BACKUP Command

Backing up your files is never fun, but it's an important part of protecting your work. In early versions of DOS, backing up your files required several steps. Before you could begin a backup, you had to format enough floppy disks to hold all of the files on the hard disk. If you ran out of formatted disks before the backup was complete, you had to format more disks and start the backup procedure from the beginning.

DOS 3.3 added the /F switch to instruct BACKUP to format a disk automatically, if necessary. DOS 4.0 made /F a default so that you don't even have to specify the switch. DOS 5 also adds support for 2.88M disks.

The syntax used for the BACKUP command is as follows:

> **BACKUP source destination** */S /M /A /F:size /F:date /T:time*
> */L:pathname*

The elements of the syntax line are described in the following listing:

Switch	Action
/S	Backs up subdirectories
/M	Backs up only those files that have changed since the last backup
/A	Adds backed-up files to an existing backup disk
/D:date	Backs up only files modified since the specified date
/T:time	Backs up only files modified since the specified time
/L:pathname	Creates a log entry to record the backup operation
/F:size	Formats the target backup disk

Using the /F Switch To Set Specific Disk Format Size *(also DOS 4)*

Although the /F switch added in DOS 3.3 tried formatting a floppy disk if necessary, you were unable to specify the size of the disk. Because many people use double-density disks (either 360K or 720K) in high-density drives (either 1.2M or 1.44M), and because formatting defaults to the drive size, this automatic format wasn't very useful.

In DOS 4 and DOS 5, you can specify the disk size by using the /F switch. You have control and can use lower density disks without worrying about running out of correctly formatted disks before completing a backup.

> *Note:* With DOS 4, the /F switch became the default for BACKUP. The default still attempts to format a floppy disk at the drive's capacity. If you use disks with a lower capacity than your disk drive, be sure to specify the correct capacity by using the /F:size parameter.

For example, if you want to back up all the files on drive C: to unformatted 720K floppy disks in your 1.44M drive A:, you can do so by using the following command:

BACKUP C:*.* A: /S /F:720

Support for 2.88M Disks

The /F switch has a new feature that enables you to specify 2.88M as the floppy disk size, if supported by your hardware. By using 2.88M disks, you can fit on one disk eight times as many files as on a 360K floppy.

Creating a DOSKEY Macro for BACKUP

Like many other common tasks that require you to enter several parameters, you may want to use a DOSKEY macro to back up files to disks lower in density than the disk drive. To create the macro BACKLOWA, add the following line to your AUTOEXEC.BAT file:

DOSKEY BACKLOWA=BACKUP C:*.* A: /S /F:720

Replace the *720* with *360* if you use 360K disks in a 1.2M disk drive.

Using the DISKCOPY Command

Another disk-related command enhanced in DOS 5 is DISKCOPY. Use this command only to copy floppy disks; you cannot use it to copy hard disks. DISKCOPY automatically formats the destination disk if the disk is unformatted or formatted with a different capacity than the source disk.

The following syntax is used with the DISKCOPY command:

   DISKCOPY *drive1: drive2: /1 /V*

/1 enables you to copy only one side of a disk, and /V verifies that the contents of the disk are copied properly.

Using the New /V Switch

Use the /V switch to verify that the copy is correct. Using this switch slows down the disk-copying process, but eliminates the need to follow the two-step process of first using DISKCOPY and then DISKCOMP to ensure accuracy.

The amount of time required to copy a disk varies, depending on the disk capacity. Higher density disks hold more information and therefore take longer to copy. A reasonable estimate, however, is that using the DISKCOPY /V switch slows the process by about 20 percent. Using the DISKCOPY command followed by DISKCOMP takes nearly twice as long as using DISKCOPY without the /V switch, and over one-and-a-half times as long as DISKCOPY with the /V switch.

The DOS command VERIFY ON does not produce the same result as DISKCOPY's /V switch. The VERIFY ON command verifies that data was not written to a bad disk sector, but does not verify that the data is correct. DISKCOPY's /V switch, however, performs the same verification as DISKCOMP does. The primary difference is that the source disk does not need to be reread when DISKCOPY verifies the target copy.

Although DISKCOPY makes an otherwise exact copy of the source disk, the target disk receives a new volume serial number. Programs can use the volume serial number to determine if a disk has been changed.

Because the volume serial number capacity was new to DOS 4, however, few programs use this information yet. The DOS utility programs like DISKCOMP, for example, do not check the volume serial number.

> ***Technical note:*** A program reads the volume serial number by reading in the boot sector of the disk using Interrupt 25H, Absolute Disk Read. The volume serial number is stored as a double word between the extended boot-record signature (29H) and the 11-byte volume label. The batch file commands do not enable you to read the number.

DISKCOPY takes very few arguments and really doesn't present a good opportunity for enhancement with a DOSKEY macro.

Summary

Chapter 9 examined four DOS commands that you can use to maintain your files—ATTRIB, REPLACE, BACKUP, and DISKCOPY. DOS 5 enhances each of these commands significantly. This chapter also gave examples of DOSKEY macros that you can use to customize these commands and make them more convenient to use.

Using Additional New and Enhanced Commands

10

Microsoft includes several command enhancements in DOS 5 that are not included in the areas examined so far. These enhancements are important, however, so this chapter gives you the information you need to use them effectively. This chapter covers the SETVER and GRAPHICS commands, and lists the features new to the DEBUG program.

Understanding SETVER

As DOS evolved, programmers developed software to take advantage of each version's new features. To prevent a user from trying to run a program on a version of DOS that lacked the necessary features, programmers relied frequently on a DOS function call to determine the version of DOS currently in use.

The DOS function call, however, has one shortcoming. DOS versions are almost entirely upward compatible; that is, a program that runs under DOS 2.11 will run under DOS 5. Programmers often check for a specific DOS version rather than one equal to or higher than the required version. When you upgrade DOS versions, for example, programs that you have been using may suddenly give you an error message such as `Incorrect DOS version`.

Technical note: Programs check the DOS version by using function 30h of interrupt 21h. This function returns both the major and minor version numbers of the DOS version currently in use. Microsoft recommends that programs accept the DOS version if it is equal to or greater than the required version. Some programmers, however, test only for a DOS version equal to the required version.

Only a few programs—among them, the utility programs that come with DOS (DISKCOPY.COM, for example)—fail to run on a higher version of DOS. Because some utility programs write data directly to disk without using DOS services, you should *always* use DOS utilities from the correct DOS version. Using SETVER to allow earlier versions of utility programs to work with DOS 5 is not recommended.

Syntax of the SETVER Command

The syntax for the SETVER command, depending on what you want the command to do, is as follows:

Action	*Format*
To install SETVER>EXE in the CONFIG.SYS file	**DEVICE=***C:\DOS***\SETVER.EXE**
To display table	**SETVER** *drive:*
To add entry	**SETVER** *drive:* **filename n.nn**
To delete entry	**SETVER** *drive:* **filename /DELETE /QUIET** or **SETVER** *drive:* **filename /D /QUIET**

Note: You cannot use wild cards in the file-name argument. You must specify each program individually.

The DOS Version Table

Because DOS is upwardly compatible, Microsoft provides a program called SETVER.EXE that builds a version table. This table lists the names of various programs and the DOS version they require. Microsoft provides a default version table containing entries for several programs. To see the current version table, type the following command:

SETVER

The following version table is displayed:

```
WIN200.BIN      3.40
WIN100.BIN      3.40
WINWORD.EXE     4.10
EXCEL.EXE       4.10
HITACHI.SYS     4.00
MSCDEX.EXE      4.00
REDIR4.EXE      4.00
NET.EXE         4.00
NET.COM         3.30
NETWKSTA.EXE    4.00
DXMA0MOD.SYS    3.30
BAN.EXE         4.00
BAN.COM         4.00
MSREDIR.EXE     4.00
METRO.EXE       3.31
IBMCACHE.SYS    3.40
REDIR40.EXE     4.00
DD.EXE          4.01
DD.BIN          4.01
LL3.EXE         4.01
REDIR.EXE       4.00
SYQ55.SYS       4.00
SSTDRIVE.SYS    4.00
```

Note: To see the version table for programs on a particular drive, include the drive letter followed by a colon (:) after the SETVER command, as in the following:

SETVER A:

When you use SETVER to display the current version table, you do not need to reboot your PC because no changes have been made to the table. If you make changes, either by adding or deleting entries, you must reboot so that the changes take effect.

> ***Note:*** SETVER.EXE must be installed on a device driver through CONFIG.SYS before you can use SETVER from the command line. When you instal DOS 5, SETVER.EXE is installed in CONFIG.SYS. Type **CONFIG.SYS**, however, to display your configuration file on-screen. If SETVER.EXE is not included in the CONFIG.SYS file, add the line **DEVICE=dc:pathc\SETVER.EXE**, in which dc:pathc\ is the location of SETVER.EXE.

Using SETVER To Run Older Programs under DOS 5

Suppose that you use a program called DUMBPROG.EXE that "requires" DOS 3.10, and you want to continue using this program when you upgrade to DOS 5. When you try to use this program, however, DUMBPROG displays the message `Incorrect DOS version` and returns to the DOS prompt.

Before SETVER, your only choices were to abandon DUMBPROG, to ask the manufacturer for an updated version, or to return to your old version of DOS. SETVER, however, enables you to "trick" DUMBPROG into thinking it's still running under DOS 3.10. To add your program to the version table, enter the following command:

SETVER C:DUMBPROG.EXE 3.10

After issuing this command, you must reboot your system in order for the new version table to take effect. After you do so, DUMBPROG will run just as it did before your DOS upgrade.

Note: Although the remote possibility exists that a program really cannot run properly under a newer version of DOS, problems you encounter are more likely to be caused by a program that is really a number of related programs, instead of a single program. If you encounter difficulties after using SETVER, make sure that you have included all COM and EXE files that make up the program. For example, if DUMBPROG.EXE is a menu program that runs DUMB1.EXE, DUMB2.EXE, or DUMB3.EXE, depending on your menu selections, each of these programs probably will require its own entry in the version table.

Keep in mind, however, the earlier warning about disk utility programs. You should be wary of using SETVER with disk utility programs, especially if you have changed your hard disk's partition size to allow for a volume larger than 32M. If a disk utility program assumes that a hard disk must be smaller than 32M, the program may destroy data when run on a larger hard disk.

Removing a program from the version table also is easy. Suppose that DUMBPROG.EXE is updated to run under DOS 5. To remove the DUMBPROG.EXE entry from the version table, issue the following command:

SETVER C:DUMBPROG.EXE /DELETE

Remember to reboot your PC after using SETVER so that the new version table takes effect.

If you make a mistake when entering a program into the SETVER version table, you can correct it. Suppose that DUMBPROG.EXE really needs DOS 3.20, not DOS 3.10. To correct your error, just reissue the command with the proper DOS version indicated, as in the following:

SETVER C:DUMBPROG.EXE 3.20

Again, remember to reboot your PC to make the new version table current.

You may not need to use SETVER often, but it does give you the opportunity to use new DOS 5 features even with older programs.

Note: Each entry in SETVER's version table uses 16 bytes of conventional memory. Although this is a small amount, you may want to delete entries for programs you don't use. Before doing this, however, you should print a copy of the table using the following command:

SETVER >PRN

Label the printout "Original SETVER version table" and keep it with your DOS 5 documentation. This enables you to read any programs that you have deleted from the table.

Using the SETVER /QUIET Switch

The /QUIET switch enables batch files to modify the version table without displaying SETVER's messages. If you do not include this switch, SETVER displays the following message:

```
Version table successfully updated.
The version change will take effect the next time you
restart your system
```

Using the GRAPHICS Command

Your PC may have one or more different screen modes, depending on the type of video controller and monitor installed on your PC. The original MDA (Monochrome Display Adapter) has a single, text-only display mode. The CGA (Color Graphics Adapter) adds six additional modes, including three graphics modes. The EGA (Enhanced Graphics Adapter), MCGA (Multi-Color Graphics Array), and VGA (Video Graphics Array) adapters add many more graphics modes.

Most PC users sooner or later want to print the graphics shown on their screens. Unfortunately, the Print Screen key (PrtSc on some keyboards) was intended to send text, not graphics, to a printer. The primary reason for this lies in the way printers respond to commands. Graphics printing is much more complex than printing text. Because printing graphics requires control of each dot placed on the page, the commands are quite detailed. Graphics printing also is affected by the many different types of printers with different graphics command sets that are available.

Syntax of the GRAPHICS Command

The syntax for the GRAPHICS command is as follows:

> **GRAPHICS** *type profile /r /b /lcd /printbox:id*

The following listing describes the action performed by the parameters.

Parameter	Description
type	Specifies printer type
profile	File containing information of supported printers
/r	Prints black and white as seen on-screen
/b	Prints the background in color for COLOR4 and COLOR8 printers
/lcd	Prints an image using LCD aspect ratio
/printbox:id	Selects the print box size

Support for Additional Printers *(also DOS 4)*

Despite the fact that many different types of printers are available, until DOS 4, support was provided only for certain IBM brand PC printers. DOS 5 adds support for many new types of printers by making use of a graphics printer profile file. This file, called GRAPHICS.PRO, is a text file that contains the information GRAPHICS.COM needs to send the correct commands for printing graphics screens to the printer.

Earlier versions of GRAPHICS.COM contained the printer information within GRAPHICS.COM itself. By moving this data to an external text file, Microsoft makes adding graphics screen-printing capabilities to new printers much easier. In fact, a printer manufacturer can simply provide a replacement for the GRAPHICS.PRO file to enable its customers to use GRAPHICS.COM for screen printing.

As an example of the advantages that GRAPHICS.PRO provides, Table 10.1 lists the number of HP printer models now supported, in addition to the IBM brand printers already supported, by DOS.

Table 10.1
Printers Supported by GRAPHICS.PRO in DOS 5

Printer type	Model name
COLOR1	IBM Color Printer with black ribbon that prints in gray scales
COLOR4	IBM Color Printer with RGB (red, green, blue) ribbon that produces four colors
COLOR8	IBM Color Printer with CMY (cyan, magenta, yellow, and black) ribbon, that produces eight colors
GRAPHICS	IBM Graphics Printer Model 2
	IBM ProPrinter and ProPrinter II
	IBM ProPrinter XL (8 1/2-inch paper)
	IBM ProPrinter X24
	IBM ProPrinter XL24 (8 1/2-inch paper)
	IBM Pageprinter
	IBM Quietwriter II
	IBM Quietwriter III
THERMAL	IBM PC Convertible Printer
GRAPHICSWIDE	IBM Quietwriter II (13 1/2-inch paper)
	IBM ProPrinter XL (13 1/2-inch paper)
	IBM ProPrinter XL24 (13 1/2-inch paper)

Printer type	Model name
HPDEFAULT	Any Hewlett-Packard PCC printer
DESKJET	A Hewlett-Packard DeskJet printer
LASERJETII	A Hewlett-Packard Laserjet II printer
PAINTJET	A Hewlett-Packard PaintJet printer
QUIETJET	A Hewlett-Packard QuietJet printer
QUIETJET PLUS	A Hewlett-Packard QuietJet Plus printer
RUGGED WRITER	A Hewlett-Packard ThinkJet printer
RUGGED WRITERWIDE	A Hewlett-Packard Rugged Writerwide printer
THINKJET	A Hewlett-Packard ThinkJet printer

Assume that you have an HP Laserjet II printer connected to your PC and you want to print a graphics screen. Before you load the program that produces the screen, issue the following command:

GRAPHICS LASERJETII

After you type the command, your printer should print the current screen anytime you press the Print Screen key.

The /R Switch

Computer screens often have many more black areas than white areas. In fact, the standard DOS screen has white letters on a black background. Unless you add the /R switch to the GRAPHICS command, the black-and-white areas of the screen are reversed when the screen is printed. This effect normally is what you want; but if not, add the /R switch after the printer's name.

Remember that using the /R switch results in black printing as black, and white as white. If you print a standard DOS screen, your printer will try to cover most of the page with black. Printer ribbons and toner cartridges don't last too long when printing in this manner.

Comparison with Screen Capture Programs

GRAPHICS is not a screen capture program. Its sole purpose is to print the current screen immediately. Screen capture programs, such as those used to produce screens for Que's books, offer more functions than GRAPHICS does. By using screen capture programs, for example, you can capture, edit, and save a screen to print later. These programs give greater flexibility in the size of the printed image, as well as a much greater range of output devices. If all you need is an occasional screen dump for documentation, however, the "free" GRAPHICS command may meet your needs.

Using DEBUG

DEBUG is a program primarily intended for use by programmers to examine and modify programs. Using DEBUG without proper study can be dangerous because of its ability to write directly to your disk, bypassing the DOS file system, and its capability to destroy programs. This book is not intended to teach you how to use DEBUG. The following material examines the changes to DEBUG, but does not recommend that you use these new features unless you have a full understanding of DEBUG, your PC hardware, and the DOS file system.

Syntax of DEBUG

The syntax for DEBUG is as follows:

> **DEBUG** *filename arglist*

The following list describes the parameters' actions:

Parameter	Action
filename	Name of a file to load when debug is started
arglist	Arguments to pass to program file name when it is loaded

Unlike most DOS commands, most directives to DEBUG are entered *after* DEBUG is loaded. The command syntax represents only the commands needed to load DEBUG. Table 10.2 lists the commands used after DEBUG is loaded.

Table 10.2
DEBUG Commands

Command	Action
A	Assembles 8086/8087/8088 mnemonics instructions into a machine language program
C	Compares two portions of memory and displays any differences
D	Displays the contents of a portion of memory in both hexadecimal and ASCII displays
E	Enters data into memory, starting at a specified address, by overwriting any existing data
F	Fills a range of memory with specified values and overwrites any existing data
G	Executes the program that was loaded into memory along with DEBUG
H	Performs hexadecimal arithmetic by showing the sum and difference of the two numbers entered
I	Reads and displays one byte from the specified port
L	Loads a file or absolute disk sectors into memory
M	Moves a block of memory to another memory location
N	Assigns file names for the Load and Write commands and assigns parameters to the file being debugged
O	Sends a byte value to a specified output port
P	Executes a loop, a repeated string instruction, a software interrupt, or a subroutine call to completion

continues

Table 10.2 *(Continued)*

Command	Action
Q	Ends the Debug session and returns you to DOS
R	Displays the contents of one or more registers and enables you to change a register's contents
S	Searches a portion of memory for specified hexadecimal or ASCII values and displays the address or addresses at which the value was found
T	Executes instructions in the program being debugged and displays the contents of all registers, flags, and the decoded instruction
U	Disassembles bytes and displays the corresponding source code statements
W	Writes the current file to disk
XA	Allocates expanded memory (EMS) pages
XD	Deallocates expanded memory pages
XM	Maps allocated expanded memory pages
XS	Displays the status of expanded memory pages and handles (also DOS 4)

New DEBUG Commands

DEBUG has five new commands—one for general use and four relating to expanded (EMS) memory. The following sections briefly describe these new commands.

The Proceed Command (P)

The Proceed command causes a loop, a repeated string instruction, a software interrupt, or a subroutine call in the program being debugged to execute to completion. You also can specify the address of the first instruction to be executed and the number of instructions to execute. If you do not specify an address, the default is to begin at the current address shown in CS:IP. If you do not specify the number of instructions to execute, the default is to execute a single instruction (which may, in turn, execute a loop, a repeated string instruction, a software interrupt, or a subroutine call).

The Proceed command cannot be used to trace through ROM.

The Allocate Expanded Memory Command (XA)

This command allocates a specified number of 16K expanded memory (EMS) pages. If the memory is available and is allocated successfully, DEBUG displays a message showing the number (in hexadecimal) of the EMS handle created. If the memory is not available, DEBUG displays an error message.

The Deallocate Expanded Memory Command (XD)

This command deallocates expanded memory assigned to a specified handle. If the memory assigned to the handle is properly deallocated, DEBUG displays a message showing which memory handle was affected. If the memory was not deallocated, DEBUG displays an error message.

The Map Expanded Memory Command (XM)

This command causes a logical expanded memory page belonging to a specified handle to be mapped into a physical expanded memory page. If the operation is successful, DEBUG displays a message specifying which logical page belonging to the specified EMS handle was mapped into which physical memory page.

The Display Expanded Memory Status Command (XS)

This command displays the expanded memory status information, including EMS handles and their allocated logical and physical memory pages. This information shows how much memory has been allocated to each EMS handle.

Summary

In Chapter 10, you examined some of the miscellaneous DOS commands either added or enhanced in DOS 5. These commands improve the way DOS functions and give you more control over the operation of your system.

Chapter 11 introduces the new DOS full-screen editor, EDIT, which you may find to be a great improvement over EDLIN.

EDIT: Using the Full-Screen Editor

Previous versions of DOS have used the line-oriented editor, EDLIN, to edit text files such as batch files. Although useful for editing small files, EDLIN is far from easy to use. In this chapter, you see EDLIN compared to EDIT, showing why you no doubt will choose to use EDIT over EDLIN. You also see the features that EDIT offers; those that an easy-to-use text editor should offer. You see how editing your DOS configuration is even easier using the new, full-screen editor. You learn to edit two text files that DOS uses most—CONFIG.SYS and AUTOEXEC.BAT.

Understanding EDIT's Features

Perhaps you have been using EDLIN as your text editor for creating batch files and other text files for some time. Perhaps you have been using your word processor to create text files. The next few sections compare EDLIN to EDIT, showing why you may want to abandon using EDLIN and learn to use EDIT. After you become familiar with EDIT, you may decide that this easy-to-use utility gets the job of creating text-only files done just as efficiently as your word processor, only without the hassle of having to convert the word processing file into an ASCII file.

EDLIN versus EDIT

For compatibility reasons, DOS 5 still includes the EDLIN editor. EDLIN works well with redirection for processing files. For example, if you make the same types of changes to text files, such as search and replace text, or you format lines in a certain way, you may automate editing with EDLIN.

You may create a file—MODIFY.TXT, for example—that contains EDLIN commands. The commands in MODIFY.TXT may search for certain characters in a text file and replace those characters with ASCII graphics characters used to make boxes.

Suppose that you create a file, GREETING.BAT, that must be modified to include graphics characters. Using EDLIN and redirection, you may type the following command:

EDLIN GREETING.BAT < MODIFY.TXT

EDLIN would load GREETING.BAT into memory and modify the file by using the commands stored in MODIFY.TXT.

Although using EDLIN in this automatic mode is quite handy, this single feature cannot make you ignore the features that EDIT offers in the way of text editing. Consider the number of steps that you have to perform manually to edit a file in EDLIN versus editing a file using EDIT. Consider editing the following AUTOEXEC.BAT batch file:

```
@ECHO OFF
\CLS
PROMPT Current Directory is - $P$_Your command? -
PATH C:\DOS;C:\WIN30;C:\;C:\DOS\BATCH;C:\123R3
MOUSE /S100
SET RECOGNIZ= -SW
SET DIRCMD=/P /O:GNE /A:-D
DOSKEY DEL=C:\DOS\DEL.COM $1
DOSKEY CD=C:\DOS\NORTON\NCD.EXE $1
```

Suppose that you want to change the name of the Windows directory in the PATH from C:\WIN30 to C:\WINDOWS. Using EDLIN, you need to issue the following series of commands:

1. Enter **EDLIN AUTOEXEC.BAT**

2. Press L to list the line numbers.

3. Press 4 to begin editing line 4.

4. Move the cursor 19 places to the right using the right-arrow key.

5. Press the Del key twice to delete the *30*.

6. Press the Ins key to enter insert mode.

7. Type **DOWS**.

8. Press the Ins key to leave insert mode.

9. Press the F3 key to complete the line.

10. Press Enter.

11. Press E to end and save the modified file and the unmodified file, which is now called AUTOEXEC.BAK. Later you can delete AUTOEXEC.BAK at the DOS prompt.

Using EDIT, the following procedure is somewhat easier.

1. Enter **EDIT AUTOEXEC.BAT**

2. Move the cursor to the *3* in *30* in the fourth line.

3. Press the Del key twice to delete the *30*.

4. Type **DOWS**

5. Press Alt-F for the file menu.

6. Press X to exit.

7. Press Enter to save the modified file at the Save before exiting prompt.

Because EDIT doesn't create a BAK file, you don't have to bother deleting it. From this simple example, you can see that EDIT is much easier to use. If you had made more extensive changes, EDIT's advantage would have been even clearer.

Another weighty difference between EDLIN and EDIT is the way in which you issue commands. With EDLIN, you must remember single letter commands and the sequence in which a command must be issued. With EDIT, however, the commands are issued from an easy-to-follow menu. If a command requires additional information, such as with search and replace, a box appears on-screen prompting you for the needed information.

The biggest difference between EDIT and EDLIN is that EDLIN is a line-oriented editor while EDIT is screen oriented. This means that the EDLIN user who wishes to change a line first must determine the correct line number, specify that line number, and then edit the line. The EDIT user, on the other hand, simply moves the cursor to the point where the change is going to be made and types the correction.

Starting EDIT

Starting EDIT is an easy procedure. From the DOS Shell, select Editor. When you start Editor, you are prompted for the file to edit. You may type the file name, including the optional drive and path where the file is located. To start EDIT from the command line, type **EDIT** (assuming that EDIT is in the current directory or is in your search path). When you type **EDIT**, you also may include the file to edit. In addition, when starting from the command line, you may use EDIT's useful switches. Notice the following command line for EDIT:

> **EDIT** *filename /B /G /H /NOHI*

The switches that you may use with EDIT alter the appearance of EDIT on the screen. /B is used to display EDIT when you have a single color monitor attached to a color video adapter. /G enables quick screen updates on a CGA monitor. /H causes EDIT to display the maximum number of lines for your monitor. The /H switch really affects EGA monitors that can produce 43 lines on the screen and VGA monitors that can display 50 lines on the screen. Finally, /NOHI is used for monitors that are not able to display high-intensity characters. The /NOHI switch is most appropriate for LCD screens, such as those used on a laptop computer.

Understanding the EDIT Screen

When you start EDIT without loading a file to edit, you are prompted to press either Enter to see instructions for using EDIT, or to press Esc to begin using EDIT. After pressing Esc, you see the screen shown in figure 11.1.

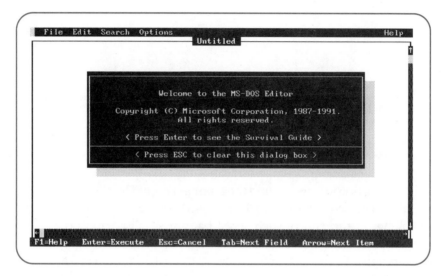

Fig. 11.1. *Select to view the Survival Guide or to begin editing after you start EDIT.*

At the top of the screen is EDIT's menu bar with the pull-down menus: File, Edit, Search, Options, and Help. The next line is the title bar—the name of the file that you are editing. If no file is loaded to edit, you see the word Untitled (as shown in fig. 11.2).

The very bottom of the screen shows the message/status line. This line displays messages, such as activities that you may perform. Notice that you initially are instructed to press F1 for help, or to press the Alt key to activate the menus. If a menu is activated, the message line tells you the action when you select a menu option.

At the right of the message/status line is useful information—the lock key indicators and line:column indicator. The lock key indicators show C if Caps Lock is on, and N if Num Lock is on. The line:column indicator displays where the cursor is located.

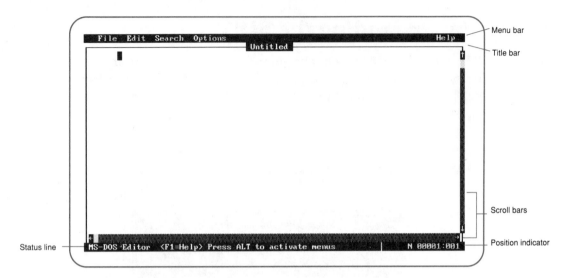

Fig. 11.2. The main EDIT screen.

Notice that borders are around the editing screen. The right and bottom borders are scroll bars, which are used for vertical and horizontal scrolling. At the end of each scroll bar are scroll arrows pointing in opposite directions. The scroll arrows are for use with a mouse to scroll through the file that you are editing. Within each scroll bar is the scroll box. The scroll box shows you your position within the file. The scroll box also may be used with the mouse to scroll through the file.

Using the Mouse and the Keyboard

Using EDIT is easy whether you are using the keyboard only, or a combination of the keyboard and a mouse. The use of drop-down menus and quick-keys add to the ease of use of this editor.

Moving the Cursor

As you use EDIT, aside from typing, you will most likely move the cursor. Table 11.1 shows you all the cursor-movement keys to aid you in quickly moving through the file.

Table 11.1
Cursor-Movement Keys for EDIT

Key(s)	Action
Arrow keys	Moves the cursor one character or one line; also scrolls the screen if the edge is reached
Ctrl-Left Arrow	Moves the cursor one word to the left
Ctrl-Right Arrow	Moves the cursor one word to the right
Home	Moves the cursor to the beginning of the line
End	Moves the cursor to the end of the line
Ctrl-Enter	Moves the cursor to the beginning of the next line
Ctrl-Q-E	Moves the cursor to the top of the screen
Ctrl-Q-X	Moves the cursor to the bottom of the screen
Ctrl-Up Arrow or Ctrl-W	Scrolls up one line
Ctrl-Down Arrow or Ctrl-Z	Scrolls down one line
PageUp	Scrolls up one screen
PageDown	Scrolls down one screen
Ctrl-Home or Ctrl-Q-R	Moves to the beginning of the file
Ctrl-End or Ctrl-Q-C	Moves to the end of the file
Ctrl-PageUp	Scrolls left one screen
Ctrl-PageDown	Scrolls right one screen

Using the mouse makes moving the cursor a breeze—especially if you are moving the cursor a great distance through the file. Using a mouse, point to one of the scroll arrows on either end of the scroll bars and click the mouse button. To see text below the last currently visible line, click the lower scroll arrow. To see text above the current screen, click the upper scroll arrow. If text lines are too long for the current display (EDIT allows lines up to 256 characters), use the right and left scroll arrows.

You also may move more than one line or column at a time using the mouse. You can drag the scroll box in the scroll bar, for example, to move great distances in a file. By clicking the mouse with the mouse pointer in the shaded areas of the scroll bar, you may scroll an entire screen, similar to pressing the PgUp or PgDn keys or Ctrl-PgUp or Ctrl-PgDn key combinations.

Editing Text

Besides moving the cursor and typing text, you also must remove and insert text. As you are editing text in EDIT, you can use the keys shown in table 11.2.

Table 11.2
Keys for Inserting and Deleting Text

Key(s)	Function
Backspace or Ctrl-H	Deletes a character to the left of the cursor
Del or Ctrl-G	Deletes the character at the cursor
Ctrl-T	Deletes the word at the cursor
Ctrl-V	Toggles overwriting of existing characters
Ins	Inserts characters into existing text

Copying, Moving, and Deleting Blocks of Text

Although editing usually involves single characters or words, you may have to clear, copy, or move blocks of text. With EDIT, you can easily select blocks of text and then manipulate those blocks.

If you want to move a text block, clear a text block, or copy a text block, you first must select the block. EDIT makes this very easy by enabling you to select any amount of text—from a single character, to a word, a line, or even the entire file.

To select text using the keyboard, move the cursor to the first character you want to select (using the arrow keys or other cursor-movement keys mentioned above), hold down one of the Shift keys, move the cursor to the last character you want to select, and then release the keys. The selected text remains highlighted. To cancel the selection, press any cursor-movement key.

To select text using the mouse, move the mouse pointer to the first character of the text you want to select. Hold down the left mouse button and move the cursor to the last character you want to select. Release the mouse button, and the selected text remains highlighted. To cancel a selection, click the mouse button while the cursor is anywhere in the EDIT window (but not in the menus).

After you select your text, you must choose whether to make a copy of the selected text, cut the text for moving, or just delete the text. If you copy or cut the block, the block is saved in the *clipboard*, which is an area of memory for holding text in transition. You then may paste the text from the clipboard back to the file you are editing.

To copy a block, you copy and paste. To move a block, you cut and paste. Although these are options that you may select from the EDIT menu, you may use certain keystrokes to perform these operations, as shown in table 11.3.

Table 11.3
Copying, Moving, or Clearing Blocks of Text

Command	*Shortcut keystrokes*
Cut	Shift-Delete
Copy	Ctrl-Insert
Paste	Shift-Insert
Clear	Delete

This gives you a good idea of how to use EDIT to manipulate text. As mentioned earlier, one of the nice features of EDIT is that commands may be selected from menus. Before using the menus, however, you should be familiar with the contents of the menus.

Using the Drop-Down Menus

Drop-down menus get their name based on their operation. When you select a menu, the menu "drops" below the menu name. The menu remains on the screen, closing only when you make a selection, press Esc, or click the mouse outside of the menu, somewhere in the editing screen.

Selecting the drop-down menus with EDIT may be done from the keyboard or with the mouse. Pressing the Alt key activates the menu bar, as shown in figure 11.3.

Pressing the Alt key actually makes two things happen. First, as shown in figure 11.3, the File menu option appears in reverse video. This is the menu selector bar. You may move the selector bar by pressing the right- and left-arrow keys on the keyboard, or by using the mouse. After you move the selector bar to the correct menu, pressing either the up- or down-arrow keys causes the menu to drop down.

Second, when you press Alt, the first letter of each menu is highlighted. By pressing one of the highlighted letters, you can pull down that menu.

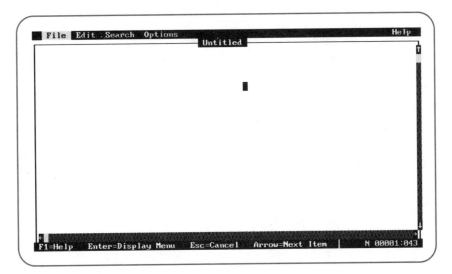

Fig. 11.3. Activating the menu bar.

You also can activate a menu in two simple keystrokes. Press and hold the Alt key, press the first letter of the menu, and then release both keys. The appropriate menu will drop down.

Using the mouse, simply move the mouse pointer to the menu desired and click the left button. The menu will drop down.

After a menu has dropped down, you may make selections from the menu (see fig. 11.4). Notice that a selection bar is in the menu. This selection bar may be moved using the up- and down-arrow keys. Press Enter after you select the correct menu option, or simply press the highlight letter of the menu option. Using a mouse, point to the menu option and click the left mouse button.

Some menu options contain an ellipsis (...). This means that another menu, usually in the form of a dialog box, will appear on the screen (see fig. 11.5). You must supply additional information in this dialog box for the command to be carried out.

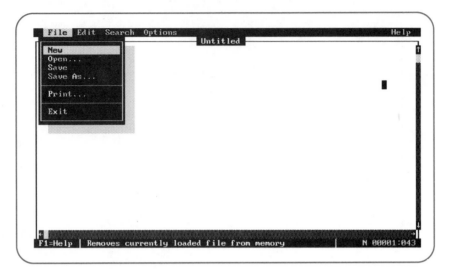

Fig. 11.4. *The File drop-down menu.*

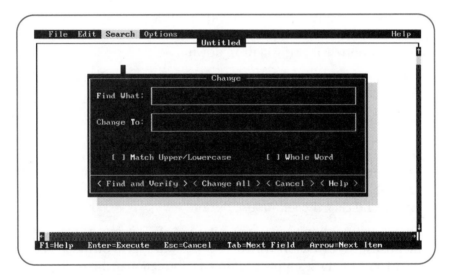

Fig. 11.5. *The Change dialog box from the Search menu command.*

Menus enable you to perform a variety of commands. Table 11.4 shows all the menus, commands, and a description of each command.

Table 11.4
EDIT Menu Commands

Menu	Command	Description
File	New	Clears the current file, if any; enables you to save the file if not already saved; and enables a new file to be created
	Open...	Loads a file from disk into memory for editing
	Save	Saves the current file to disk by the same name as was retrieved or selecting a name if a new file
	Save as...	Saves the current file in memory by a different name
	Print...	Prints the current file in memory to the printer
	Exit	Exits EDIT, enabling you to save a file if it has not already been saved
Edit	Cut	Removes the highlighted text from the file, keeping the last cut text in temporary memory
	Copy	Copies the highlighted text into temporary memory without removing the highlighted text
	Paste	Places cut or copied text from the temporary memory into the current file loaded into memory, starting at the current cursor position
	Clear	Similar to Cut without placing text in temporary memory

continues

Table 11.4 *(Continued)*

Menu	Command	Description
Search	Find...	Locates text in the file
	Repeat Last Find	Repeats the last search that was conducted
	Replace...	Locates text in the file and replaces it with other text
Options	Display...	Changes the colors of the screen
	Help Path	Specifies where the EDIT help file can be found

Using Context-Sensitive Help for EDIT

A handy feature of EDIT is on-line, context-sensitive help. At any time while using EDIT, press F1 and help appears. Suppose that you have the Search menu pulled down, and the Change menu option selected. Pressing F1 shows help on the Change command (see fig. 11.6). After you read the help, you either can press Enter or click OK with the mouse to close the help box.

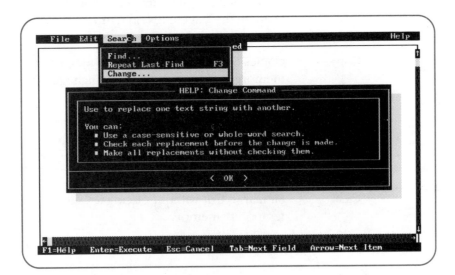

Fig. 11.6. Help on the Change command.

The Help menu is in the menu bar. This menu gives you more than context-sensitive help. Actually, the selections from the Help menu are much like having documentation on disk. Table 11.5 displays the menu options on the Help menu with a brief description of what the option shows you.

Table 11.5
Options on the Help Menu

Menu Option	Description
Getting Started	Provides complete help on each command, menu, and dialog box. Displays help for using Help and EDIT's start-up commands.
Keyboard	Displays help on keystrokes to use for performing tasks
About...	Displays the version of EDIT and copyright information.

Help is interactive—similar to using hypertext. Within help are additional topics that you may select. Notice that in figure 11.7, after selecting Getting Started, several topics are displayed with arrows on either side of the topics.

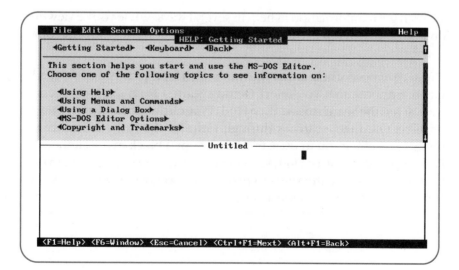

Fig. 11.7. *The Getting Started help screen with additional topics highlighted.*

You may get additional information on each topic in one of two ways. Using the keyboard, tab to each topic, then press Enter. Using the mouse, point to each topic and double-click the mouse. For example, double-clicking MS-DOS Editor Options calls up the help screen shown in figure 11.8.

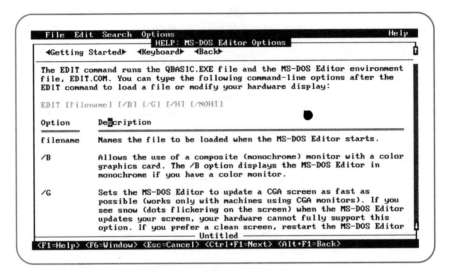

Fig. 11.8. *Selecting the MS-DOS Editor Options from the Getting Started help screen.*

You can get to information in help in several ways. While you're viewing on-line help, you can use the keys in table 11.6 to move from one topic to another.

One nice feature of help is that you may search for topics using the Search menu. Suppose that you select Getting Started from the Help menu. Next, select the Search menu, then Find. Type **clipboard** and press Enter, or select OK. EDIT searches through Help for the first occurrence of Clipboard, telling you to use Ctrl+Ins to copy a block to the clipboard. Pressing F3 (Repeat Last Find) searches for the next occurrence, then the next, and so on. You then are not restricted to following the structure of Help to get a quick question answered.

Table 11.6
Keys Used To Move from One Help Topic to Another

Key	Action
Tab	Moves to the next topic
Shift-Tab	Moves to the previous topic
Any letter	Moves to the next topic beginning with that letter
Shift-any letter	Moves to the previous topic beginning with that letter
Alt-F1	Displays the Help window for a previously viewed topic
Ctrl-F1	Displays the next topic in the Help file
Shift-Ctrl-F1	Displays the previous topic in the Help file

Using EDIT

Now that you have seen some of the features of EDIT, you can use EDIT to modify CONFIG.SYS and AUTOEXEC.BAT for DOS 5. You also will see some of the DOS 5 features used for optimizing memory.

> *Note:* For the following examples, the files AUTOEXEC.BAT and CONFIG.SYS are modified to include DOS 5 features that, in some cases, require your PC to have either an 80386, 80386SX, or 80486 processor. Even if your system doesn't have one of these CPUs, you still should follow along with the examples to learn how to use EDIT.

The actual commands being added to the files in these examples aren't as important as understanding how EDIT works. If you want to try out these examples but don't wish to modify your actual AUTOEXEC.BAT and CONFIG.SYS files, follow these steps before beginning the examples:

1. Make certain that the current directory is C:\ by typing the following command:

   **CD **

2. Copy AUTOEXEC.BAT to EXAMPLE.BAT using the following command:

   COPY AUTOEXEC.BAT EXAMPLE.BAT

3. Copy CONFIG.SYS to EXAMPLE.SYS using the following command:

   COPY CONFIG.SYS EXAMPLE.SYS

Now, when the example calls for AUTOEXEC.BAT, substitute the EXAMPLE.BAT file instead. Likewise, when the example calls for CONFIG.SYS, substitute EXAMPLE.SYS. In this way, your original AUTOEXEC.BAT and CONFIG.SYS files remain unchanged and you can experiment using EDIT to modify text files.

Modifying CONFIG.SYS with EDIT

If you haven't loaded EDIT, do so now. Select Open from the File menu. Type the name of the file to open—CONFIG.SYS—in the Open dialog box at the File Name prompt (see figure 11.9). Press Enter or click OK to open the file for editing.

EDIT loads CONFIG.SYS and changes the title bar to indicate that CONFIG.SYS is the name of the file currently being edited. Figure 11.10 shows a typical CONFIG.SYS file.

Note: For this example, you are modifying CONFIG.SYS to include DOS 5 features which require that your PC have an 80286, 80386, 80386SX, or 80486 processor. Specifically, HIMEM.SYS requires an 80286 or higher with extended memory. Also, the DOS=HIGH command requires an 80286 or higher with extended memory (to also use the UMB parameter on an 80286 requires the NEAT chipset). The EMM386.EXE device driver requires an 80386 or higher with extended memory. The SMARTDRV.SYS device driver requires either extended or expanded memory.

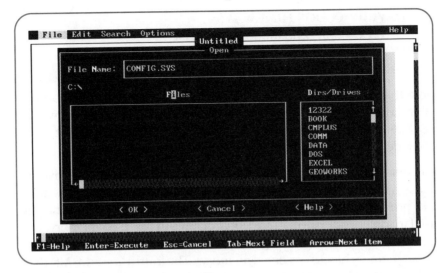

Fig. 11.9. The File Open dialog box.

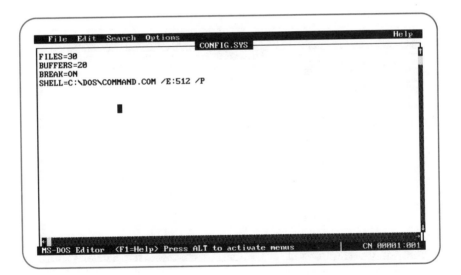

Fig. 11.10. A CONFIG.SYS file.

After the CONFIG.SYS file is loaded, the cursor should be at row 1, column 1. Use the arrow keys or your mouse to move the cursor there if necessary. Now, add the following lines of directives above the current first line:

DEVICE=C:\DOS\HIMEM.SYS
DEVICE=C:\DOS\EMM386.EXE RAM
DOS=HIGH,UMB
DEVICE=C:\DOS\SMARTDRV.SYS 1024 512

Note that EDIT, unlike EDLIN, doesn't require any special action to insert lines: just start typing and press Enter at the end of each new line. EDIT already is in insert mode; existing text is moved to the right when you type, and moved down when you press Enter.

The first line that you added enables the extended memory driver to manage memory above 1M. The second line allocates EMS 4.0 memory and provides upper memory blocks—reserved memory that may be used to load device drivers and TSR programs in reserved memory. The third line loads DOS in the high memory area and provides a link to the upper memory blocks (reserved memory). The fourth line adds MS-DOS disk caching, allocating as much as 1024K of memory for the cache. Your screen now should look like figure 11.11.

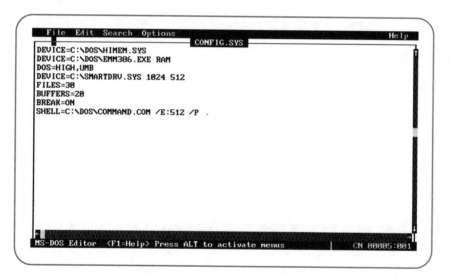

Fig. 11.11. CONFIG.SYS after adding new lines.

Because disk-caching programs such as SMARTDRV.SYS do their own buffering, you really don't need to allocate much memory space to BUFFERS. (See Chapter 4 for a more complete explanation of the BUFFERS command.) You therefore may change BUFFERS=20 to something smaller, such as BUFFERS=3.

You can use several methods to change the line. One of those methods enables you to select text and then type your replacement text. Alternatively, you can simply delete the existing text and then type new characters, but the first method takes fewer keystrokes.

Move the cursor to the *2* following the BUFFERS= statement. Hold down the shift key and move the cursor to the right until *20* is highlighted, as shown in figure 11.12. Using a mouse, point to the *2*, press and hold the left mouse button, drag the mouse until *20* is selected, and then release the mouse button.

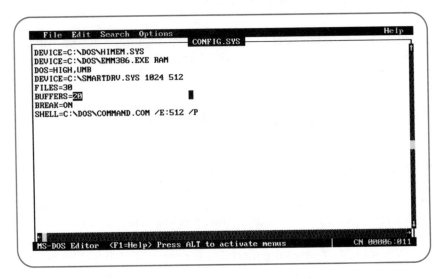

Fig. 11.12. Highlighting characters for editing.

To replace the entire highlighted text, type the new characters—in this case the number *3*. Your screen now should look like figure 11.13.

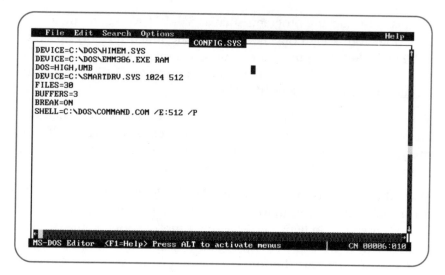

Fig. 11.13. Replacing the highlighted text.

CONFIG.SYS now has been modified to take advantage of some of the DOS 5 enhancements. Next, you will change the AUTOEXEC.BAT file.

Modifying AUTOEXEC.BAT with EDIT

Using the same commands that you used to open CONFIG.SYS, open AUTOEXEC.BAT. Notice that EDIT displays the message Loaded file is not saved. Save it now? before loading AUTOEXEC.BAT. This means that you made changes to CONFIG.SYS but forgot to save the modified file. EDIT displays this message anytime you load a file or exit EDIT, and the current file has not been saved. To save your changes, press Enter or click Yes and EDIT saves the modified version of CONFIG.SYS before loading AUTOEXEC.BAT.

As you learn more about DOS 5, you no doubt will have many ideas about what should be contained in your CONFIG.SYS and AUTOEXEC.BAT files. For the purposes of using EDIT, however, just change one existing line and add two new lines to AUTOEXEC.BAT. Figure 11.14 shows a typical AUTOEXEC.BAT file after being loaded into EDIT.

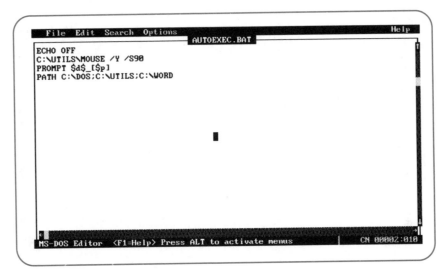

Fig. 11.14. *A typical AUTOEXEC.BAT file.*

Note: The LOADHIGH command used in the following example requires an 80286 or higher processor with extended memory. If your system does not provide high memory, the command is ignored and the programs instead are loaded into conventional memory.

Using the same methods you learned editing CONFIG.SYS, change the following line:

    C:\UTILS\MOUSE /Y /S90

    to

    LOADHIGH C:\UTILS\MOUSE /Y /S90

and then add the following two lines:

    SET DIRCMD= /P /O:GNE

    LOADHIGH C:\DOS\DOSKEY DEL=DEL $1 /P

After you make these changes, the file should look like figure 11.15.

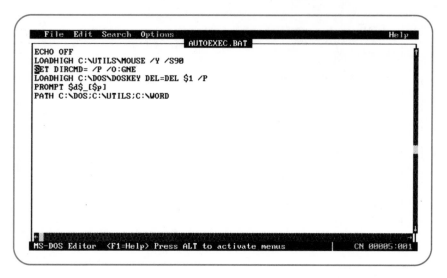

Fig. 11.15. *AUTOEXEC.BAT modified for DOS 5.*

Before exiting EDIT, save AUTOEXEC.BAT. Exit from EDIT by pressing Alt, File, and eXit. As mentioned earlier, EDIT warns you if you try to exit before saving a modified file. You can, in fact, use this as a shortcut. Press Alt and select File, then Exit and press Enter to save the modified file, and then exit EDIT.

Summary

As a DOS user, you may be familiar with EDLIN—using this utility to create and modify small files, such as batch files. Although EDLIN still is included with DOS and has some uses, you probably will prefer to use EDIT when creating files.

This chapter showed you the new EDIT features, including full-screen editing with the menu-driven editor and the added capability to cut, copy, and paste text. EDIT also supports a mouse, or provides short-cut keys to increase editing speed.

In the next chapter, you learn how to use QBasic, the Quick Basic interpreter. You will find that QBasic's interface is quite familiar because it is the same interface used by EDIT.

QBasic: A Revised BASIC

This chapter introduces the QBasic interpreter and explains how it replaces the existing BASICA or GW-BASIC interpreters. QBasic is Microsoft's name for the BASIC interpreter. This name is intended to differentiate it from the compiler, QuickBASIC. QBasic shares many of QuickBASIC's features and provides a good starting point for PC users who are considering purchasing QuickBASIC.

Highlighting QBasic's Features

QBasic provides a complete BASIC programming environment. QBasic provides the following major features:

- A smoothly integrated environment that boasts a full-screen editor, debugger, and file manager, all accessible through pull-down menus

- Programs that retain the interactive convenience of an interpreter

- Language enhancements, such as user-defined procedures, local variables, multi-line block structures, and alphanumeric labels, which bring structured coding to BASIC

- A "smart" editor that finds syntax errors as you type and reformats the instructions into a standardized appearance

- Compatibility with IBM's BASICA and Microsoft's GW-BASIC

- Support for most hardware peripherals, including a mouse, math coprocessor, and color video (CGA, EGA, and VGA)

- Much larger program and data capacity—160K instead of 64K

- A complete on-line reference to QBasic's language, syntax, and environment

- Provides support for IEEE formatted numeric values

Comparing QBasic to BASICA, GW-BASIC, and QuickBASIC

A computer can only execute instructions written in machine language, the fundamental language that a computer understands. Program instructions written in other languages, such as BASIC, must be translated into machine language. BASICA and GW-BASIC are interpreted languages. QuickBASIC is a compiled language that executes with the interactive convenience of an interpreter.

QuickBASIC: An Interpreter/Compiler

Interpreters work incrementally. The first line of the program is translated, as you complete it, into machine-language instructions, and the computer directly executes those instructions. The interpreter then translates the next line of your program, and the computer executes the resulting machine-language instructions. This translation and execution process continues throughout your program.

The advantage of an interpreter is that it allows for interaction. You can interrupt a running program at any time, print the values of variables, and then resume execution. Because each line translates incrementally, you can enter new lines when you stop the program. This capability is of great benefit to program development and debugging.

Interpreters, however, execute programs relatively slowly. Line-by-line translation means that an instruction inside a loop must be translated repeatedly with each pass through the loop.

A *compiler* represents an entirely different translation approach. A compiler translates an entire program into a separate file known as an *object file*. This object file is almost, but not quite, in machine language. Next, a program known as a *linker* combines the object file with the necessary support routines (and possibly other object files) to produce a file that contains true machine-language instructions. Finally, the computer runs the machine-language file.

When you use a compiler, the program lines you type are not interactive. For example, if you issue a command such as **PRINT "Hello world"**, a compiler requires you to compile and link the program before the command can be executed. The final executable program produced by a compiler is usually an EXE program, not a BAS file. Changing a compiled EXE program is much more difficult than changing an interpreted BASIC program.

The chief advantage of using a compiler is that it executes quickly because the final file is completely in machine language. Compilation takes some time; but, generally, the time spent compiling, linking, and running a program is about one-fifth the time that would be required if you used an interpreter.

QuickBASIC actually is a hybrid designed to achieve the best of both worlds. QuickBASIC uses a technology known as *threaded interpretation*. Each line you type in the QuickBASIC editor is translated immediately into an intermediate form known as *pseudocode*. This pseudocode, which you never see, corresponds closely to machine language.

When you run the program, QuickBASIC rapidly converts the pseudocode into true machine language. The net execution speed resembles any true compiler. The pseudocode, however, still has connections with your original BASIC instructions. As a result, you can interact with your programs just as you can with BASICA.

QBasic can be called an interpreted version of the QuickBASIC compiler. Like most current major software applications, QBasic runs from a central menu system. From these menus, you can access commands for editing or saving files, for debugging or executing the program, and for getting on-line help.

QBasic Improves upon BASICA and GW-BASIC

BASICA and GW-BASIC are poor choices for developing long programs. (This major drawback made many professional programmers choose to use other languages such as C and Pascal.) The following list shows some of these programs' limitations:

- Variables are global to the entire program. If you use a variable called VAR1 at one point in a program, for example, this variable will exist throughout the program. You cannot change the value of VAR1 in a subroutine without changing VAR1 for the whole program.

  As a result, inadvertent conflicts can develop easily in two parts of the same program. Moving a piece of code from one section to another—or from one program to another—requires careful avoidance of variable-naming clashes.

- Block structures are inadequate. IF..., DEF FN, and other structures are limited to a single line. Using several lines for a block improves the readability and clarity of a program, but BASICA and GW-BASIC force you to fit such information in a single line.

- Each line must have a line number. To merge program components from different sources, you must resolve the merged line numbers.

  Suppose that you want to merge two programs that have lines numbered from 100 to 200. Before you can do this, you have to renumber one of the programs.

- User-defined subprograms are lacking. Except for the primitive DEF FN and GOSUB, you cannot create independent functions and subprograms that can be called from the main program. You therefore are unable to create program modules to perform specific tasks or to save these modules in a library to be used as needed.

- A program cannot be larger than 64K.

QBasic corrects these shortcomings and makes BASIC a structured language comparable to C or Pascal. In addition to correcting these

BASICA and GW-BASIC flaws, the developers of QBasic have given the program (and QuickBASIC) several other language enhancements:

- TYPE...END TYPE blocks are permitted. These blocks, which are similar to C "structures" and Pascal "records," make it easier for users to consolidate different pieces of related information. This can be particularly helpful if you are developing or maintaining database applications.

- QBasic has new control structures such as SELECT CASE and DO...LOOP. These structures greatly simplify the development of menus and other interactive program modules.

- QBasic supports true recursion. Recursion permits a procedure to call itself. By supporting recursion, QBasic makes it possible for programs handling complex procedures to be simpler and more compact.

- Binary mode is used for reading and writing disk files. This enhancement enables QBasic to read and write to any type of disk file.

- Alphanumeric line labels are used, and line numbers are optional. This change makes it easier to read and understand QBasic programs.

- Long integer (32 bit) data type is employed. QBasic can handle a wider range of values because of this change.

- Programs can be much larger—up to 160K

QBasic Runs Most BASICA and GW-BASIC Programs

In most cases, you can load BASICA and GW-BASIC programs into QBasic and run them without modification. QBasic does not support the BASICA commands—such as AUTO, LIST, and RENUM—that affect the program itself. Some BASICA instructions require modification.

Unsupported BASICA and GW-BASIC Keywords

A few BASICA and GW-BASIC keywords are not included in QBasic. In most cases, these keywords are not needed because of QBasic's more advanced programming environment. In other cases, QBasic provides a better way of performing the same task. The following keywords are not included in QBasic:

AUTO	EDIT	MERGE	RENUM	CONT
LIST	MOTOR	SAVE	DEF USR	LLIST
NEW	LOAD	USR	DELETE	

Most of the BASICA and GW-BASIC keywords that QBasic doesn't support—AUTO, EDIT, MERGE, RENUM, CONT, LIST, SAVE, LLIST, NEW, LOAD, and DELETE—are commands a programmer may issue from the command line and do not usually appear in a program. The MOTOR command, also unsupported, is a command you are unlikely to encounter, unless you use a cassette recorder for program or data storage.

The final two unsupported keywords, DEF USR and USR, merit closer attention because they specify the address and call assembly language programs. Microsoft has long recommended using the CALL statement instead of DEF USR and USR. If you have been using CALL, you will not have a problem switching to QBasic. If you have used DEF USR and USR in your BASICA or GW-BASIC programs, you will have to rewrite those sections, using CALL ABSOLUTE statements instead.

In most cases, however, you should be able to load and run a BASICA or GW-BASIC program into QBasic without any problem. Because both BASICA and GW-BASIC normally save programs in a form (called *tokenized*) that the QBasic editor cannot read, you must save the program as an ASCII file before QBasic can load the program. To save the BASICA or GW-BASIC program as ASCII, use the *A* option. For example, to save TESTPROG as ASCII, issue the command **SAVE "TESTPROG.BAS", A**. Next, use the /MBF option when starting QBasic. This enables QBasic to read and write BASICA and GW-BASIC data files.

Unsupported QuickBASIC Keywords

QBasic is much closer to QuickBASIC than to BASICA and GW-BASIC. Even so, the following QuickBASIC keywords are not included in QBasic:

ALIAS	EVENT	LOCAL	SETMEM	BYVAL
$INCLUDE	SADD	SIGNAL	CDECL	Int86
Interrupt	UEVENT	COMMAND$	Int86X	InterruptX

If you already use QuickBASIC, you may not see any benefit in switching to QBasic, so the fact that these QuickBASIC keywords are unsupported should be no problem to you. If, however, you are using a book on QuickBASIC, such as Que's *Using QuickBASIC 4*, to learn QBasic, you should be aware of these differences.

Using QBasic on Your PC

QBasic provides a complete replacement for the existing BASIC interpreters on all IBM and compatible PCs. In the past, IBM provided one version of BASIC for their systems, while Compaq, Northgate, and other manufacturers of compatible equipment provided a different version. With the advent of QBasic, Microsoft has merged these two versions into one and has greatly simplified the task of upgrading multiple systems from different vendors.

QBasic Replaces GW-BASIC and BASICA

Microsoft developed GW-BASIC for IBM-compatible computers. GW-BASIC runs completely in RAM (random-access memory). If you want to load GW-BASIC, the entire program must reside on either your hard disk or on a floppy disk.

One advantage of GW-BASIC is that, as a disk-based program, it is easy to update because you can replace the entire program with a new file.

A disadvantage of GW-BASIC is that some PC vendors charged extra for the program or did not make the program available for their systems. Because Microsoft did not provide a direct means of licensing either DOS or GW-BASIC except through PC vendors, if the manufacturer of your compatible system went out of business, you were just out of luck.

BASICA, on the other hand, runs only on IBM computers because part of the language is contained in IBM-proprietary ROM (read-only memory) chips. The features and functionality of BASICA and GW-BASIC are identical. If you know one program, you know the other.

One advantage of BASICA is that it can be loaded quickly, because the program is partially contained in ROM. In fact, many IBM models automatically load the ROM portion of BASICA (also known as "cassette BASIC") if the PC is unable to access the disk drives or, on a floppy-disk system, no disk is in drive A:.

A disadvantage of BASICA is that it is difficult to update. Because BASICA is contained partially in ROM, changing the heart of the program requires a hardware update.

With the introduction of DOS 5, Microsoft has replaced both of the older interpreters with QBasic. After you install DOS 5 on your system, whether you have a true IBM-built PC or compatible does not matter.

Exploring QBasic's New Features

QBasic has a number of new features that are much easier to use than the older versions of BASIC. If you have used BASICA or GW-BASIC, you will find that QBasic offers many improvements.

Line Numbers No Longer Required

The feature you notice immediately, if you have programmed in one of the older versions of BASIC like BASICA or GW-BASIC, is that QBasic does not require line numbers.

Most programming languages don't require line numbers. BASICA and GW-BASIC require line numbers only because BASIC was developed as a tool to teach programming. Line numbers were included primarily to assist the teacher and student and had no inherent purpose as far as the computer was concerned.

When programming with the older versions, you had to be certain that you added a line number before typing in a line. If you did not, the BASIC interpreter assumed that you were issuing a direct command for immediate execution, rather than adding a line to your program.

The required line numbers also made it more difficult to make program modules stand out visually as separate sections.

Like many of the other modernizations Microsoft includes in QBasic, dropping the requirement of line numbers makes the language easier to use.

> *Note:* Line numbers are now optional—not prohibited. Older BASIC language programs that have line numbers still can be loaded and run under QBasic (as long as they don't use any of the nonsupported keywords discussed earlier).

Full-Screen Editor Available

Another immediately noticeable change is the full-screen editor. As figure 12.1 shows, when you load QBasic, you are immediately in the Editor. The QBasic Editor also is used as the DOS editor, EDIT (see Chapter 11). As you can see, the QBasic Editor also provides a help dialog box immediately after loading the program.

The opening screen displays a message inviting you to visit a help screen called the *Survival Guide*. As you see in figure 12.2, this screen guides you through the basic steps of using menus and gaining more comprehensive help.

> *Tip:* The Survival Guide displays the keyboard methods of using the QBasic menu and help system. The QBasic editor is even easier to use with a mouse. To use a mouse instead of the keyboard, load your mouse driver (such as MOUSE.COM) before loading QBasic (you'll probably include the command to load the driver in AUTOEXEC.BAT or CONFIG.SYS, depending on the type of mouse driver) and double-click the pointer on your selection.

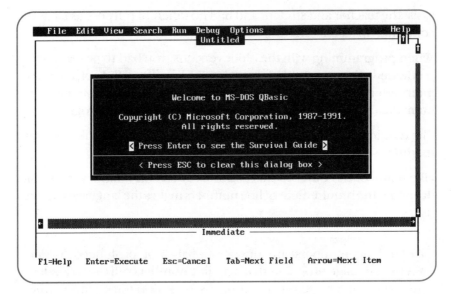

Fig. 12.1. *The QBasic opening screen.*

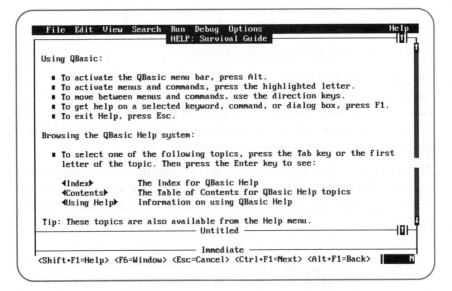

Fig. 12.2. *The QBasic Survival Guide.*

Notice in figure 12.2 that three items are contained between left and right pointing arrowheads—Index, Contents, and Using Help. The arrowheads indicate that you can select one of these topics for further information. In fact, whenever you see topics enclosed between arrowheads in a QBasic help screen, the arrowheads are an indicator that you can choose to receive further information on that topic.

If you haven't used QBasic Help before, the Using Help option is a good place to start. Move the cursor to Using Help and press Enter. If you use a mouse, place the pointer on Using Help and double-click the left mouse button.

Selecting Using Help displays the first of two pages of help screens. To see the second page, you can use the Page Down key, use the down-arrow key to move the cursor, or use your mouse by pointing at the down arrow at the bottom of the scroll bar at the right edge of the screen. Figures 12.3 and 12.4 show the two pages of help on Using Help.

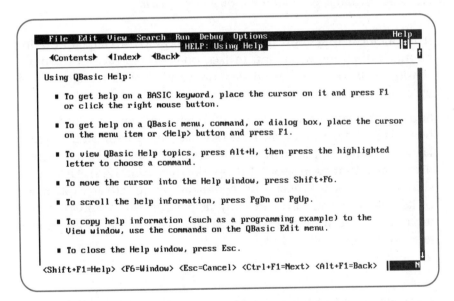

Fig. 12.3. First page of information on Using Help.

Note: Many QBasic help screens have more information than can be displayed on a single screen. Unless the first page of help provides all the information you need, you should use Page Down to check for additional information.

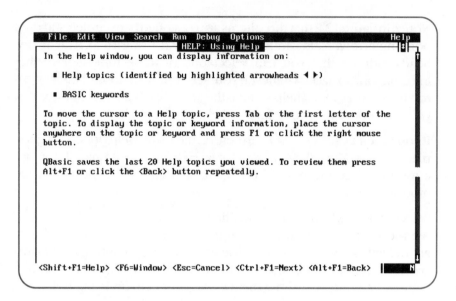

Fig. 12.4. Second page of information on Using Help.

If the on-line help system only showed you how to use Help, it wouldn't be much of an improvement. In fact, on-line help provides context-sensitive help for any of the QBasic commands. You don't have to look up commands in the manual any more.

Suppose that you are working on a program and you want to find out how to use the IF statement. To do so, place the cursor on the QBasic keyword IF in your program's text, press the F1 key, and a help screen displaying information about IF drops down (see fig. 12.5). This screen shows the complete syntax of the command, along with an explanation of its function. You also can copy help information and paste the information into your programs. You then can edit the information as needed.

Using the File Menu To Print On-Line Help Topics

If you find that you have trouble remembering information presented by QBasic's help system, you can print help information for a permanent record.

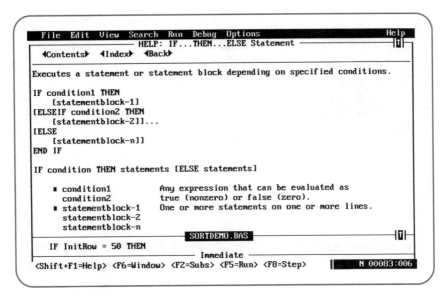

```
  File  Edit  View  Search  Run  Debug  Options                    Help
 ──────────────── HELP: IF...THEN...ELSE Statement ─────────────────
   ◄Contents►  ◄Index►  ◄Back►
 ──────────────────────────────────────────────────────────────────
 Executes a statement or statement block depending on specified conditions.

 IF condition1 THEN
     [statementblock-1]
 [ELSEIF condition2 THEN
     [statementblock-2]]...
 [ELSE
     [statementblock-n]]
 END IF

 IF condition THEN statements [ELSE statements]

     ■ condition1         Any expression that can be evaluated as
       condition2         true (nonzero) or false (zero).
     ■ statementblock-1   One or more statements on one or more lines.
       statementblock-2
       statementblock-n
 ───────────────────────────── SORTDEMO.BAS ───────────────────────
   IF InitRow = 50 THEN
 ───────────────────────────── Immediate ──────────────────────────
 <Shift+F1=Help> <F6=Window> <F2=Subs> <F5=Run> <F8=Step>    N 00083:006
```

Fig. 12.5. Help information on the IF statement.

To print the text of a help screen, perform the following steps:

1. Press the Alt key to activate the menu bar and select File. You also can use the mouse to access QBasic's menus and make selections.

   When you select File, the drop-down File menu is displayed (see fig. 12.6).

2. Select Print and the Print dialog box is displayed.

3. Indicate whether you want to print Selected Text Only or Current Window by moving the dot from one check box to the other with the up- or down-arrow keys, or your mouse pointer.

   You may want to leave the selection set to Current Window so that the entire help text is printed.

4. Select OK by pressing the Tab key and then Enter (or by clicking OK with your mouse). The help text then will be printed.

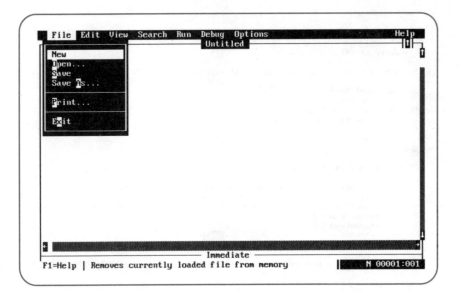

Fig. 12.6. *The drop-down File menu.*

QBasic's on-line help system provides assistance with all areas of using QBasic. Printing out a hard copy of selected help topics can help you learn how to use the new features of QBasic.

Using Other Editor Menus

Although the QBasic editor is the same full-screen editor introduced in Chapter 11, when loaded as QBasic's editor, it has different menus and a few other important differences. The other QBasic editor menus—Edit, View, Search, Run, Debug, and Options—are discussed in the following paragraphs.

The Edit menu has the same initial selections as EDIT, the full-screen DOS text editor, but adds two new QBasic-related items—New SUB and New FUNCTION (see fig. 12.7). These two items are used to open new windows for subprograms and functions.

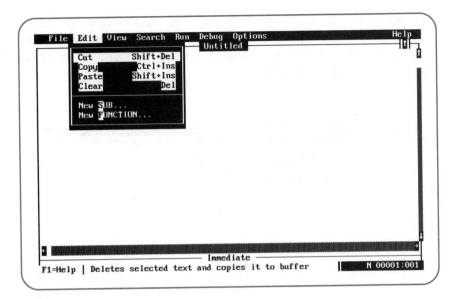

Fig. 12.7. *The QBasic Edit menu.*

The View menu is an addition that EDIT does not display. The View menu gives you options for viewing the current program, as shown in figure 12.8.

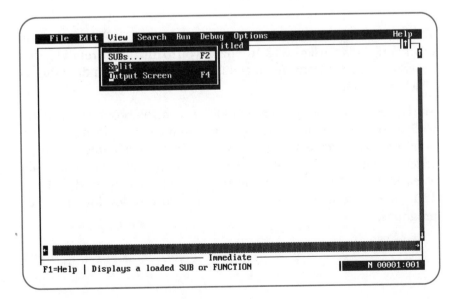

Fig. 12.8. *The QBasic View menu.*

The Search menu, which works exactly like the EDIT Search menu, enables you to find and optionally replace text. If you have used word processing software, the commands in the Search menu, shown in figure 12.9, should be familiar.

Fig. 12.9. The QBasic Search menu.

The Run menu is another addition not displayed by EDIT. Selections on this menu, shown in figure 12.10, enable you to run the currently loaded program, restart it from the beginning, or continue from the point at which you stopped.

The Debug menu, another QBasic addition, controls program execution so that you can find and correct programming errors. Using its selections, you can execute a single program statement at a time, execute a series of program steps, or execute the program until a particular point is reached. The Debug menu selections, which are displayed in figure 12.11, are powerful tools you can use to help you develop error-free programs.

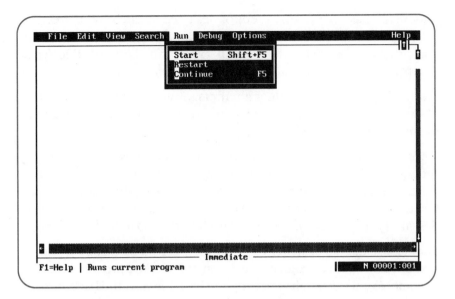

Fig. 12.10. *The QBasic Run menu.*

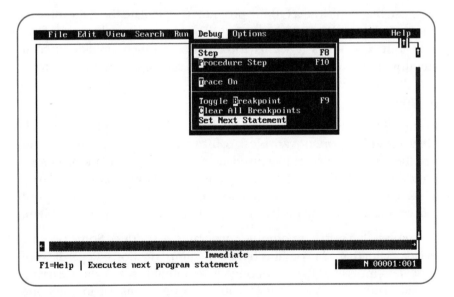

Fig. 12.11. *The QBasic Debug menu.*

Although QBasic has a "smart" editor designed to catch and correct, or at least point out, syntax errors, your QBasic programs still may possibly contain errors. One reason for this is that you can make two distinct types of errors while designing and entering programs.

Syntax errors, which the editor attempts to catch, are errors in the use of the language or, possibly, spelling errors. You may, for example, misspell PRINT as PRIMT.

Logic errors represent incorrect or incomplete development of the program's actions (or logic). The program's syntax may be correct, but the results may not be what you expect. In such cases, the editor does not find anything wrong, because you did not make any of the errors it was designed to find. Clearly, you need another method to find logic errors.

The QBasic debugger helps you find logic errors by enabling you to suspend and resume program execution, to execute a program one line at a time, to trace through your program both forward and backward, to watch the values of variables as the program executes, and to set conditions (or "breakpoints") that will halt program execution.

Suppose that you write a QBasic program to calculate the daily interest due on loans made by your company. The program works most of the time, but sometimes it seems to calculate a much smaller interest amount than you normally collect. You can see no obvious logic errors, and the editor didn't find any syntax errors when you typed in the program.

Using QBasic's debugger, you can step through the program and watch the values of important variables. You can, for example, make certain that the total interest due increased after each day's calculation. As your program runs, you can have the current value of the variable displayed in a small window. Then, as you execute the program while trying out different scenarios, you probably will be able to determine the problem.

Remember that very few computer programs are perfect. Some people, in fact, claim that all programs have some imperfections. Regardless of your view, tools like QBasic's debugger are valuable when you are trying to eliminate problems either in your own programs, or in someone else's. By giving you control over how fast and how far a program runs, what conditions cause it to stop running, and by showing you precisely what the program is doing while it is running, the debugger makes a sometimes difficult task much easier.

The final selection, the Options menu, adds one item not on the EDIT Options menu: Syntax Checking. When a dot appears to the left of Syntax Checking, QBasic checks each program line as you enter it to make sure that you have not made any syntax errors typing the line (see fig. 12.12). Although Syntax Checking cannot prevent logic errors, it can help by ensuring that the statements you type at least match QBasic's language requirements.

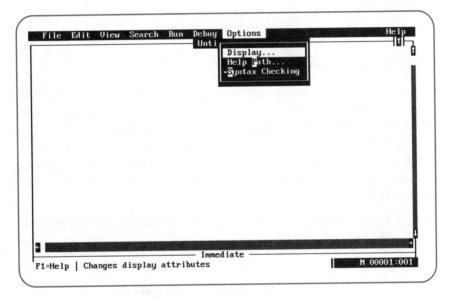

Fig. 12.12. *The QBasic Options menu.*

The Immediate Window Assists Command Execution

The Immediate Window executes BASIC instructions directly. When you type a BASIC instruction in the Immediate Window, the instruction runs instantly. You can do the following things with the Immediate Window:

- Calculate and display the value of any numeric or string expression

- Display the value of a program variable after running or interrupting a program

- Change the value of a variable and then resume execution of an interrupted program

- Test a small section of code before you add it to your program

If you have experience with BASICA or GW-BASIC, the Immediate Window is similar to their direct mode. With BASICA or GW-BASIC, any instruction you type without a line number executes immediately. In QBasic, any instruction you type in the Immediate Window executes immediately.

New Commands and Keywords

QBasic represents a major improvement over GW-BASIC and BASICA not only in the programming environment, but also in the many new commands and keywords QBasic offers. The following tables list the new commands and keywords by function. As you look over these tables, remember that, with the few exceptions mentioned earlier, QBasic continues to support all existing GW-BASIC and BASICA commands and keywords.

Table 12.1 shows the new commands and keywords that control file input and output.

Table 12.1
New File Commands and Keywords

Command or Keyword	Function
ACCESS	Sets File I/O Mode to READ, WRITE, or READ-WRITE
APPEND	File I/O Mode that places file pointer at the end of the file
BINARY	File I/O Mode that opens a file in binary mode and allows access to any byte position in the file
FILEATTR	Returns information on the attributes of an open file

Command or Keyword	Function
FREEFILE	Returns the next available file number
OUTPUT	File I/O Mode that opens a file for sequential output
RANDOM	File I/O Mode that opens a file for random access
SEEK	Returns or sets file pointer position

Table 12.2 shows the new commands and keywords used for string and numeric conversions.

Table 12.2
String and Number Conversions

Command or Keyword	Function
CLNG	Rounds a numeric expression to a long integer
CVDMBF & CVSMBF	Converts Microsoft-binary-format numeric strings to IEEE-format numbers
DEFLNG	Defines a long integer
LCASE$	Converts strings to lowercase
LTRIM$	Removes leading spaces from strings
MKDMBF$ & MKSMBF$	Converts IEEE-format numbers to Microsoft & binary-format numeric strings
MKL$	Converts long integers to 4-byte strings
MOD	Returns modulus (remainder)
RTRIM$	Removes trailing spaces from strings
UCASE$	Converts strings to uppercase

Table 12.3 shows the new commands and keywords used to control program execution and flow.

Table 12.3
Program Control

Command or Keyword	Function
CALL ABSOLUTE	Transfers control to a machine language procedure
DO..LOOP	Repeats a block of program statements until specified conditions are met
EXIT	Exits a DO or FOR loop
SELECT CASE	Conditionally executes program statements depending on an expression's value
SLEEP	Suspends program for specified period of time
TIMER	Enables, disables, or suspends timer event trapping

Table 12.4 examines QBasic's new commands and keywords that manipulate arrays.

Table 12.4
Arrays

Command or Keyword	Function
$DYNAMIC	Allocates storage for dynamic arrays
LBOUND	Returns the smallest available subscript for an array
REDIM	Declares or resizes a dynamic array
$STATIC	Allocates storage for a static array
UBOUND	Returns the largest available subscript for an array

Table 12.5 includes the miscellaneous commands and keywords new to QBasic.

Table 12.5
Miscellaneous New Commands and Keywords

Command or Keyword	Function
CONST	Declares a symbolic constant
DECLARE	Declares a function or SUB procedure
DOUBLE	Declares a double-precision floating point variable
FUNCTION	Defines a function procedure
SHARED	Provides SUBPROGRAM or FUNCTION access to module-level variables
STATIC	Declares a local variable
SUB	Defines a SUB procedure
TYPE	Creates a user-defined type
VARSEG	Returns the segment address of variable

Learning QBasic

You do not have to spend much time learning QBasic if you have some experience with BASICA, GW-BASIC, or some other version of BASIC. You do have to learn the QBasic environment—the fundamentals of entering, editing, and running a program with the menu system. After an hour or two, you should be able to write and run programs comfortably. You should, of course, begin exploring the new language features that QBasic offers.

Summary

This chapter introduced some of the exciting new features of QBasic that make the program such an improvement over GW-BASIC and BASICA. This chapter showed you the new, full-screen editor, QBasic's new commands and keywords, and how to use your existing BASIC language programs with QBasic. You also saw how many of the new features, such as the program debugger and the word processor-like editor, enable you to easily create your own QBasic programs.

Command
Reference

This Command Reference includes all DOS commands that have been enhanced or added since DOS 3.3. If a command has been enhanced, then only the new information is given with the command. Giving only new information will enhance your awareness of the new features of DOS 5.

Icons are used to show you when the command was enhanced or added. You easily can determine if the command was enhanced with DOS 4 or with DOS 5. You also can tell if the command was enhanced with DOS 4 and then again with DOS 5.

Each command is presented in the same format: next to the command name is a listing of the DOS versions with which the command can be used. You then see either the term *internal*, indicating a command built into DOS, or the term *external*, indicating a disk-resident command. In the line immediately below the command name, you first see a short description of the command function.

The syntax required to invoke the command is displayed next. Any enhanced or new switches used with the command are given with information about their correct use in the command line.

The Notes contain additional comments, background information, or suggestions for using the command effectively. This section highlights any enhanced or new features and sometimes mentions existing command features and how they relate to the new features of the command.

An example is shown for all commands. With some commands, the example shows necessary uses of the command, along with other uses of the command.

Command Reference Conventions

Great effort has been taken to make the Command Reference as easy as possible to use. To understand fully the syntax lines discussed, you must be familiar with a few conventions. These conventions signal key properties of the terms shown in the command line, indicating what is mandatory or merely optional, and what components of the syntax line are variable. Conventional substitute forms also stand in place of the variable terms you will use.

Expressing File Names

To represent a file name, you see the following:

> *d:path***filename.ext**

The *d:* represents a drive designation and can be any valid drive letter available on your computer.

path represents a single subdirectory or a path of subdirectories on a valid drive. This shows the path to the file.

filename.ext represents the full file name and its extension. When specifying a file name, you must give the extension if one exists. When a file has no extension, you omit this portion of the file name specification. The **.ext** always is shown in the syntax line as a reminder to supply this if, in fact, the name bears an extension.

When the syntax specifies an external command, you see a command line that resembles the following:

*dc:pathc***command_name**

The *dc:* represents the *drive* that contains the command. Again, this can be any valid drive letter that is on your computer.

pathc represents the subdirectory or *path* of subdirectories that leads to the command.

command_name is any valid DOS command. **FORMAT**, for example, may replace **command_name** in an actual line. When entering the command name, you do not need to specify the extension.

If FORMAT.COM resides in drive C: in the subdirectory path \DOS\DISK, the syntax line

*dc:pathc***FORMAT**

means that you can type

C:\DOS\DISK\FORMAT

to start formatting a disk.

Using Upper- and Lowercase Letters

In any syntax line, not all elements of the syntax can be represented in a literal manner. For example, *filename.ext* can represent any file name with any extension. *filename.ext* also may represent any file name with no extension at all. Command names and switches, however, can be represented in a literal way. To activate FORMAT.COM, you must type **FORMAT**.

Any literal text that you can type in a syntax line is shown in uppercase letters. Any text you can replace with other text (variable text) is shown in lowercase letters.

As an example, the syntax line

FORMAT d:

means that you must type **FORMAT** to format a disk. The **d:**, however, can be replaced by any valid disk drive letter. If **d:** is to be drive A:, then you type the following:

FORMAT A:

Mandatory versus Optional

Not all parts of a syntax line are essential when typing the command. You must be able to distinguish mandatory parts of the syntax line from those that are optional. Any portion of a syntax line that you see in **bold** letters is mandatory; whatever you see in *italic* is optional.

Typing the drive and path that contain a command is not always mandatory. For example, if FORMAT.COM is in the \DOS directory on drive C:, and your current directory is C:\DOS, you do not need to type the drive and path to start FORMAT.COM. In this instance, the syntax form can omit this information:

*C:\DOS***FORMAT**

If you have FORMAT.COM residing on a drive and directory other than that shown in this example, the syntax would be represented as

*dc:pathc***FORMAT**

in which *dc:pathc* is variable text and optional, and **FORMAT** is literal text to type and is mandatory.

Pulling It All Together

Look at the following sample syntax line:

*dc:pathc***FORMAT d:** */V:label /F:size /Q /U /?*

The drive and path pointing to the command are both optional and variable, indicated by the italic, lowercase type. All of the switches are optional. The switches are in uppercase, signifying literal text. A few options for the /V and /F switches are variable.

The only mandatory items in the syntax line are the command **FORMAT** and the drive to format, **d:**.

APPEND

V3.3, V4, V5—External

4.0 Instructs DOS to search the directories on the disks you specify for nonprogram or nonbatch files, or both.

Syntax

*dc:pathc***APPEND** */X:ON /X:OFF /PATH:ON /PATH:OFF /?*

dc:pathc are the disk drive and directory that hold the command.

Switches

/X:ON	Same as /X. Enables searching the APPEND path for nonexecutable files besides data files.
/X:OFF	Turns this feature off; the APPEND path is searched for nonexecutable files only.
/PATH:ON	Enables searching the APPEND path for a program file that is not found in the specified directory.
/PATH:OFF	Turns off search for files that have drive or path specified.
/?	Displays syntax help on-screen.

Notes

The first time you execute APPEND, the program loads from the disk and installs itself in DOS. APPEND then becomes an internal command and is not reloaded from the disk until you restart DOS. You can give the /X and /E switches only when you first invoke APPEND. You cannot give any path names with these two switches.

Because you may prefer to alter APPEND after you load it into memory, Microsoft added to DOS 4 the capability to disable the /X switch and the search path. Because /X may cause problems for programs that use Search First, Find First, and EXEC functions, such as BACKUP and RESTORE, you can disable /X without rebooting the computer.

Examples

To suspend APPEND from searching the append path for executable program files, use the following form:

APPEND /X:OFF

To suspend APPEND from searching the APPEND path when a program with a specific path is not found (C:\WP\WORD.EXE), use the following form:

APPEND /X:OFF /PATH:OFF

ASSIGN
V2, V3, V4, V5—External

5.0 Instructs DOS to use a disk drive other than one specified by a program or command.

Syntax

*dc:pathc***ASSIGN d1=d2** ... */STATUS /?*

dc:pathc are the disk drive and directory that hold the command.

d1 is the letter of the disk drive the program or DOS normally uses.

d2 is the letter of the disk drive that you want the program or DOS to use instead of the usual drive.

The three periods (...) represent additional disk drive assignments.

Switches

/STATUS   Displays all current drive assignments.

/?   Displays syntax help on-screen.

Notes

ASSIGN reroutes a program, causing it to use a disk drive that is different from the one the program intends. A program "thinks" that it is using a certain disk drive, when in fact the program is using another drive.

Aside from the help switch (/?) added with DOS 5, the /STATUS switch also is added. Using this switch shows all the drive assignments that have been made. With previous versions of DOS, you had to rely on your memory to remember which drive assignments had been made.

When using ASSIGN to determine the assignment status, you do not have to use the long form of the switch, /STATUS. You also can use /S, the short form of the switch.

Examples

To assign all activity for drive A: to drive C:, use the following form:

ASSIGN A = C

or

ASSIGN A=C

To view current drive assignments made, type the following command:

ASSIGN /STATUS

or

ASSIGN /S

To clear any previous drive reassignments, type the following command only:

ASSIGN

ATTRIB   V3, V4, V5—External

5.0   Displays, sets, or clears the read-only or archive attributes of a file.

Syntax

dc:pathc**ATTRIB** +*S* –*S* +*H* –*H d:path**filename.ext* /?

dc:pathc\\ are the disk drive and directory that hold the command.

+*S* sets a file's system file attribute on.

+*H* sets a file's hidden attribute on.

–*S* sets a file's system file attribute off.

–*H* sets a file's hidden attribute off.

d:path\\ are the disk drive and directory that hold the files for which the attribute will be displayed or changed.

filename.ext is the name of the file(s) for which the attribute will be displayed or changed. Wild cards are permitted.

Switch

/?   Displays syntax help on-screen.

Notes

DOS 5 delivers more control over a file's attributes. You can make a file a system file, or you can hide a file. Setting either attribute hides the file from view and makes the file inaccessible to a program. Only files that have their system or hidden attribute set on with ATTRIB may have the respective attributes set off.

Examples

Use the following to set the hidden and system attributes on for the file MEMO.TXT:

ATTRIB +H +S MEMO.TXT

To turn off the hidden and system attributes of MEMO.TXT, type the following:

ATTRIB -H -S MEMO.TXT

To turn on the hidden attribute of MEMO.TXT, type:

ATTRIB +H MEMO.TXT

BACKUP

Backs up one or more files from a hard disk or floppy disk onto another disk.

Syntax

*dc:pathc***BACKUP** **d1:***path\filename.ext* **d2:** */F:size* */?*

dc:pathc are the disk drive and directory that hold the command.

d1:*path* are the hard disk or floppy disk drive and the directory to be backed up.

filename.ext specifies the file you want to back up. Wild cards are permitted.

d2: is the hard or floppy disk drive that receives the backed up files.

Switches

/F:size	Formats the destination floppy disk according to the *size* specified. If you use a 1.2M disk drive, but only 360K floppy disks, you can specify /F:360 to format the 360K disk in the 1.2M drive.
/?	Displays syntax help on-screen.

Notes

Backing up to floppy disks with BACKUP from a version of DOS prior to V3.3 requires you to first format enough floppy disks before invoking the BACKUP command. If you format too few floppy disks, you will need to stop BACKUP, format more floppy disks, then restart BACKUP. With DOS 3.3, however, the addition of the /F switch enabled formatting floppy disks in the middle of a BACKUP.

Beginning with DOS 4, BACKUP automatically formats unformatted floppy disks without using the /F switch. However, the /F switch is modified to enable you to specify the capacity of the destination, or target, floppy disks. The *size* that you specify is the same as the sizes you use with FORMAT. Therefore, if you use only 360K floppy disks for the backup operation, and your drive is a 1.2M drive, specify the switch /F:360 and all unformatted floppy disks will be formatted at the proper capacity.

Because DOS 5 supports 2.88M floppy disks, using DOS 5 you can specify 2880, 2880K, 2880KB, 2.88, 2.88M, or 2.88MB with the /F switch to format 2.88M floppy disks.

Examples

To back up the entire hard disk C: to floppy disks in drive A:, using 720K floppy disks in a 1.44M drive, type the following command:

BACKUP C:\ A: /S /F:720

To back up all files as of a specified date, using 360K floppy disks in a 1.2M drive, type the following:

BACKUP C:\ A: /S /D:08/21/89 /F:360

CHKDSK   V1, V2, V3, V4, V5—External

Checks the directory and the file allocation table (FAT) of the disk and reports disk and memory status. CHKDSK also can repair errors in the directories or in the FAT.

Syntax

*dc:pathc***CHKDSK** */?*

dc:pathc are the disk drive and directory that hold the command.

d: is the disk drive to be analyzed.

Switch

/?   Displays syntax help on-screen.

Notes

CHKDSK, beginning with DOS 4, shows you the following items of information:

- Volume name and creation date (only disks with volume labels)
- Total disk space
- Number of files and bytes used for hidden or system files
- Number of files and bytes used for directories
- Number of files and bytes used for user (normal) files
- Bytes used by bad sectors (flawed disk space)
- Bytes available (free space) on disk
- Total bytes in each allocation unit
- Total allocation units on the disk
- The available allocation units on the disk
- Bytes of total memory (RAM)
- Bytes of free memory

An allocation unit is equal to a cluster.

The CHKDSK command basically works the same as it does for many versions of DOS; CHKDSK is used to report disk space usage and repair certain problems with file allocation. With DOS 4, however, a few new lines were added to its report. These lines report information about allocation units—the size of an allocation unit, total allocation units, and available allocation units. An allocation unit, 1 cluster, is disk space allocated to files, made up of multiple sectors. This is the minimum unit allocated by DOS.

Pay particular attention to the number of available allocation units. Although CHKDSK may show that you have 5,064,704 bytes of free disk space, or 2473 available allocation units, you may run out of disk space sooner than you think if you create small files (files smaller than one allocation unit).

For example, on a 40M hard disk, 1 allocation unit is normally 2048 bytes (2K). Whether you save a file that is 1 byte or 2000 bytes, 2048 bytes are used up. When you run out of allocation units, you run out of disk space.

Example

To analyze the current disk drive, type the following command:

CHKDSK

COMMAND   V2, V3, V4, V5—External

Invokes an additional copy of COMMAND.COM, the command processor.

Syntax

*dc:pathc***COMMAND** *cttydevice /MSG /?*

dc:pathc are the disk drive and the directory that hold the command.

cttydevice is the device to be used for input and output. Refer to the CTTY command.

Switches

/MSG   Loads all error messages into memory. Must be used with /P.

/?   Displays syntax help on-screen.

Notes

COMMAND.COM is the command processor that you interface with when you type at the DOS prompt. Besides containing a few commands, such as DIR and CLS, COMMAND.COM parses the commands that you type at the DOS prompt and starts the programs that you request.

One change made to DOS 4 is the capability to set the *ctty* device when starting COMMAND.COM. With DOS versions prior to DOS 4, you had to use the CTTY command after COMMAND.COM was loaded. With DOS 4 and more recent versions, you can specify the device to be used for input and output by COMMAND.COM when you start COMMAND.COM.

If you are using DOS 5 with a floppy-disk system, you may specify the /MSG switch in the SHELL directive of CONFIG.SYS. Using this switch loads all error messages in memory. If an error occurs, the disk with COMMAND.COM does not have to reside in the drive. An additional 1K of RAM is required to use this switch.

Examples

To start COMMAND.COM, assigning COM2 as the *ctty* device, type the following form:

COMMAND COM2

To load COMMAND.COM as the command processor, loading messages into memory, issue the following CONFIG.SYS directive (use when booting from a floppy disk):

SHELL=A:\COMMAND.COM /MSG /P

COMP V1, V2, V3, V4, V5—External

 Compares two sets of disk files. This command is not available with some DOS versions. If COMP is not available on your version of DOS, see the FC command.

Syntax

*dc:pathc***COMP** *d1:path1\filename1.ext1*
d2:path2\filename2.ext2 /D /A /L /N:*line* /C /?

dc:pathc are the disk drive and the directory that hold the command.

d1:path1 are the drive and the directory that contain the first set of files to be compared.

filename1.ext1 is the file name for the first set of files. Wild cards are permitted.

d2:path2 are the drive and the directory that contain the second set of files to be compared.

filename2.ext2 is the file name for the second set of files. Wild cards are permitted.

Special Terms:

d1:path1\filename1.ext1 is the *primary* file set.

d2:path2\filename2.ext2 is the *secondary* file set.

Switches

/D	Displays the hexadecimal values of the differing characters.
/A	Displays the actual differing characters.
/L	Displays the line number of the differing characters.
/N:*line*	Compares the number of lines in a file. *line* is the number of lines to compare.
/C	Makes the comparison of the files so that they are not case sensitive.
/?	Displays syntax help on-screen.

Notes

COMP is the utility for comparing files. Use the command to verify that files on which you used the COPY command are correct. Also, use COMP to check a known good program copy against a questionable copy.

COMP normally displays the hexadecimal value of the mismatched characters. You then must determine which characters do not match. DOS 5 enables you to display either the decimal values of the mismatched characters or the actual characters themselves. DOS 5 also enables you to display which lines in the files contain the mismatch. If you are matching ASCII files, the /C switch is useful. This switch enables a noncase-sensitive compare. Also useful with an ASCII file is the /N switch, which enables you to compare only a portion of the file.

Examples

To compare the file IBM.LET to IBM.BAK and display the actual mismatched characters, type the following form:

COMP IBM.LET IBM.BAK /A

To compare the first 10 lines of the files IBM.LET and IBM.BAK, type the following command:

COMP IBM.LET IBM.BAK /N:10

Configuration Subcommand
BUFFERS   V2, V3, V4, V5—Internal

`4.0` `5.0` Sets the number of disk buffers set aside by DOS in memory.

Syntax

BUFFERS = nn,*mm*

nn is the number of buffers to set, in the range of 1 to 99.

mm is the number of sectors, from 1 to 8, that can be read or written at a time. The default is one.

Switch

(none)

Notes

Beginning with DOS 4, BUFFERS can be installed with a secondary cache, also called lookahead buffers. The purpose of the secondary cache is to read up to 8 more sectors into memory while the disk is being read. When DOS is requested to read the disk again, the information that is called for most likely is already contained in the secondary cache, eliminating the need to access the disk as often. If you use a disk cache, such as SMARTDRV.SYS, do not use the secondary cache.

With DOS 4, you can place BUFFERS in expanded memory, using the /X switch. This switch is not supported in DOS 5.

With DOS 5, if you are using at least an 80286 computer with 1M of RAM, BUFFERS can be created in the high memory area, provided that you load DOS high. This frees conventional memory for use by applications programs.

BUFFERS is an important directive to increase disk drive performance. How you use BUFFERS, however, is related directly to the type of computer that you use and to the amount of memory that is contained in your computer. If your computer has 1M of RAM or less, and no expanded memory, you will want to utilize the potential of BUFFERS. If, however, your computer has expanded memory, or has extended memory greater than 1M, you are better off using a disk cache, such as SMARTDRV.SYS, supplied with DOS 5.

Example

To set your CONFIG.SYS file so that DOS uses 20 disk buffers and 8 secondary-cache buffers, enter the command in the following form:

BUFFERS = 20,8

Configuration Subcommand
DEVICEHIGH   V5—Internal

Enables loading device drivers into reserved memory on 80386SX, 80386, and 80486 computers.

Syntax

DEVICEHIGH *SIZE=hexbyte dd:pathd***filenamed.extd**

SIZE=hexbyte is the least amount of reserved memory that must be available for the device driver to be loaded into memory. *hexbyte* is the actual size in bytes expressed as a hexadecimal value.

dd:pathd are the disk drive and path in which the device driver is located.

filenamed.extd is the actual file name and extension of the device driver.

Switch

(none)

Notes

DEVICEHIGH uses reserved memory (memory between 640K and 1M in RAM) to locate device drivers and TSR programs. Locating device drivers and TSRs in reserved memory rather than conventional memory leaves more room for your programs to operate. Relocating device drivers in reserved memory requires that you use an 80386SX, 80386, or 80486 computer with at least 1M of RAM.

Before you can use DEVICEHIGH, however, you must install HIMEM.SYS and EMM386.EXE as device drivers. These device drivers must precede the DEVICEHIGH directive in your CONFIG.SYS file.

In addition, you must enable a link between your conventional memory and the upper memory blocks. This is done with the DOS=UMB CONFIG.SYS directive.

Example

To install SMARTDRV.SYS in reserved memory, allocating 512K of XMS memory for a disk cache, use the following lines in your CONFIG.SYS file:

```
DEVICE = C:\DOS\HIMEM.SYS
DEVICE = C:\DOS\EMM386.EXE RAM
DOS = HIGH,UMB
DEVICEHIGH C:\DOS\SMARTDRV.SYS 512
```

This assumes that your DOS utility files are found on drive C: in the directory \DOS, and that you have 512K of extended memory that you can allocate to SMARTDRV.SYS. (You should have at least 2M of RAM to use these lines in your CONFIG.SYS file.)

Configuration Subcommand
DOS

5.0 Loads DOS into the high memory area or controls a link between conventional memory and reserved memory.

Syntax

> **DOS = HIGH | LOW**
>
> or
>
> **DOS = UMB | NOUMB**
>
> or
>
> **DOS = HIGH | LOW, UMB | NOUMB**

HIGH is used to locate a portion of DOS into the high memory area.

LOW is the default setting and causes DOS to reside entirely in conventional memory.

UMB establishes and maintains a link between conventional memory and the upper memory blocks in reserved memory.

NOUMB is the default setting and disconnects a link between conventional memory and the upper memory blocks in reserved memory.

Switch

(none)

Notes

If you use DOS 5 on an 80286, 80386SX, 80386, or 80486 computer with at least 1M of RAM, you can enable DOS to relocate a portion of itself into the high memory area. Doing so frees up conventional memory for your programs to use. If your computer uses the 8088 or 8086 microprocessor, however, you cannot use this feature. Specifying HIGH with DOS tells DOS to relocate itself in the high memory area, while LOW tells DOS to load itself in conventional memory.

If you use an 80386SX, 80386, or 80486 computer with at least 1M of RAM, you can enable DOS to relocate memory into the reserved area between 640K and 1M by using HIMEM.SYS and EMM386.EXE (using the RAM or NOEMS parameter). Doing so enables DOS to load device drivers and memory-resident programs into the reserved area, freeing conventional memory that programs can use. DOS, however, must maintain a link between conventional memory and reserved memory. This link is maintained by the UMB option of DOS.

Examples

To enable DOS to relocate portions of itself into the high memory area, use the following form:

DOS = HIGH

To enable DOS to relocate portions of itself into the high memory area and maintain a link between conventional and reserved memory, use the following form:

DOS = HIGH, UMB

Configuration Subcommand
DRIVPARM
V4, V5—Internal

Defines or changes the parameters of a block device, such as a disk drive.

Syntax

DRIVPARM = /I

Switch

/I   Used if you have a 3 1/2-inch floppy disk drive connected internally to your floppy drive controller, but your ROM BIOS does not support a 3 1/2-inch drive.

Notes

You have great flexibility in adding block devices to your computer. Make sure that you specify the correct type of device, number of heads, and number of sectors. Incorrect values can cause the device to work either incorrectly or not at all.

Example

To specify an internal 3 1/2-inch, 1.44M drive that will be drive B: and will support change-line, use the following form:

DRIVPARM /D:1 /C /F:7 /I

Configuration Subcommand
INSTALL
V4, V5—Internal

4.0   Starts terminate-and-stay-resident (TSR) programs from CONFIG.SYS. Example programs to start with INSTALL are FASTOPEN, KEYB, NLSFUNC, and SHARE.

Syntax

INSTALL = *dc:pathc***filename.ext** *options*

dc:pathc are the disk drive and the directory that hold the command.

filename.ext is the name of the file, which can be FASTOPEN.EXE, KEYB.EXE, NLSFUNC.EXE, SHARE.EXE, or some other valid terminate-and-stay-resident program.

options are any parameters the **filename.ext** command requires to function.

Switch

(none)

Notes

INSTALL enables DOS to load some programs from CONFIG.SYS. You may use INSTALL if you want a program to load only once, each time you start DOS.

Example

To start SHARE.EXE in your CONFIG.SYS file by using INSTALL, type the following form:

INSTALL = C:\DOS\SHARE.EXE

This directive assumes that SHARE.EXE is in the directory \DOS on drive C:.

Configuration Subcommand
REM
V4, V5—Internal

4.0 Places remarks or hidden statements in the CONFIG.SYS file.

Syntax

REM *remark*

Switch

(none)

Notes

REM statements can be useful in the CONFIG.SYS file to document commands in the file. For example, if you place the DRIVPARM command in your CONFIG.SYS file, you also can place a REM statement on the line before the DRIVPARM command to explain the type of drive you are installing.

Example

To place a remark in your CONFIG.SYS file to explain another entry, you can type a line similar to the following:

REM internal 3 1/2-inch, 1.44M, B:, change-line
DRIVPARM /D:1 /C /F:7 /I

Notice that the REM statement explains the DRIVPARM line.

DEL
V1, V2, V3, V4, V5—Internal

`4.0` Deletes files from the disk.

DEL, an alternative command for ERASE, performs the same functions as ERASE. See ERASE for a complete description.

DELOLDOS
V5—External

`5.0` Removes all DOS files of versions prior to DOS 5 from the hard disk.

Syntax

*dc:pathc*__DELOLDOS__ */B /?*

dc:pathc are the disk drive and directory that hold the command.

Switches

/B   Forces black and white screen mode.

/?   Displays syntax help on-screen (DOS 5 only).

Notes

When you upgrade to DOS 5, your old version of DOS is preserved on your hard disk, and with the Uninstall disks that the DOS 5 Setup program creates. After you are sure that the upgrade is working correctly, and there are no incompatibilities with programs that you are using, you may delete the old version of DOS from your hard disk. Deleting the old version of DOS frees up additional storage room on your disk.

Examples

To remove the old version of DOS from your disk, use the following form:

DELOLDOS

DIR

5.0 Lists any or all files and subdirectories in a disk directory.

Syntax

DIR */A:attrib* */O:sort* */S* */B* */L* */?*

Switches

/A:attrib Displays only files that are assigned an attribute that you specify. The settings for *attrib* are given in the following table:

Attrib	Description
(/A only)	Displays all directory entries, even system and hidden
H	Displays hidden files
–H	Displays files that are not hidden
S	Displays system files
–S	Displays files that are not system files
D	Displays subdirectories
–D	Displays only files (no subdirectory names)
A	Displays files for archiving
–A	Displays files that are archived
R	Displays read-only files
–R	Displays files which can be read and written to

/O:*sort*	Displays the directory in sorted order. The settings for *sort* are given in the following table:

Sort	Description
(/O only)	Directory entries sorted alphabetically, listing subdirectories before files (0-9, A-Z)
N	Sorts alphabetically by root name (0-9, A-Z)
–N	Sorts reverse-alphabetically by root name (Z-A, 9-0)
E	Sorts alphabetically by extension (0-9, A-Z)
–E	Sorts reverse-alphabetically by extension (Z-A, 9-0)
D	Sorts by date and time, earliest to latest
–D	Sorts by date and time, latest to earliest
S	Sorts by size, smallest to largest
–S	Sorts by size, largest to smallest
G	Lists subdirectories before files
–G	Lists subdirectories after files

/S	Lists all files in the current directory and all subsequent directories.
/B	Lists root name and extension with period; FILENAME.EXT. No other information is listed, such as size, date, and time created.
/L	Lists file names and subdirectory names in lowercase.
/?	Displays syntax help on-screen.

Notes

The DIR command shows all the information that it always has, with the new addition of the total bytes of files listed. Additionally, when you display a wide directory listing with the /W switch, subdirectories are displayed in square brackets. This enables you to distinguish subdirectories easily from file names.

Using DOS 5 gives you greater control over the listing of files. You may list files with only certain attributes, for example. Listing files that may be archived enables you to determine which files you can back up or XCOPY when you specify all archived files. You also can sort files in many different ways, which enables you to better manage your files. When you use the /S switch, you can view the files in the current directory as well as the files in subsequent directories.

Using the /B switch enables you to easily create a list of files for batch file processing. For example, look at the following command:

DIR /B > DIRLIST.TXT

This command creates a file DIRLIST.TXT that contains one file name per line—each line contains the root name, a period, and the file extension.

Examples

To list all files in the \DOS directory from oldest to newest, type the following form:

DIR \DOS /O:d

To list all files in the \DOS directory, and subsequent directories, type the following form:

DIR \DOS /S

DISKCOPY
V1, V2, V3, V4, V5—External

Copies the entire contents of one floppy disk to another on a track-for-track basis, making an exact duplicate. DISKCOPY works only with floppy disks.

Syntax

*dc:pathc***DISKCOPY d1: d2:** */V /?*

dc:pathc are the disk drive and the directory that hold command.

d1: is the floppy disk drive that holds the source disk.

d2: is the floppy disk drive that holds the destination disk.

Switches

/V   Verifies the copy. Although this switch slows down the copy procedure, you may want to use this switch when copying important disks.

/?   Displays syntax help on-screen.

Special Terms:

The disk you copy from is the *source* or first disk.

The disk you copy to is the *destination* or second disk.

Notes

DISKCOPY makes exact copies of floppy disks of identical size and density. Using the /V switch, you verify the disk as you are copying. Using this switch eliminates the need to use DISKCOMP, which saves time.

Example

If you want to create, in drive B:, a duplicate of a disk placed in drive A:—and verify as you copy—type the following form:

DISKCOPY A: B: /V

DOSKEY   V5—External

5.0   Enables you to recall a history of DOS commands, edit DOS command lines, and create macros.

Syntax

*dc:pathc***DOSKEY** */REINSTALL /BUFSIZE=bytes /MACROS /HISTORY /INSERT ¦ OVERSTRIKE macroname=macrotext /?*

dc:pathc are the drive and subdirectory in which DOSKEY is located.

macroname is the name assigned to the command or commands to perform.

macrotext is the command or commands that are performed when typing the *macroname* and pressing Enter.

Switches

/REINSTALL	Starts a second copy of DOSKEY.
/BUFSIZE=bytes	Sets aside memory for DOSKEY to store commands and macros. The value of *bytes* is the actual amount of memory to set aside. The default is 1024 bytes, or 1K bytes.
/MACROS	Lists all the macros created with DOSKEY.
/HISTORY	Lists all commands stored in memory from earliest to latest.
/INSERT ¦ OVERSTRIKE	Enables insert mode or overstrike mode, respectively. Insert mode enables you to insert characters while editing a command line, rather than typing over characters in the line.
/?	Displays syntax help on-screen.

Notes

DOS ordinarily remembers the last command typed at the command line. DOSKEY, however, stores a history of commands in memory. The number of commands retained in memory depends on the buffer size, which is normally 1K of memory. When the buffer is full, the oldest command is eliminated, which makes room for a new command. The buffer also contains macros as well as a history of commands.

You can use several keys to recall a command in the history. The keys and their functions are as follows:

Key	Function
↑	Displays the last command in the history
↓	Displays the next command in the history. When the last command is reached, the first command is redisplayed.
PgUp	Displays the first command in the history
PgDn	Displays the last command in the history

In addition to DOS' standard editing keys, several keys and key combinations are used to edit a command on the command line. The additional keys that you may use are as follows:

Key	Function
←	Moves the cursor one character to the left
Ctrl-←	Moves the cursor one word to the left
→	Moves the cursor one character to the right
Ctrl-→	Moves the cursor one word to the right
Home	Moves the cursor to the first character in the command line
End	Moves the cursor after the last character in the command line
Esc	Erases the current command line
F7	Lists all commands in the history, numbering each command, and indicating the current command
Alt-F7	Erases all the commands in the history
F9	Enables you to specify the number of the command in the history to make current. The command numbers can be seen by pressing F7.
F10	Lists all macros in memory
Alt-F10	Erases all macros in memory

With DOSKEY, you can create macros in a manner similar to creating batch files. By typing the name of a macro and pressing Enter, you may perform several commands. When you create macros, a few characters are created by dollar sign equivalents, as follows:

Code	Description
$g or $G	Same as >. Used for redirecting output
$l or $L	Same as <. Used for redirecting input
$b or $B	Same as ¦. Used for piping
$t or $T	Separates macro commands
$$	Use the dollar sign in the command line
$1 through $9	Replacable parameters. Same as %1 through %9 in a batch file.
$*	A replaceable parameter that represents all information that you type on the command line following the macro name

When creating a macro, you can include any valid DOS command, including batch files. You may start a batch file from a macro. However, you cannot start a macro from a batch file.

Examples

To start DOSKEY, use the following form:

DOSKEY

To create a macro for moving files, use the following form:

DOSKEY MOVE=COPY $1 $2 $T DEL $1

To list all macros in memory, use the following form:

DOSKEY /MACROS

You can create a batch file that consists of commands that you typed from the command line. From the DOS command line, for example, type the commands necessary to start Lotus 1-2-3 and copy the file you work on to a floppy disk in drive A:. You then can use DOSKEY to create a batch file as follows (each line shown is typed at a DOS prompt):

Press Alt-F7 to clear the command history.

> **CD \123**
> **123**

(type /Quit to exit 1-2-3 and return to the DOS prompt)

> **CD **
> **COPY C:\SALES\JUNSALES.WK1 A:**
> **DOSKEY /HISTORY > 123.BAT**

The commands that you typed change the directory to \123 and start 1-2-3. When you exit 1-2-3, you then return to the root directory and copy the sales file that you worked on to a floppy disk for a backup. Using redirection with DOSKEY, you create a batch file in what can be called "learn mode."

`4.0` `5.0` # DOSSHELL   V4, V5—External

Starts the Shell that accompanies DOS.

Syntax

To start DOS Shell in text mode, use the following form:

> *dc:pathc***DOSSHELL** */T:screen /B /?*

To start DOS Shell in graphics mode, use the following form:

> *dc:pathc***DOSSHELL** */G:screen /B /?*

To start DOS Shell in the default screen mode, use the following form:

> *dc:pathc***DOSSHELL**

dc:pathc are the disk drive and subdirectory in which DOSSHELL is located.

Switches

/T:screen   Displays DOS Shell in text mode, using the resolution described by the screen.

/G:screen   Displays DOS Shell in graphics mode, using the resolution described by the screen.

Switch	*Monochrome/CGA*	*EGA*	*VGA*
/T:L	25 lines	25 lines	25 lines
/T:M	x	43 lines	43 lines
/T:M1	x	43 lines	43 lines
/T:M2	x	43 lines	50 lines
/T:H	x	43 lines	43 lines
/T:H1	x	43 lines	43 lines
/T:H2	x	43 lines	50 lines
/G:L	25 lines	25 lines	25 lines
/G:M	x	43 lines	30 lines
/G:M1	x	43 lines	30 lines
/G:M2	x	43 lines	34 lines
/G:H	x	43 lines	43 lines
/G:H1	x	43 lines	43 lines
/G:H2	x	43 lines	60 lines

/B   Starts DOS Shell in black and white rather than color.

/?   Displays syntax help on-screen.

Notes

DOSSHELL changed between DOS 4 and 5. In DOS 4, DOSSHELL is a batch file used to start the shell. DOSSHELL contains all the switches needed to start the shell in the correct configuration for your computer. DOSSHELL in DOS 5, however, is a command file (COM). When installing DOS, DOSSHELL is configured for your computer system.

Example

To start the shell, use the following form:

DOSSHELL

To start the Shell in the highest resolution on a VGA display, type the following:

DOSSHELL /G:H2

EDIT

5.0 EDIT is a full-screen editor, included with DOS for creating ASCII files, such as batch files.

Syntax

*dc:pathc***EDIT** *d:path\filename.ext* /B /G /H /NOHI /?

dc:pathc are the disk drive and subdirectory in which EDIT is located.

d:path\filename.ext are the location and file name of the file to load into EDIT when EDIT starts.

Switches

/B	Puts EDIT in Black & White screen colors.
/G	Quickly writes to a CGA monitor (this switch may cause "snow" on some monitors).
/H	Displays EDIT in the maximum lines that your screen supports (43 for EGA and 50 for VGA).
/NOHI	Uses reverse video rather than high-intensity characters (for LCD screens).
/?	Displays syntax help on-screen.

Notes

EDIT is a full-screen editor that works much like the editor in QBasic, the BASIC interpreter that is included with DOS 5. EDIT performs many of the same tasks as EDLIN, but is much easier to use than EDLIN. Edit prints an open file, cuts and pastes text, offers on-line help, and supports a mouse.

Examples

To start EDIT, use the following form:

EDIT

To start EDIT and load the AUTOEXEC.BAT file from the root directory of drive C:, use the following form:

EDIT C:\AUTOEXEC.BAT

To start EDIT, load MEM.TXT, and set EDIT to display the maximum number of lines that your display supports, use the following form:

EDIT MEM.TXT /H

EMM386

V5—External

5.0 Enables your 80386SX, 80386, or 80486 computer to convert extended memory into EMS 4.0 expanded memory and to control that expanded memory. EMMS386 also converts some extended memory to reserved memory.

Syntax

As a device driver:

DEVICE = *dc:pathc***EMM386.EXE** *ramval W=ON ¦ OFF Ms FRAME=xxxx /Pxxxx /Pn=xxxx X=xxxx-xxxx B=xxxx L=xmsmem A=regs H=hhh RAM ¦ NOEMS*

As a command:

dc:pathc**EMM386** *ON ¦ OFF ¦ AUTO W=ON ¦ OFF /?*

dc:pathc\\ are the disk drive and subdirectory in which EMM386 is located.

Device Driver parameters:

ramval is the amount of RAM (in 1K bytes) to assign as EMS 4.0 memory. Enter a value from 16 to 32768 as a multiple of 16 (16, 32, 48,...,32752, 32768). Any number that you enter, however, is rounded to the nearest 16th. The default is 256.

W=ON | OFF enables or disables support for the Weitek Coprocessor. The default is W=OFF.

Ms specifies the segment base address. *s* is a number that is used to represent the address. This is the beginning address of the EMS page frame. The numbers and associated addresses (listed in hexadecimal) are as follows:

1	C000
2	C400
3	C800
4	CC00
5	D000
6	D400
7	D800
8	DC00
9	E000
10	8000
11	8400
12	8800
13	8C00
14	9000

FRAME=xxxx specifies directly the beginning address of the EMS page frame. *xxxx* may be one of the addresses listed under *Ms*.

/Pxxxx specifies directly the beginning address (same as *FRAME=xxxx* above).

Pn=xxxx defines an address for a page segment. *n* may be the numbers 0, 1, 2, 3, 254, 255. To remain compatible with EMS 3.2, P0 through P3 must be contiguous addresses. You cannot use this option if you use *Ms*, *FRAME=xxxx*, or */Pxxxx*.

X=xxxx-xxxx specifies that a range of memory should not be used for the EMS page frame. *xxxx-xxxx* are the ranges to keep free.

B=xxxx specifies the lowest address to use for bank switching. The default is 4000.

L=xmsmem specifies the number of 1K bytes that will remain as extended memory, rather than being converted to EMS memory. *xmsmem* is the value of 1K bytes of memory. For 1M to remain as extended memory, use the options L=1024.

A=regs allocates the number of alternate registers that EMM386 may use. Although the default number is 7, you can specify a number from 0 to 254 for *regs*.

H=hhh enables you to change from the default 64 handles that EMM386 uses. *hhh* may be a number from 2 to 255.

RAM ¦ NOEMS is used to allocate reserved memory; that is, place some extended memory in open areas in the 640K to 1M address space. Although *RAM* leaves room for an EMS page frame in the reserved area, *NOEMS* does not leave room for the EMS page frame.

Command parameters:

ON enables expanded memory.

OFF disables expanded memory.

AUTO enables expanded Weitek Coprocessor support when a program requests it.

W=ON ¦ OFF enables or disables, respectively, Weitek Coprocessor support.

Switch

/?   Displays syntax help on-screen.

Notes

EMM386.EXE can be used from the DOS command line only when EMM386.EXE is installed as a device driver from the CONFIG.SYS file. To install EMM386.EXE from CONFIG.SYS, add, at the least, the following line to your CONFIG.SYS file:

DEVICE=C:\DOS\EMM386.EXE

The preceding statement assumes that EMM386.EXE is located in the \DOS subdirectory on drive C:. When installed, 256K of extended memory is used as EMS 4.0 expanded memory. EMM386 will set up its own page frame, without any additional instructions from you.

You can place device drivers and TSR programs into reserved memory by using either the RAM or the NOEMS options of EMM386. The RAM option remaps extended memory into the 640K to 1M range, which leaves room for the EMS page frame. The NOEMS option enables you to place 64K additional memory in the reserved area; however, you cannot use extended memory as expanded memory. Use NOEMS only if you do not want to enable expanded memory but you prefer additional memory be allocated to the UMBs. Normally, however, you will want to use the RAM option.

EMM386, when used from the DOS command line, controls the settings of the counterpart device driver.

Examples

To install EMM386 from CONFIG.SYS (assuming that EMM386.EXE is in C:\DOS), allocating 1M or EMS memory and enabling reserved memory, use the following form:

DEVICE=C:\DOS\EMM386.EXE 1024 RAM

To install EMM386 from CONFIG.SYS (assuming EMM386.EXE is in C:\DOS) as a UMB provider only, use the following form:

DEVICE=C:\DOS\EMM386.EXE NOEMS

To temporarily disable expanded memory, use the following form:

EMM386 ON

To enable Weitek Coprocessor support, use the following form:

EMM386 W=ON

ERASE

4.0 Removes one or more files from the directory.

Syntax

ERASE *d:path***filename.ext** */P* */?*

or with its alternative command:

DEL *d:path***filename.ext** */P* */?*

d:path are the disk drive and the directory that hold the file(s) to be erased.

filename.ext is the name of the file(s) to be erased. Wild cards are permitted.

Switches

/P	With DOS 4 or 5, this switch prompts you before erasing the file with the message `filename.ext, Delete (Y/N)?`
/?	Displays syntax help on-screen.

Notes

ERASE, or its short form DEL (for DELETE), removes files. The directory entry for each erased file is altered so that DOS knows the file is not in use. The space occupied by each file erased from the disk is freed. You can use the UNDELETE command to restore deleted files.

The /P switch enables you to delete files selectively. You are prompted before ERASE deletes each file that you specify.

Example

To erase all the files in C:\MEMOS using DOS 4 or 5—and be prompted before each file is erased—type the following form:

ERASE C:\MEMOS /P

or

DEL C:\MEMOS /P

EXPAND

5.0 Copies a compressed, unusable file from the original DOS disks to an uncompressed, usable form.

Syntax

*dc:pathc***EXPAND** *d1:path1***filename.ext ...**
dd:*pathd\\filenamed.extd* **/?**

dc:pathc are the disk drive and directory that hold the command.

d1:path1 is the letter of the disk drive and path where the compressed file is located.

filename.ext is the name of the compressed file.

The three periods (...) represent additional compressed file specifications.

dd:*pathd\\filenamed.extd* is the drive or path or new file name to which the compressed file should be expanded.

Switch

/? Displays syntax help on-screen.

Notes

Files stored on the original DOS 5 disks are stored as compressed files. This enables more data to be stored on fewer disks than files that are not compressed. Before you can use one of the files on the disks, however, you first must decompress the file.

When you use SETUP to install DOS, the files are decompressed as they are transferred to the correct disks. Suppose that you delete a file accidentally, however, or for some reason a file gets corrupted. You must transfer the file from the original DOS disk. You use EXPAND to transfer the file, decompressing it as you transfer the file. EXPAND can be considered as another form of COPY—however, EXPAND is a "one-way" copy.

Examples

To expand FORMAT.COM from the 5 1/4-inch Disk 1 to C:\DOS\, type the following:

EXPAND A:FORMAT.CO_ C:\DOS\FORMAT.COM

FASTOPEN
V3.3, V4—External

Keeps directory information in memory so that DOS can quickly find frequently needed files.

Syntax

*dc:pathc***FASTOPEN d:**=*nnn . . . /X /?*

dc:pathc are the disk drive and the directory that hold the command.

d: is the name of the disk drive that contains directory information to be held in memory.

nnn is the number of directory entries to be held in memory (10 to 999).

. . . designates additional disk drives in the forms **d:**=*nnn*.

Switches

/X   Tells DOS to use expanded memory to store the information buffered by FASTOPEN.

/?   Displays syntax help on-screen.

Notes

FASTOPEN was added to DOS 3.3 and retained in DOS 4 and 5. This command caches directory information on files and can be used on any disk drive.

If you give *nnn*, the value must be between 10 and 999, inclusively. FASTOPEN's minimum value is 10 or the maximum level of your deepest directory plus 1, whichever value is greater.

If your computer has expanded memory, you can use the /X switch. This places the buffer space in expanded memory, which frees more conventional memory.

Examples

To keep in expanded memory the location of up to 90 files residing on drive C:, use the following form:

FASTOPEN C:=90 /X

To load FASTOPEN from CONFIG.SYS, buffering the location of up to 40 files from drive C: and drive D:, use the following form:

INSTALL=C:\DOS\FASTOPEN C:=40 D:=40

FIND
V2, V3, V4, V5—External

Displays from the designated files all the lines matching or not matching (depending on the switches you use) the specified string. This command also can display the line numbers.

Syntax

*dc:pathc***FIND** */I /?* **"string"** *d:path\\filename.ext...*

dc:pathc are the disk drive and the directory that hold the command.

string is the set of characters that you want to find. As shown in the syntax line, **string** must be enclosed in quotation marks.

d:path are the disk drive and the directory that hold the file.

filename.ext is the file you want to search.

Switches

/I   Enables noncase-sensitive search.

/?   Displays syntax help on-screen.

Notes

FIND is one of several filters provided with DOS 3, 4, and 5. The command can find lines that contain **string** or those that do not. FIND also can number and count lines rather than display them.

In versions of DOS prior to DOS 5, FIND performs a case-sensitive search. That is, the string in quotation marks must match exactly a string in the file for the string to be found. Using DOS 5's /I switch, however, you can find any string in a file, whether the string is uppercase, lowercase, or a mixture of each.

Example

To display each noncase-sensitive occurrence of the string *print* in the file HELP.TXT, type the following form:

FIND /I "print" HELP.TXT

FORMAT   V1, V2, V3, V4, V5—External

 Initializes a disk to accept DOS information and files; also checks the disk for defective tracks and optionally places DOS on the floppy or hard disk.

Syntax

*dc:pathc***FORMAT d:** */F:size /V:label /Q /U /?*

dc:pathc are the disk drive and the directory that hold the command.

d: is a valid disk drive name.

Switches

/F:*size*   Formats a disk to less than maximum capacity, with *size* designating one of the following values:

Drive	Allowable values for size
160K, 180K	160, 160K, 160KB, 180, 180K, 180KB
320K, 360K	All of above, plus 320, 320K, 320KB, 360, 360K, 360KB
1.2M	All of above, plus 1200, 1200K, 1200KB, 1.2, 1.2M, 1.2MB
720K	720, 720K, 720KB
1.44M	All for 720K, plus 1440, 1440K, 1440KB, 1.44, 1.44M, 1.44MB
2.88M	2880, 2880K, 2880KB, 2.88, 2.88M, 2.88MB

/V:label Transfers volume label to formatted disk. Replaces label with 11-character name for new disk.

/U Formats a disk unconditionally. Erases any data that existed previously on the disk without the capability to recover the information.

/Q Performs a quick format on the disk. Erases only the file allocation table and root directory. Does not recheck the disk for bad sectors.

/? Displays syntax help on-screen.

Notes

With versions of DOS prior to DOS 5, FORMAT destroys information previously recorded on floppy disks or hard disks; do not FORMAT a disk that contains useful information. FORMAT with DOS 5, however, can perform a safe format. When formatting a previously formatted disk, the file allocation table and root directory are saved to another location on the disk and then are cleared, and the disk is checked—previously existing data, however, is not cleared. You can rebuild an accidentally formatted disk that was formatted safely. To completely erase a disk that was used previously, issue the /U switch. An unconditional format takes about 27 percent longer than the default safe format.

With DOS 5, you also may format a disk quickly by selecting the /Q switch. This switch clears the File Allocation Table and root directory, but does not check the disk for bad sectors. To reuse a known good disk, simply quick format the disk. The quick format is nearly 80 percent quicker than the default safe format.

Examples

To quickly reformat a disk in drive A:, type the following form:

FORMAT A: /Q

To perform an unconditional format of the disk in drive B:, type the following form:

FORMAT B: /U

GRAPHICS   V2, V3, V4, V5—External

4.0 5.0   Prints the graphics-screen contents on a suitable printer.

Syntax

*dc:pathc***GRAPHICS** *printer filename /PRINTBOX:x /?*

dc:pathc are the disk drive and the directory that hold the command.

printer is the type of IBM Personal Computer printer you use. In DOS 5, the additional printers you can specify are as follows:

GRAPHICSWIDE	Graphics Printer and IBM ProPrinter with 11-inch wide carriage
HPDEFAULT	Any Hewlett-Packard PCC printer
DESKJET	Hewlett-Packard DeskJet printer
LASERJETII	Hewlett-Packard LaserJet Series II (II, IIP, IID) printer
PAINTJET	Hewlett-Packard PaintJet printer

QUIETJET	Hewlett-Packard QuietJet printer
QUIETJET PLUS	Hewlett-Packard QuietJet Plus printer
RUGGED WRITER	Hewlett-Packard Rugged Writer printer
RUGGED WRITERWIDE	Hewlett-Packard Rugged WriterWide printer
THINKJET	Hewlett-Packard ThinkJet printer

filename is the name of the file that contains printer information. If no file name is specified, DOS uses the name GRAPHICS.PRO.

Switches

/*PRINTBOX:x* Prints the image and uses the print box size *id* represented by *x*. This value must match the first entry of a Printbox statement in the printer profile, such as *lcd* or *std*.

/? Displays syntax help on-screen.

Notes

The GRAPHICS command enhances your print screen capability. When you normally press Shift-PrtSc or Print Screen, a copy of the screen is sent to your printer. If the monitor is displaying graphics, however, you cannot send a copy of the screen to the printer. With GRAPHICS loaded in memory, you are able to send graphics screens to the printer by pressing the key to print the screen. DOS 5 increases significantly the number of printers supported by GRAPHICS.

Example

To load GRAPHICS in memory so that you can print a graphics screen on an HP LaserJet II printer or compatible, type the following command:

GRAPHICS LASERJETII

HELP

5.0 Displays syntax and help on-screen for each DOS command, both internal and external.

Syntax

*dc:pathc***HELP** *command*

or

command */?*

Switch

/? Displays syntax help on-screen.

Notes

When using the many new and different commands, you can forget easily which switch works with which command, or how the syntax of a command is laid out. To give helpful reminders, Microsoft includes on-line help with DOS 5. While the help is not as extensive as, for example, this Command Reference, you may find the precise reminder that you need. Note, however, that CONFIG.SYS directives are not included in HELP.

Examples

Suppose that you forget how to use the MODE command to initialize a serial port. You can type the following:

HELP MODE

or

MODE */?*

To find a one-line description of each of the DOS commands, type the following command:

HELP

KEYB

 Changes the keyboard layout and characters to one of five languages other than American English.

Syntax

*dc:pathc***KEYB** *keycode, codepage, d:path***KEYBOARD.SYS**
/ID:*code* */E* */?*

dc:pathc are the disk drive and the directory that hold the command.

keycode is the two-character keyboard code for your location.

codepage is the three-digit code page that will be used (437, 850, 860, 863, or 865).

*d:path***KEYBOARD.SYS** are the drive and the path to the KEYBOARD.SYS file.

Switches

/ID:*code*	The code for your choice of enhanced keyboard.
/E	Specifies that you are using an enhanced keyboard. This is useful for 8088/8086 computers.
/?	Displays syntax help on-screen.

Notes

Previously, KEYB was a set of five programs, featuring one program for each of the five national languages that DOS supported. DOS 3.3 codified the five programs into one program.

When KEYB is active, it reassigns some alphanumeric characters to different keys and introduces new characters. The new layout and characters vary among the supported languages.

If you do not specify a *codepage*, DOS uses the default code page for your country. The default code page is established by the COUNTRY directive in CONFIG.SYS or, if the COUNTRY directive is not used, by the DOS default code page. KEYB attempts to activate the default code page.

If you plan to use the KEYB command with any degree of regularity, you can start the command from the CONFIG.SYS file with the INSTALL directive. Less memory is used starting KEYB this way. For more information, see "Configuration Subcommand—INSTALL" earlier in this command reference.

Example

To display the current keyboard code and codepage, type the following command:

KEYB

LOADFIX

Loads and executes a program that gives the `Packed file corrupt` **error** message when the file is executed.

Syntax

*dc:pathc***LOADFIX** *d:path***filename.ext** */?*

dc:pathc are the disk drive and directory that hold the command.

filename.ext is the name of the file to execute.

Switch

/?   Displays syntax help on-screen (DOS 5 only).

Notes

Some programs expand when loaded into memory. When loaded into the first 64K of RAM, some programs may give the error message `Packed file corrupted` and return the computer to the DOS prompt. LOADFIX can be used to load this file above the first 64K of RAM.

Example

To execute the program MESSAGE.EXE that gave the error message `Packed file corrupted`, type the following:

LOADFIX MESSAGE.EXE

or

LOADFIX MESSAGE

LOADHIGH   V5—External

Loads device drivers or memory-resident programs in memory beyond conventional memory.

Syntax

LOADHIGH *d:path***filename.ext** *prog_options* /?

or

LH *d:path***filename.ext** *prog_options* /?

d:path is the location of the device driver or memory-resident program to load high.

filename.ext is the name of the device driver or memory resident program to load high.

prog_options are any options that are required by **filename.ext**.

Switch

/?   Displays syntax help on-screen.

Notes

On 80386SX, 80386, or 80486 computers, memory can be assigned to "holes" in the range between the top of conventional memory (640K) and where extended memory begins (1M). You can place device drivers and memory-resident programs in this range, which frees the conventional memory normally used by these programs. LOADHIGH enables DOS to relocate these programs to this upper-memory area of RAM.

Before you can use LOADHIGH, you first must install
HIMEM.SYS and EMM386.EXE (using the RAM or NOEMS
parameter) as device drivers in CONFIG.SYS. You also must
include in CONFIG.SYS the statement DOS=UMB
(DOS=HIGH,UMB to load DOS into the HMA and to enable
upper memory blocks).

Programs that you load high are device drivers or terminate-and-
stay-resident (TSR) programs that you normally use—for example, FASTOPEN.EXE. You may want to include the
LOADHIGH syntax in the AUTOEXEC.BAT file so that your
device drivers or TSR programs load into upper memory each
time that you start your system.

Examples

To load your mouse driver from C:\UTILS into upper memory,
use the following form:

LOADHIGH C:\UTILS\MOUSE

or

LH C:\UTILS\MOUSE

To load FASTOPEN from C:\DOS into upper memory, buffering
40 files from drive C:, use the following form:

LOADHIGH C:\DOS\FASTOPEN C:=40

or

LH C:\DOS\FASTOPEN C:=40

MEM

V4, V5—External

Displays the amount of used and unused memory, allocated and open
memory areas, and all programs currently in the system.

Syntax

*dc:pathc***MEM** */PROGRAM /DEBUG /CLASSIFY /?*

dc:pathc are the disk drive and the directory that hold the
command.

Switches

/PROGRAM   Displays programs in memory, including the address, name, size, and type of each file for every program. Also shows current free memory. You can use /P, the shortened form of the switch.

/DEBUG   Displays programs in memory, including the address, name, size, and type of each file for every program. Also displays system device drivers and installed device drivers, as well as all unused memory. You can use /D, the shortened form of the switch.

/CLASSIFY   Displays programs in memory, including the program name and size in bytes shown in decimal and hexadecimal. Programs are shown loaded in conventional memory and, if available, reserved memory (upper memory blocks). Displays the total bytes free (conventional memory plus reserved memory) and the largest executable program size. You can use /C, the short form of the switch.

/?   Displays syntax help on-screen.

Notes

MEM displays memory usage information on-screen. MEM displays statistics for conventional memory and also for extended and expanded memory if the latter two are available. You cannot specify /PROGRAM, /DEBUG, and /CLASSIFY at the same time.

If you use a 80386SX, 80386, or 80486 PC, you can use MEM / PROGRAM or MEM /CLASSIFY extensively as you begin loading device drivers and TSRs in reserved memory. MEM /PROGRAM gives the location and size (in hexadecimal) of each program in memory. MEM /CLASSIFY displays each program in memory and how much space is being used. The difference between /PROGRAM and /CLASSIFY is that CLASSIFY easily distinguishes whether a program is loaded in conventional or reserved memory. Using the /CLASSIFY switch, MEM also displays used and available conventional and reserved memory. With this information, you can determine the order that device drivers and TSRs load into memory to make the best use of the reserved memory space.

Examples

To display the current memory usage, type the following command:

MEM

To display programs loaded in memory, type the following:

MEM /CLASSIFY

or

MEM /C

MIRROR

5.0

Saves information about a disk drive to recover accidentally lost data.

Syntax

To save information about drive and files that are deleted, use the following form:

*dc:pathc***MIRROR** *d1: d2: dn: /Tdrive-entries /1*

To save information about a drive partition, use the form:

*dc:pathc***MIRROR /PARTN**

To quit tracking deleted files, use the form:

*dc:pathc***MIRROR /U**

To display on-screen help for MIRROR, use the form:

*dc:pathc***MIRROR /?**

dc:pathc are the optional disk drive and subdirectory in which MIRROR is located.

d1:, *d2:*, and *dn:* are disk drives for which mirror information is saved.

Switches

/Tdrive-entries	Loads a portion of MIRROR that remains in memory to keep track of files that you delete. *drive* is the mandatory disk drive for which deleted files are tracked. *entries* is an optional value from 1 to 999 that specifies the maximum number of files that are remembered when deleted.
/1	Keeps MIRROR from making a backup of the mirror file when the file is updated.
/PARTN	Makes a copy of the drive's partition table.
/U	Removes from memory the memory-resident portion of MIRROR that keeps track of deleted files.
/?	Displays syntax help on-screen.

Notes

MIRROR can create up to three files that enable you to recover from possible disk tragedies. Using MIRROR creates a file called MIRROR.FIL on your hard disk that contains a copy of the root directory and file allocation table for the drive. The root directory and file allocation table are necessary to track the location of each file on the drive. MIRROR.FIL is a hidden file, protecting you from accidentally deleting the file.

MIRROR, using the /T switch, creates a file called PCTRACKR.DEL. PCTRACKR.DEL also is hidden on the disk. A portion of MIRROR remains in memory, recording deleted files and the file's location on the drive. You can retrieve deleted files saved with MIRROR. To remove the memory-resident portion of the program from memory, use the /U switch with MIRROR.

When you track deleted files, you can specify how many files can be contained in the PCTRACKR.DEL file. You can specify from 1 to 999, but the PCTRACKR.DEL default values, shown in the following list, are probably more than satisfactory:

Size of disk	Entries stored
360K	25
720K	50
1.2M/1.44M	75
20M	101
32M	202
Over 32M	303

Using the /PARTN switch with MIRROR creates the file
PARTNSAV.FIL. This file contains information from the drive's
partition table. The partition is created initially with FDISK.
Rather than saving PARTNSAV.FIL on the hard disk, however,
you are instructed to place a floppy disk in drive A:. The file will
be saved on the floppy disk. Label the floppy disk and store it in
a safe place.

UNFORMAT, a companion of MIRROR, uses these files. If you
lose information, accidentally format a disk, or if the partition
table is damaged in some way, you may be able to recover by
using UNFORMAT if you have used MIRROR previously.

Caution: The MIRROR and UNFORMAT commands are not a replacement for proper backups of your hard disk!

Examples

To record the file allocation table and root directory for the
current drive into a mirror file, use the following form:

MIRROR

To track as many as 500 deleted files for drive D:, use the
following form:

MIRROR /TD-500

To remove the memory-resident portion of MIRROR from
memory, use the following form:

MIRROR /U

To record the file allocation table for drives C:, D:, and E:, use
the following form:

MIRROR C: D: E:

To record the partition table for the current drive, use the following form:

MIRROR /PARTN

When prompted, place a floppy disk in drive A: and press Enter.

MODE   V1, V2, V3, V4, V5—External

This command has numerous forms that you can use in this reference as separate commands. Generally, MODE sets the printer characteristics, keyboard rate, the video display, and the Asynchronous Communications Adapter. MODE also is used in setting code pages for international characters. This command controls redirection of printing between parallel and serial printers. Finally, MODE controls code page switching for the console and printer. Other functions differ according to DOS implementation.

MODE   V1.1, V2, V3,
COMMUNICATIONS   V4, V5—External

5.0 Controls the protocol characteristics of the Asynchronous Communications Adapter.

Syntax

*dc:pathc***MODE COMy:** *baud, parity, databits, stopbits, P*

or

*dc:pathc***MODE COMy:** *BAUD=baud PARITY=parity DATA=databits STOP=stopbits RETRY=ret /?*

dc:pathc are the disk drive and the directory that hold the command.

y: is the adapter number (1, 2, 3, or 4); the colon after the number is optional.

baud is the baud rate (110, 150, 300, 600, 1200, 2400, 4800, 9600, or 19200).

parity is the parity checking (None, Odd, or Even; in DOS versions before 4.0, use N, O, or E).

databits is the number of data bits (7 or 8).

stopbits is the number of stop bits (1 or 2).

P represents continuous retries on time-out errors.

ret tells DOS what to do when a time-out error occurs. You can choose from the following options:

ret	*Action*
E	Returns the error when port is busy (default)
B	Returns busy when port is busy
P	Continues retrying until not busy
R	Returns ready when port is busy (infinite retry)
NONE	Takes no action

Switch

/?	Displays syntax help on-screen.

Notes

When using MODE with the communications adapters, you must enter at least the communications port. Specifying only the adapter displays the current status of the port. All other parameters are optional.

If you are using the first syntax form and you do not want to change a parameter, enter a comma for that value.

The 19200 baud rate is valid only for those computers that support 19200 baud. If you try to use the 19200 baud rate on a PC or compatible that does not support 19200 baud, DOS displays an `Invalid parameter` message and takes no further action.

If the adapter is set for continuous retries (P or RETRY=B) and the device is not ready, the computer appears to be locked up. You can abort this loop by pressing Ctrl-Break.

Examples

To set up your communications port for 9600 BAUD, even parity, 8 databits, 1 stop bit, and continuous retry, use the following form:

MODE COM1:9600,E,8,1,P

or the optional form:

MODE COM1:96,E,8,1,P

With DOS 4 or 5, you can use the following form:

MODE COM1 BAUD=9600 PARITY=EVEN DATA=8 STOP=1 RETRY=P

MODE
CONSOLE RATE/DELAY   V4, V5—External

`4.0` Adjusts the rate at which the keyboard repeats a character when a key is held down.

Syntax

*dc:pathc***MODE CON:** *RATE=x DELAY=y /?*

dc:pathc are the disk drive and the directory that hold the command.

x is a value that specifies the character-repeat rate. You can select a value between 1 and 32.

y is a value that specifies the delay between the initial pressing of the key and the start of automatic character repetition. This value can be 1, 2, 3, or 4, representing delays of 1/4 second, 1/2 second, 3/4 second, and one full second, respectively.

Switch

/?   Displays syntax help on-screen.

Notes

A keyboard repeats a character on-screen if you hold down the key. Two types of time are associated with key repeat—the amount of time elapsed after the key is pressed before the character begins repeating and the time between each repetition of the character. MODE enables you to increase and decrease the time before a key begins repeating (DELAY) and the speed at which the character is repeated (RATE).

Example

To set the keyboard rate to 10 and the delay to 2, enter the following form:

MODE CON RATE=10 DELAY=2

MODE
DISPLAY TYPE   V3, V4, V5—External

MODE dt switches the active display adapter between the monochrome display and a graphics adapter/array (Color/Graphics Adapter, Enhanced Color/Graphics Adapter, or Video Graphics Array) on a two-display system. MODE dt also sets the graphics adapter/array characteristics.

Syntax

*dc:pathc***MODE dt,***y*

or

*dc:pathc***MODE** *dt*, **S**, *T*

or

*dc:pathc***MODE CON**: **COLS**=*x* **LINES**=*y* /?

dc:pathc are the disk drive and the directory that hold the command.

dt is the display type, which may be one of the following:

Type	Function
40	Sets the display to 40 characters per line for the graphics display
80	Sets the display to 80 characters per line for the graphics display
BW40	Makes the graphics display the active display and sets the mode to 40 characters per line, black and white (color disabled)
BW80	Makes the graphics display the active display and sets the mode to 80 characters per line, black and white (color disabled)
CO40	Makes the graphics display the active display and sets the mode to 40 characters per line (color enabled)
CO80	Makes the graphics display the active display and sets the mode to 80 characters per line (color enabled)
MONO	Makes the monochrome display the active display

S shifts the graphics display to the right (R) or to the left (L) by one character.

T requests alignment of the graphics display screen with a one-line test pattern.

x specifies the number of columns that appear on the display. Either 40 or 80 columns are possible.

y specifies the number of lines that appear on the display, applicable only to EGA and VGA displays. EGA values are 25 and 43; VGA values are 25, 43, and 50.

Switch

/?	Displays syntax help on-screen.

Notes

For the first form of the command, you must enter the display type (dt); all other parameters are optional. For the second form of the command, you must enter the shift parameter **S** (either an R or an L for right or left); the display type (dt) and test pattern (T) are optional.

The S (R or L) parameter works only with the Color/Graphics Adapter; the display does not shift if you use this command with any other adapter. The T parameter, conversely, causes the test pattern to be displayed with any graphics adapter (Convertible, EGA, or VGA). If you use the parameter with the Monochrome Adapter, DOS responds with an error message.

Color is not displayed automatically when you use the CO40 or CO80 parameter for the display type. Programs that use color, however, can be displayed in color.

Examples

To set your 80-column color monitor into Black-and-White mode, type the following form:

MODE BW80

If you have a VGA display and you want to display color, 80 columns, and 50 lines of text, type the following form:

MODE CO80,50

or

MODE CON COLS=80 LINES=50

MODE
PRINTER
V1, V2, V3, V4, V5—External

4.0 Sets the IBM-compatible printer characteristics.

Syntax

> *dc:pathc***MODE LPTx**:*cpl,lpi,P*

With DOS 4 or 5, you can use the following form:

> *dc:pathc***MODE LPTx** *COLS=cpl LINES=lpi RETRY=ret /?*

dc:pathc are the disk drive and the directory that hold the command.

x: is the printer number (1, 2, or 3). The colon is optional.

cpl is the number of characters per line (80, 132).

lpi is the number of lines per inch (six or eight).

P specifies continuous retries on time-out errors.

ret tells DOS what to do when a time-out error occurs. You can choose from the following options:

ret	*Action*
E	Returns the error when port is busy (default)
B	Returns busy when port is busy
P	Continues retrying until printer is not busy
R	Returns ready when port is busy
NONE	Takes no action

Switch

/?   Displays syntax help on-screen.

Notes

You must specify a printer number, but all other parameters are optional, including the colon after the printer number. If you do not want to change a parameter, enter a comma for that parameter.

The characters-per-line and lines-per-inch portions of the command affect only IBM and Epson printers and all printers that use IBM- and Epson-compatible control codes.

Examples

To set the printer on LPT1 to 132 characters per line and 8 lines per inch, and to check continually for the printer's busy condition, type the following form:

MODE LPT1:132,8,P

or

MODE LPT1 COLS=132 LINES=8 RETRY=B

MODE
STATUS

V4, V5—External

Displays the status of a specified device or of all devices that can be set by MODE.

Syntax

*dc:pathc***MODE device /STATUS /?**

dc:pathc are the disk drive and the directory that hold the command.

device is the optional device to be checked by MODE.

Switches

/STATUS   The mandatory switch to check the status of a device or devices. If you prefer, you can enter just **/STA** rather than the complete **/STATUS**.

/?   Displays syntax help on-screen.

Notes

This command enables you to see the status of any device that you normally set with MODE. Typing **MODE LPT1 /STA**, for example, displays the status of the first parallel port.

Example

To display the current status of the console, type the following form:

MODE CON /STATUS

QBASIC

Loads the BASIC interpreter into memory for BASIC programming.

Syntax

*dc:pathc***QBASIC** *d:path\\filename.ext /H /NOHI /B /EDITOR /G /MBF /RUN d:path\\filename.ext /?*

dc:pathc are the drive and subdirectory in which QBasic is located.

d:path is optional location of the BASIC program to load into memory.

filename.ext is the name of the BASIC program.

Switches

/H	Changes the display mode to view QBasic with the maximum number of lines on the screen.
/NOHI	Enables QBasic to work with monitors that do not support high intensity video.
/B	Puts QBasic in Black-and-White mode.
/EDITOR	Starts the editor in nonprogramming mode.
/G	Enables CGA monitors to update quickly. Do not use this switch if "snow" appears on the screen.
/MBF	Enables the QBasic program statements CVS, CVD, MKS$, and MKD$ to use the Microsoft Binary Format for numbers rather than the IEEE format.

/RUN *d:path* *filename.ext*	Loads *filename.ext* in memory and starts execution.
/?	Displays syntax help on-screen.

Notes

QBasic is a comprehensive development environment for interpreted BASIC. A subset of Microsoft QuickBASIC, QBasic replaces BASIC, BASICA, and GW-BASIC from earlier versions of DOS.

Examples

To start QBasic, use the following form:

QBASIC

To start QBasic on a black-and-white monitor and load the program INVNTRY.BAS, use the following form:

QBASIC INVNTRY /B

To start QBasic, load and execute the program TRANSFER, use the following form:

QBASIC /RUN TRANSFER

REPLACE

V3.2, V3.3, V4, V5—External

Replaces files on one disk with files of the same name from another disk; adds files to a disk by copying them from another disk.

Syntax

*dc:pathc***REPLACE** *ds:paths***filenames**.*exts dd:pathd* /U /?

dc:pathc are the disk drive and the directory that hold the command.

ds:paths are the disk drive and directory that hold the replacement file(s).

filenames.*exts* are the replacement files. Wild cards are permitted.

dd:pathd are the disk drive and the directory whose file(s) will be replaced.

In the fragment *ds:paths***filenames**.*exts*, *s* represents the *source*. The source is the file that will be added to a directory or that will replace an existing file in the directory.

In the fragment *dd:pathd, d* represents the *destination*. The destination can be the file to be replaced or the disk and directory in which a new file will be added. DOS refers to the destination as the *target*.

Switches

/U	Replaces only those files of a date and time earlier than the source files.
/?	Displays syntax help on-screen.

Notes

The REPLACE command, which was added with DOS 3.2, is a semi-intelligent COPY program that can selectively update or add files to one or more directories.

You can use this command to replace one or a few files that are duplicated in several subdirectories. You also can use the command to update a major application program or even DOS itself. REPLACE is especially useful because it can search subdirectories for files to replace.

REPLACE replaces or adds files, based on the matching of file names. The command disregards drive names, directory names, and file contents, searching only for the appropriate file names and extensions. By using this exclusive search facility, you can quickly find older files and replace them with their updated versions.

Examples

To search the current directory of drive A: for files with a COM extension, and then copy over files with matching names in C:\DOS, type the following form:

REPLACE A:*.COM C:\DOS

Any COM file on drive A: is not copied if its name does not match a file in the directory C:\BIN.

To replace only matching files in C:\DOS that are dated earlier than the source files, type the following form:

REPLACE A:*.COM C:\DOS /U

RESTORE

V2, V3, V4, V5—External

5.0

Restores one or more backup files from one disk onto another. This command complements BACKUP.

Syntax

*dc:pathc***RESTORE d1:** *d2:path***filename.ext** */D /?*

dc:pathc are the disk drive and the directory that hold the command.

d1: is the disk drive holding the backup files.

d2: is the disk drive that will receive the restored files.

path is the path to the directory that will receive the restored files.

filename.ext is the file that you want to restore. Wild cards are allowed.

Switches

/D	Lists files that will be restored without actually performing the restoration.
/?	Displays syntax help on-screen.

Notes

You can use the RESTORE command only on files that you have saved with the BACKUP command. RESTORE prompts you to insert the backup disks in order. If you insert a disk out of order, RESTORE prompts you to insert the correct disk.

To view the files to be restored, issue the /D switch. This switch simulates a restoration based on file specifications and other switches that you have used. Using the /D switch, you ensure that the correct files will be restored.

Example

To view files that would be restored from the disks in drive B: to C:\REPORTS, type the following form:

RESTORE B: C:\REPORTS\ /D

SETVER

Sets a specific DOS version to be emulated with a program file.

Syntax

To implement the DOS version table, use the following form in CONFIG.SYS:

DEVICE=_dc:pathc_**\SETVER.EXE**

To add a program to the version table, use the following form from the command line:

dc:pathc**\SETVER** _d:_**filename.ext dosver**

To remove a program from the version table, use the following form from the command line:

dc:pathc**\SETVER filename.ext /DELETE /QUIET**

To view the version table, use the following form from the command line:

dc:pathc**\SETVER**

To view help for SETVER, use the following form from the command line:

> *dc:pathc***SETVER** */?*

dc:pathc is the drive and subdirectory path in which SETVER is located.

filename.ext is the program file to add to the version table.

dosver is the version of DOS to emulate, such as 3.31, or 4.01.

Switches

/DELETE	Removes a program and its associated DOS version from the version table.
/Quiet	Supresses the messages issued SETVER when using /DELETE.
/?	Displays syntax help on-screen.

Notes

SETVER enables programs requiring specific DOS versions to operate with DOS 5. To enable SETVER capabilities, you first must install SETVER.EXE as a device through CONFIG.SYS.

When you use SETVER, the current version table is affected. If you specify SETVER with no parameters, the current version table is displayed to the screen. You may use SETVER with redirection to print the contents of the version table.

You can specify a file name that already exists in the version table. However, the file name in the version table will be replaced with the new entry.

Examples

To install SETVER as a device, when SETVER.EXE is located in C:\DOS, add the following line to CONFIG.SYS:

> **DEVICE=C:\DOS\SETVER.EXE**

To view the current version table, use the following form:

> **SETVER**

To add the program WP.EXE (located in the directory C:\WORD) to the version table, specifying that the program must use DOS 3.3, use the following form:

SETVER C:\WORD\WP.EXE 3.3

To remove NOTES.EXE from the version table, use the following form:

SETVER NOTES.EXE /DELETE

SHARE   V3, V4, V5—External

4.0 5.0   Enables DOS support for file and record locking.

Syntax

*dc:pathc***SHARE** */F:name_space /L:numlocks /?*

dc:pathc are the disk drive and the directory that hold the command.

Switches

/F:name_space	Sets the amount of memory space (*name_space* bytes large) used for file sharing.
/L:numlocks	Sets the maximum number (*numlocks*) of file/record locks to use.
/?	Displays syntax help on-screen.

Notes

SHARE is the DOS 3 through 5 program for file and record locking.

You use SHARE when two or more programs or processes share a single computer's files. After SHARE is loaded, DOS checks each file for locks whenever the file is opened, read, or written. If a file is open for exclusive use, an error message results from any subsequent attempt to open the file. If one program locks a portion of a file, an error message results if another program attempts to read or write the locked portion.

You must use SHARE if you use DOS 4.0 and 4.01 and use a hard disk partition larger than 32M. The necessity of using SHARE for hard disks formatted larger than 32M was eliminated for DOS 5, however.

For convenience, you can use INSTALL in the CONFIG.SYS file to activate SHARE. See "Configuration Subcommand—INSTALL" earlier in this command reference.

Example

To install SHARE with the default file space (/F) of 2048 bytes and number of locks (/L) of 20, type the following command:

SHARE

SYS   V1, V2, V3, V4, V5—External

 Places a copy of DOS on the specified disk.

Syntax

*dc:pathc***SYS** *d2:* **d:** */?*

dc:pathc are the disk drive and the directory that hold the command.

d: is the disk drive that will receive the copy of DOS—the destination drive.

d2: is the disk drive that contains the copy of DOS to copy—the source drive.

Switch

/?   Displays syntax help on-screen.

Notes

The SYS command places a copy of IO.SYS and MSDOS.SYS (or IBMBIO.COM and IBMDOS.COM on IBM's version) on the target disk. You also must copy COMMAND.COM onto the target disk to enable the disk to load and execute the disk-operating system.

With DOS 4 and 5, the current drive no longer needs the copy of DOS to transfer the DOS system files. You may specify the drive that contains the copy of DOS to transfer. Remember, however, that the command operates backward from other commands. When you specify the drives, you specify the destination drive first and the source drive second.

Example

To place the two hidden DOS files on the empty disk in drive A:, type the following command:

SYS A:

TIME   V1.1, V2, V3, V4, V5—Internal

`4.0` Sets and shows the system time.

Syntax

TIME *hh:mm:ss.xxA | P /?*

hh is the one- or two-digit number for hours (0 to 23).

mm is the one- or two-digit number for minutes (0 to 59).

ss is the one- or two-digit number for seconds (0 to 59).

xx is the one- or two-digit number for hundredths of a second (0 to 99).

A | P may be typed to designate AM or PM. If you do not use *A* or *P*, you must enter the time in military hours.

Note: Depending on the country code's setting in your CONFIG.SYS file, a comma may be the separator between seconds and hundredths of seconds.

Switch

/?   Displays syntax help on-screen.

Notes

TIME is used to set the computer's internal 24-hour clock. The time and date are recorded in the directory whenever you create or change a file. This information can help you find the most recent version of a file when you check your directory.

You may enter the time according to the 24-hour clock or the 12-hour clock. If you enter the time according to the 12-hour clock, you must follow the time with the letters *A* or *P* for AM or PM.

Example

If you wish to set the current time to 3:15 p.m., type the following form:

TIME 15:15

or

TIME 3:15P

TREE   V2, V3, V4, V5—External

Displays on the monitor all the subdirectories on a disk and optionally displays all files in each directory.

Syntax

*dc:pathc***TREE** *d: /F /A /?*

dc:pathc are the disk drive and the directory that hold the command.

d: is the disk drive that contains the disk you want to examine.

Switches

/F	Displays all files in the directories.
/A	Graphically displays the connection of subdirectories using nongraphic ASCII characters.
/?	Calls on-screen syntax help.

Notes

The TREE command displays all directories on a disk so that you do not need to enter every directory, run a DIR command, and search for every <DIR> file (subdirectory). The /F option also displays the name of every file in every directory.

TREE shows one directory or file name on a line and can scroll quickly off the screen. To copy the entire tree, you can redirect the output to the printer.

Examples

To display a listing of all directories and subdirectories of the current disk drive, type the following command:

TREE

If you want the graphic display of your directory system to be created with nongraphic characters, type the following form:

TREE /A

UNDELETE   V5—External

5.0   Restores files that have been deleted.

Syntax

To restore deleted files using the delete tracking file created with MIRROR, use the following form:

*dc:pathc***UNDELETE** *dd:pathd\\filenamed.extd /LIST /DT /DOS /ALL /?*

dc:pathc are the drive and subdirectory in which UNDELETE is located.

dd:pathd\\filenamed.extd are the drive and subdirectory location of the file *filenamed.extd* to restore.

Switches

/LIST	Displays the files that may be recovered. If you specify a file (or files) to be recovered, the file name limits the list.
/DT	Specifies UNDELETE to restore files based on the information in the delete tracking file created by the MIRROR command.
/DOS	Specifies UNDELETE to restore files based on the directory contents. You must confirm each file before it is restored. If a delete tracking file exists, it is ignored.
/ALL	Recovers all files without prompting. UNDELETE will use the delete tracking file, if one exists. Otherwise UNDELETE will use the standard DOS directory. If the DOS directory is used, then the missing first character will be replaced by the # character. If a second file name conflicts with an already-restored file, then % will replace the first character.
/?	Displays syntax help on-screen.

Notes

The UNDELETE command accompanying DOS 5 is a greatly needed command. With this command, you may restore deleted files by using either the delete tracking file or the standard DOS directory.

When you delete a file, the first character in the file name is removed. If you undelete using the \DOS switch, you are prompted to give the actual character that will replace the missing first character. If you use the /ALL switch and a delete tracking file does not exist, each deleted file is restored without prompting. The character # is placed as the first character in the file. Thus, the deleted BETTER.TXT is undeleted as #ETTER.TXT.

If both BETTER.TXT and LETTER.TXT are deleted, BETTER.TXT is restored as #ETTER.TXT, and LETTER.TXT is restored as %ETTER.TXT. To overcome possible file name conflicts, UNDELETE replaces with the following characters in order: # % & - 0 1 2 3 4 5 6 7 8 9.

Although UNDELETE enables you to recover accidentally deleted files, do not use this command as a replacement for backing up important data. Always keep up-to-date backups of your data.

Examples

To undelete the file LTR0915.DOC using the delete tracking file, type the following form:

UNDELETE LTR0915.DOC /DT

To undelete all files in the C:\DATA directory using the DOS directory, without prompting before a file is restored, type the following form:

UNDELETE C:\DATA*.* /ALL

UNFORMAT   V5—External

5.0 Reconstructs a formatted hard disk.

Syntax

To test or recover erased files or a formatted disk, use the following form:

*dc:pathc***UNFORMAT** *d1: /U /J /P /L /TEST*

To recover a disk whose partition is lost, use the following form:

   *dc:pathc***UNFORMAT /PARTN**

To display on-screen help for UNFORMAT, use the following form:

   *dc:pathc***UNFORMAT /?**

dc:pathc are the drive and subdirectory in which UNFORMAT is located.

d1: is the drive in which UNFORMAT will be performed.

Switches

/U	Unformats the hard disk without using files created by MIRROR.
/J	Tests the files created by MIRROR to verify that they are up-to-date with information on the disk. The /J switch does not unformat the disk.
/L	Lists on-screen all files and subdirectories that UNFORMAT finds. When used with the /PARTN switch, the partition table is displayed to the screen.
/P	Lists on the printer all files and subdirectories that UNFORMAT finds. When used with the /PARTN switch, the partition table is displayed to the printer.
/TEST	Performs a simulated unformat of the disk.
/PARTN	Restores a hard disk's partition table with the PARTNSAV.FIL created by MIRROR.
/?	Displays syntax help on-screen.

Notes

UNFORMAT attempts to recover a formatted disk, using the files created by MIRROR. If no files created by MIRROR exist on the drive, UNFORMAT still attempts to restore the disk.

Unformatting a disk without MIRROR files is slower and not as reliable as unformatting a disk that has up-to-date MIRROR files.

To prepare to use UNFORMAT, format a floppy disk using the /S switch (making the disk bootable) and transfer the UNFORMAT.EXE file to the floppy disk. Also, transfer to the newly formatted disk any device drivers that are necessary for the computer's operation, including the CONFIG.SYS and AUTOEXEC.BAT files. In the case that the hard disk gets formatted, you then may boot from the floppy disk and perform the UNFORMAT.

Before using UNFORMAT, you probably should use UNFORMAT with the /J or /TEST switches. This enables you to determine if the MIRROR files are up-to-date, or if the UNFORMAT will be performed to your expectations.

Caution: The MIRROR and UNFORMAT commands are not a replacement for proper backups of your hard disk!

Examples

To evaluate the mirror files on drive A: with the actual disk information, use the following form:

UNFORMAT A: /J

To perform a simulated UNFORMAT on the disk in drive A:, use the following form:

UNFORMAT A: /TEST

To UNFORMAT drive D:, use the following form:

UNFORMAT D:

Index

S

Computer Books From Que Mean PC Performance!

Spreadsheets

1-2-3 Database Techniques	$29.95
1-2-3 Graphics Techniques	$24.95
1-2-3 Macro Library, 3rd Edition	$39.95
1-2-3 Release 2.2 Business Applications	$39.95
1-2-3 Release 2.2 PC Tutor	$39.95
1-2-3 Release 2.2 QueCards	$19.95
1-2-3 Release 2.2 Quick Reference	$ 8.95
1-2-3 Release 2.2 QuickStart, 2nd Edition	$19.95
1-2-3 Release 2.2 Workbook and Disk	$29.95
1-2-3 Release 3 Business Applications	$39.95
1-2-3 Release 3 Workbook and Disk	$29.95
1-2-3 Release 3.1 Quick Reference	$ 8.95
1-2-3 Release 3.1 QuickStart, 2nd Edition	$19.95
1-2-3 Tips, Tricks, and Traps, 3rd Edition	$24.95
Excel Business Applications: IBM Version	$39.95
Excel Quick Reference	$ 8.95
Excel QuickStart	$19.95
Excel Tips, Tricks, and Traps	$22.95
Using 1-2-3/G	$29.95
Using 1-2-3, Special Edition	$27.95
Using 1-2-3 Release 2.2, Special Edition	$27.95
Using 1-2-3 Release 3.1, 2nd Edition	$29.95
Using Excel: IBM Version	$29.95
Using Lotus Spreadsheet for DeskMate	$22.95
Using Quattro Pro	$24.95
Using SuperCalc5, 2nd Edition	$29.95

Databases

dBASE III Plus Handbook, 2nd Edition	$24.95
dBASE III Plus Tips, Tricks, and Traps	$24.95
dBASE III Plus Workbook and Disk	$29.95
dBASE IV Applications Library, 2nd Edition	$39.95
dBASE IV Programming Techniques	$24.95
dBASE IV Quick Reference	$ 8.95
dBASE IV QuickStart	$19.95
dBASE IV Tips, Tricks,and Traps, 2nd Edition	$24.95
dBASE IV Workbook and Disk	$29.95
Using Clipper	$24.95
Using DataEase	$24.95
Using dBASE IV	$27.95
Using Paradox 3	$24.95
Using R:BASE	$29.95
Using Reflex, 2nd Edition	$24.95
Using SQL	$29.95

Business Applications

Allways Quick Reference	$ 8.95
Introduction to Business Software	$14.95
Introduction to Personal Computers	$19.95
Lotus Add-in Toolkit Guide	$29.95
Norton Utilities Quick Reference	$ 8.95
PC Tools Quick Reference, 2nd Edition	$ 8.95
Q&A Quick Reference	$ 8.95
Que's Computer User's Dictionary	$ 9.95
Que's Wizard Book	$ 9.95
Quicken Quick Reference	$ 8.95
SmartWare Tips, Tricks, and Traps 2nd Edition	$24.95
Using Computers in Business	$22.95
Using DacEasy, 2nd Edition	$24.95
Using Enable/OA	$29.95
Using Harvard Project Manager	$24.95
Using Managing Your Money, 2nd Edition	$19.95

Using Microsoft Works: IBM Version	$22.95
Using Norton Utilities	$24.95
Using PC Tools Deluxe	$24.95
Using Peachtree	$27.95
Using PFS: First Choice	$22.95
Using PROCOMM PLUS	$19.95
Using Q&A, 2nd Edition	$23.95
Using Quicken: IBM Version, 2nd Edition	$19.95
Using Smart	$22.95
Using SmartWare II	$29.95
Using Symphony, Special Edition	$29.95
Using Time Line	$24.95
Using TimeSlips	$24.95

CAD

AutoCAD Quick Reference	$ 8.95
AutoCAD Sourcebook 1991	$27.95
Using AutoCAD, 3rd Edition	$29.95
Using Generic CADD	$24.95

Word Processing

Microsoft Word 5 Quick Reference	$ 8.95
Using DisplayWrite 4, 2nd Edition	$24.95
Using LetterPerfect	$22.95
Using Microsoft Word 5.5: IBM Version, 2nd Edition	$24.95
Using MultiMate	$24.95
Using Professional Write	$22.95
Using Word for Windows	$24.95
Using WordPerfect 5	$27.95
Using WordPerfect 5.1, Special Edition	$27.95
Using WordStar, 3rd Edition	$27.95
WordPerfect PC Tutor	$39.95
WordPerfect Power Pack	$39.95
WordPerfect Quick Reference	$ 8.95
WordPerfect QuickStart	$19.95
WordPerfect 5 Workbook and Disk	$29.95
WordPerfect 5.1 Quick Reference	$ 8.95
WordPerfect 5.1 QuickStart	$19.95
WordPerfect 5.1 Tips, Tricks, and Traps	$24.95
WordPerfect 5.1 Workbook and Disk	$29.95

Hardware/Systems

DOS Tips, Tricks, and Traps	$24.95
DOS Workbook and Disk, 2nd Edition	$29.95
Fastback Quick Reference	$ 8.95
Hard Disk Quick Reference	$ 8.95
MS-DOS PC Tutor	$39.95
MS-DOS Power Pack	$39.95
MS-DOS Quick Reference	$ 8.95
MS-DOS QuickStart, 2nd Edition	$19.95
MS-DOS User's Guide, Special Edition	$29.95
Networking Personal Computers, 3rd Edition	$24.95
The Printer Bible	$29.95
Que's PC Buyer's Guide	$12.95
Understanding UNIX: A Conceptual Guide, 2nd Edition	$21.95
Upgrading and Repairing PCs	$29.95
Using DOS	$22.95
Using Microsoft Windows 3, 2nd Edition	$24.95
Using Novell NetWare	$29.95
Using OS/2	$29.95
Using PC DOS, 3rd Edition	$24.95
Using Prodigy	$19.95

Using UNIX	$29.95
Using Your Hard Disk	$29.95
Windows 3 Quick Reference	$ 8.95

Desktop Publishing/Graphics

CorelDRAW Quick Reference	$ 8.95
Harvard Graphics Quick Reference	$ 8.95
Using Animator	$24.95
Using DrawPerfect	$24.95
Using Harvard Graphics, 2nd Edition	$24.95
Using Freelance Plus	$24.95
Using PageMaker: IBM Version, 2nd Edition	$24.95
Using PFS: First Publisher, 2nd Edition	$24.95
Using Ventura Publisher, 2nd Edition	$24.95

Macintosh/Apple II

AppleWorks QuickStart	$19.95
The Big Mac Book, 2nd Edition	$29.95
Excel QuickStart	$19.95
The Little Mac Book	$ 9.95
Que's Macintosh Multimedia Handbook	$24.95
Using AppleWorks, 3rd Edition	$24.95
Using Excel: Macintosh Version	$24.95
Using FileMaker	$24.95
Using MacDraw	$29.95
Using MacroMind Director	$29.95
Using MacWrite	$24.95
Using Microsoft Word 4: Macintosh Version	$24.95
Using Microsoft Works: Macintosh Version, 2nd Edition	$24.95
Using PageMaker: Macinsoth Version, 2nd Edition	$24.95

Programming/Technical

Assembly Language Quick Reference	$ 8.95
C Programmer' sToolkit	$39.95
C Quick Reference	$ 8.95
DOS and BIOS Functions Quick Reference	$ 8.95
DOS Programmer's Reference, 2nd Edition	$29.95
Network Programming in C	$49.95
Oracle Programmer's Guide	$29.95
QuickBASIC Advanced Techniques	$24.95
Quick C Programmer's Guide	$29.95
Turbo Pascal Advanced Techniques	$24.95
Turbo Pascal Quick Reference	$ 8.95
UNIX Programmer's Quick Reference	$ 8.95
UNIX Programmer's Reference	$29.95
UNIX Shell Commands Quick Reference	$ 8.95
Using Assembly Language, 2nd Edition	$29.95
Using BASIC	$24.95
Using C	$29.95
Using QuickBASIC 4	$24.95
Using Turbo Pascal	$29.95

For More Information, Call Toll Free!

1-800-428-5331

All prices and titles subject to change without notice. Non-U.S. prices may be higher. Printed in the U.S.A.

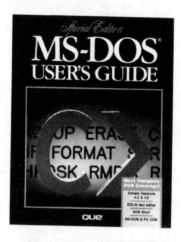

Teach Yourself
With QuickStarts From Que!

The ideal tutorials for beginners, Que's QuickStart books use graphic illustrations and step-by-step instructions to get you up and running fast. Packed with examples, QuickStarts are the perfect beginner's guides to your favorite software applications.

1-2-3 Release 2.2 QuickStart, 2nd Edition
Releases 2.01 & 2.2

Order #1207	$19.95 USA

0-88022-612-9, 400 pp., 7 3/8 x 9 1/4

1-2-3 Release 3.1 QuickStart, 2nd Edition
Releases 3 & 3.1

Order #1208	$19.95 USA

0-88022-613-7, 400 pp., 7 3/8 x 9 1/4

dBASE IV QuickStart
dBASE IV

Order #873	$19.95 USA

0-88022-389-8, 384 pp., 7 3/8 x 9 1/4

dBASE IV QuickStart, 2nd Edition
Through Version 1.1

Order #1209	$19.95 USA

0-88022-614-5, 400 pp., 7 3/8 x 9 1/4

Excel QuickStart
IBM Version 1 & Macintosh Version 2.2

Order #957	$19.95 USA

0-88022-423-1, 334 pp., 7 3/8 x 9 1/4

MS-DOS QuickStart, 2nd Edition
Version 3.X & 4.X

Order #1206	$19.95 USA

0-88022-611-0, 400 pp., 7 3/8 x 9 1/4

Q&A QuickStart
Versions 3 & 4

Order #1264	$19.95 USA

0-88022-653-6, 400 pp., 7 3/8 x 9 1/4

Quattro Pro QuickStart
Through Version 2.0

Order #1305	$19.95 USA

0-88022-693-5, 450 pp., 7 3/8 x 9 1/4

WordPerfect QuickStart
WordPerfect 5

Order #871	$19.95 USA

0-88022-387-1, 457 pp., 7 3/8 x 9 1/4

Windows 3 QuickStart
Ron Person & Karen Rose

This graphics-based text teaches Windows beginners how to use the feature-packed Windows environment. Emphasizes such software applications as Excel, Word, and PageMaker and shows how to master Windows' mouse, menus, and screen elements.

Version 3

Order #1205	$19.95 USA

0-88022-610-2, 400 pp., 7 3/8 x 9 1/4

WordPerfect 5.1 QuickStart
Que Development Group

This is a fast-paced introduction to 5.1 essentials. Numerous illustrations demonstrate document production, pull-down menus, table design, equation editing, file merging, and mouse use.

WordPerfect 5.1

Order #1104	$19.95 USA

0-88022-558-0, 500 pp., 7 3/8 x 9 1/4

To Order, Call:
(800) 428-5331 OR (317) 573-2510

Find It Fast With Que's Quick References!

Que's Quick References are the compact, easy-to-use guides to essential application information. Written for all users, Quick References include vital command information under easy-to-find alphabetical listings. Quick References are a must for anyone who needs command information fast!

Complete Coverage From A To Z!

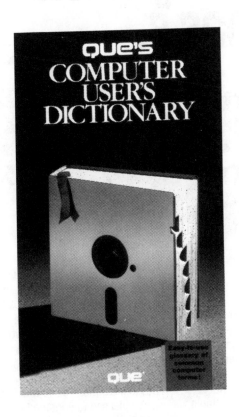

que's COMPUTER USER'S DICTIONARY

The Ultimate Glossary Of Computer Terms—Over 200,000 In Print!

Que's Computer User's Dictionary
Que Development Group

This compact, practical reference contains hundreds of definitions, explanations, examples, and illustrations on topics from programming to desktop publishing. You can master the "language" of computers and learn how to make your personal computers more efficient and more powerful. Filled with tips and cautions, *Que's Computer User's Dictionary* is the perfect resource for anyone who uses a computer.

IBM, Macintosh, Apple, & Programming

Order #1086   **$9.95 USA**

0-88022-540-8, 500 pp., 4 3/4 x 8

To Order, Call:
(800) 428-5331 OR (317) 573-2510

Welcome to the high-speed, high-productivity world of MS-DOS 5.

MS-DOS 5

Professor Egghead would like to eggspress his appreciation for your purchase of MS-DOS 5 at Egghead by offering you these special rebates. Eggzamine the following pages carefully for these super values!

Congratulations on your decision to upgrade your PC's performance with the most efficient, most flexible, and most eggciting operating system for IBM/compatible computers! With MS-DOS 5, you can now take maximum advantage of large, memory-intensive applications; work within a visually oriented, intuitive graphical environment; and *still* benefit from increased computing speed and file-access times. MS-DOS 5 shatters the restrictive bonds of the C> prompt forever, freeing you from many tedious command strings and making sophisticated file- and memory-management as easy as clicking and dragging an icon.

We at Egghead are eggcited, too, at the opportunity to be part of this revolutionary breakthrough. We believe that no PC should be without MS-DOS 5, and that's why you'll find it at your local Egghead store at the lowest price available—anywhere!

But we want to do even more! So, to introduce you to MS-DOS 5, we're pleased to eggstend to you the Eggsclusive Rebate offers you'll find on the following pages. These products are specially selected to help you eggsplore the power and ease-of-use of this superb graphical operating system. And, as your eggsperience and computing needs eggspand, remember that Egghead is your headquarters for MS-DOS 5—the only DOS worth owning!

Double your hard-disk capacity in minutes!

Caught in the squeeze between limited hard-disk space and the requirements of high-powered applications and graphical user interfaces? STACKER software lets you make the most of your hardware through state-of-the-art file compression, to give you an average of up to twice the available hard-disk space! Plus, STACKER's disk-caching function allows you to take advantage of increased storage capacity without significant impact on processing or file-access speed. Automatic installation is quick and simple, giving you real-time data compression that's compatible with MS-DOS 5 (and all DOS versions 3.0 and higher), Microsoft Windows 3.0, and most popular utilities and memory managers. New from Stac Electronics.

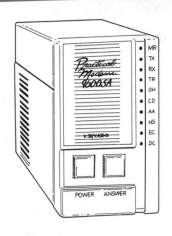

Your Choice of Norton Software Products

Name: _____

Company name (if applicable): _____

Address: _____

City: _____

State/Province: _____

ZIP/Postal Code: _____

Telephone: (___) _____

Here's how to get your software rebate:

Proof of Purchase: Include your original Egghead identified cash-register receipt (if you purchased through our retail store) or your original packing slip (if you purchased through our corporate accounts program). On the receipt/packing slip, circle the product name.
Rebate Certificate: Fill in the information requested at left. Please print clearly. Place in an envelope, along with the receipt/packing slip, and mail to Egghead Discount Software Awards Center, P.O. Box 1610, Minneapolis, MN 55440-1620. Allow 6–8 weeks for processing.
Important: One rebate per product purchased. We reserve the right to require further proof of purchase. Purchases must be made between June 11, 1991 and December 31, 1991, with mail-in rebate postmarked within 30 days of purchase. No photocopied receipts, packing slips, or rebate certificates will be accepted. Rebate offers good in U.S. and Canada; rebates will be paid in U.S. funds.

Discount
EGGHEAD SOFTWARE
America's Software Eggsperts.

Product: The Norton Utilities
The Norton AntiVirus
The Norton Backup
The Norton Commander

NewWave for Windows

Name: _____

Company name (if applicable): _____

Address: _____

City: _____

State/Province: _____

ZIP/Postal Code: _____

Telephone: (___) _____

Here's how to get your software rebate:

Proof of Purchase: Include your original Egghead identified cash-register receipt (if you purchased through our retail store) or your original packing slip (if you purchased through our corporate accounts program). On the receipt/packing slip, circle the product name.
Rebate Certificate: Fill in the information requested at left. Please print clearly. Place in an envelope, along with the receipt/packing slip, and mail to Egghead Discount Software Awards Center, P.O. Box 1610, Minneapolis, MN 55440-1620. Allow 6–8 weeks for processing.
Important: One rebate per product purchased. We reserve the right to require further proof of purchase. Purchases must be made between June 11, 1991 and December 31, 1991, with mail-in rebate postmarked within 30 days of purchase. No photocopied receipts, packing slips, or rebate certificates will be accepted. Rebate offers good in U.S. and Canada; rebates will be paid in U.S. funds.

Discount
EGGHEAD SOFTWARE
America's Software Eggsperts.

Product: H-P NewWave
for Windows

PM 9600 SA v.32/v.42 External Modem

Name: _____

Company name (if applicable): _____

Address: _____

City: _____

State/Province: _____

ZIP/Postal Code: _____

Telephone: (___) _____

Here's how to get your rebate:

Proof of Purchase: Include your original Egghead identified cash-register receipt (if you purchased through our retail store) or your original packing slip (if you purchased through our corporate accounts program). On the receipt/packing slip, circle the product name.
Rebate Certificate: Fill in the information requested at left. Please print clearly. Place in an envelope, along with the receipt/packing slip, and mail to Egghead Discount Software Awards Center, P.O. Box 1610, Minneapolis, MN 55440-1620. Allow 6–8 weeks for processing.
Important: One rebate per product purchased. We reserve the right to require further proof of purchase. Purchases must be made between June 11, 1991 and December 31, 1991, with mail-in rebate postmarked within 30 days of purchase. No photocopied receipts, packing slips, or rebate certificates will be accepted. Rebate offers good in U.S. and Canada; rebates will be paid in U.S. funds.

Discount
EGGHEAD SOFTWARE
America's Software Eggsperts.

Product: Practical Peripherals
PM 9600 SA v.32/v.42
External Modem

WordStar

Name: _____

Company name (if applicable): _____

Address: _____

City: _____

State/Province: _____

ZIP/Postal Code: _____

Telephone: ( ) _____

Here's how to get your software rebate:

Proof of Purchase: Include your original Egghead identified cash-register receipt (if you purchased through our retail store) or your original packing slip (if you purchased through our corporate accounts program). On the receipt/packing slip, circle the product name.

Rebate Certificate: Fill in the information requested at left. Please print clearly. Place in an envelope, along with the receipt/packing slip, and mail to Egghead Discount Software Awards Center, P.O. Box 1610, Minneapolis, MN 55440-1620. Allow 6–8 weeks for processing.

Important: One rebate per product purchased. We reserve the right to require further proof of purchase. Purchases must be made between June 11, 1991 and December 31, 1991, with mail-in rebate postmarked within 30 days of purchase. No photocopied receipts, packing slips, or rebate certificates will be accepted. Rebate offers good in U.S. and Canada; rebates will be paid in U.S. funds.

Discount
EGGHEAD SOFTWARE.
America's Software Eggsperts.

Product: WordStar

Great American Business Value Pack

Name: _____

Company name (if applicable): _____

Address: _____

City: _____

State/Province: _____

ZIP/Postal Code: _____

Telephone: ( ) _____

Here's how to get your software rebate:

Proof of Purchase: Include your original Egghead identified cash-register receipt (if you purchased through our retail store) or your original packing slip (if you purchased through our corporate accounts program).

Rebate Certificate: Complete the registration card in either the Money Matters or Payroll box, affix the sticker located on the front of the Business Value Pack to the registration card, and mail with receipt/packing slip to The Great American Rebate Offer, P.O. Box 863, Amherst, NH 03030. You should receive your rebate by mail within 30 days.

Important: This special offer is good for the purchase of the Business Value Pack only. One rebate per product purchased and one rebate per home/business address. Offer expires December 31, 1991. Mail-in rebate only, not payable in store. Not good with any other One-Write Plus offer. Offer not open to distributors or dealers. Valid only in U.S. and Canada. Cash redemption value: 1/100th of one cent.

Discount
EGGHEAD SOFTWARE.
America's Software Eggsperts.

Product: Great American Business Value Pack

Your Choice: Individual Training Software Packages

Name: _____

Company name (if applicable): _____

Address: _____

City: _____

State/Province: _____

ZIP/Postal Code: _____

Telephone: ( ) _____

Here's how to get your software rebate:

Proof of Purchase: Include your original Egghead identified cash-register receipt (if you purchased through our retail store) or your original packing slip (if you purchased through our corporate accounts program). On the receipt/packing slip, circle the product name.

Rebate Certificate: Fill in the information requested at left. Please print clearly. Place in an envelope, along with the receipt/packing slip, and mail to Egghead Discount Software Awards Center, P.O. Box 1610, Minneapolis, MN 55440-1620. Allow 6–8 weeks for processing.

Important: One rebate per product purchased. We reserve the right to require further proof of purchase. Purchases must be made between June 11, 1991 and December 31, 1991, with mail-in rebate postmarked within 30 days of purchase. No photocopied receipts, packing slips, or rebate certificates will be accepted. Rebate offers good in U.S. and Canada; rebates will be paid in U.S. funds.

Discount
EGGHEAD SOFTWARE.
America's Software Eggsperts.

Product: Individual Training: dBASE IV, Lotus 1-2-3 Rel. 2.2, WordPerfect 5.**1**